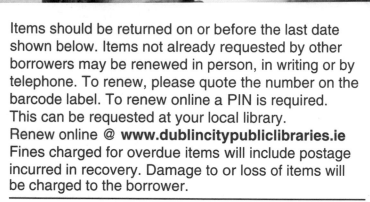

Donncha with Mag and Jack Lynch, during the recording of RTÉ Television's *The West Clare Wren*, in the couple's cottage in Kilbaha, County Clare, in November 1979.

Front cover photograph:
In the hidden Ireland at Bellevue, Ballyhogue, on the banks of the River Slaney.

Back cover photograph:
"Napoleon Bonaparte" on his horse 'Marengo' which he bought at Cahirmee Fair in Buttevant. His visit was a feature of the RTÉ television series *Donncha's Travelling Roadshow* in 1979.

DONNCHA Ó DÚLAING

DONNCHA'S WORLD

The Roads, the Stories and the Wireless

In conversation with
Declan Lyons

With Irish Wolfhound, Lia, outside Adare Manor, County Limerick, during *Donncha at Adare*, the six-part RTÉ television series featuring a variety of musical acts performing in Adare Manor in November 1980.

THREE SISTERS PRESS

Vera and Donncha 1957 in the Arcadia Ballroom during the
Ford years; With Vera, Feargal and Ruairí at Shannon Airport in
the late 60s; Donncha Óg on his graduation in 1990, with UCC
President Prof. Michael Mortell; Outside the house where he was
born on Convent Road, Doneraile, with son, Ruairí, 2014; Beloved
family pet, Rua, in the 1970s; The Late Late Toy Show with Sinéad
Ní Dhúlaing second from right; Ruairí's wife, Anne, and daughter,
Aisling; Ruairí and son, Cian.

All the grandchildren: Vera, the proudest of grandmothers with Aisling, Ruairí, Diarmuid, Bláthnaid, Fionnán, Sinéad, Caolfhionn and Cian; Grandsons, Ruairí and Fionnán at Croke Park; Commercials Hurling Club where 10-year-old grandson, Diarmuid, plays U13 hurling, from left, his dad, Donal, Vera, Donncha, Diarmuid, Feargal, and Caolfhionn; Granddaughters, Aisling and Caolfhionn, with Aidan Murphy; Long-time visitor to Ó Dúlaing's garden in Donnybrook; Descendants of Daithí Lacha; Diarmuid and his U13 Schools' medal in Croke Park, 2014; At the Garden of Remembrance with grandchildren, Caoilfhionn and Diarmuid; Granddaughters, Sinéad and Bláthnaid.

Overleaf: Studying Corkman jokes at Siamsa Cois Laoi '81.

SIAMSA COIS LAOI

CONTENTS

Opposite: Blisters in Nenagh, 1982.

In the Phoenix Park with Dónal during the 1982 Dublin City Marathon.

Above: Preparation and calculations.

Debating the pecking order.

Presentation by Golden Vale to Donncha at the start of the Brian Boru March in April 1988. Around the house and mind the dresser - in Sligo town during the 32-county Walk.

Knitting for MS Ireland.

1 FIRST STEPS

... The nurse, together with Dr. O'Sullivan, the local doctor, put in place a tough regime to keep me in this world as long as possible. It was prescribed that I be dipped continuously into baths of hot water. Ending up in hot water was to become a metaphorical motif for the rest of my life ...

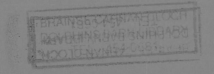

Donncha 1935 - the longest journey begins with a single step.

MEMORY IS AN UNCERTAIN thing. This book is my memories, incomplete, exaggerated, changed with time and polished over my many years. Wrestling with the slippery snake of reminiscence, I took courage from Marcel Proust, the renowned French writer, on the topic of memories, who notes:

> *"...that I could not discern between my oldest, instinctive memories, those others, inspired more recently by a taste or a scent, and those which are actually the memories of another, from whom I had acquired them at second hand – no fissures, indeed, no geological faults, but at least those veins, those streaks of colour which in certain rocks, in certain marbles, point to differences of origin, age and formation."*

There is much that I have forgotten, buried in some cobwebbed recess of the mind, crumbling gradually to nothingness. But, as Samuel Beckett points out, it is only because we forget things that we have memories. Memories expand to fill space and time. I have vivid, pictorial recall of my early years that could fill volumes while there are times that are memory deserts from which it is difficult to dredge up even the smallest nugget.

I'll begin though in a time that is rich in warm memories for me, in Doneraile, my birthplace.

I was born in the midst of turmoil. It was the 15th of March, 1933 and the great depression gripped world economies. There was a bank crisis in the United States that saw nearly five-hundred banks closed in the first quarter of the year. Adolph Hitler was laying down the foundations for his dictatorship. Joseph Stalin strengthened his iron grip on Russia and was manufacturing a famine to crush Ukrainian dreams of independence. In Ireland, the Fianna Fáil government began a trade war with our neighbour and former adversary, Britain.

My birth was a small personal drama relative to these major events but it was traumatic and dramatic. I was born early and sickly. The parish midwife, Nurse Herlihy, was on hand to ease my entry into this world but predicted that it would be a short visit as she feared I wouldn't last longer than a half day in it. I was quickly baptised Denis Patrick Dowling in St. Mary's Church, Doneraile, as was the custom for any baby thought too delicate for this world. The nurse, together with Dr. O'Sullivan, the local doctor, put in place a tough regime to keep me in this world as long as possible. It was prescribed that I be dipped continuously into baths of hot water. Ending up in hot water was to become a metaphorical motif for the rest of my life.

While the nurse and doctor concentrated on matters medical, my anxious parents turned to the rock of faith to find salvation for their first-born. They were devout in their beliefs and promised to forego alcohol and my mother swore to give up smoking if only I could be saved. The nuns from the local Presentation Convent sent Sister Kevin with Lourdes' water to sprinkle on this poor ailing infant, and this was sprinkled conscientiously, along with the continuing bathings.

It was some form of liquid that saved me: the abstinence from one; the immersion in another, or the sprinkling with the third. Or indeed, it was most likely a combination of all three. Thus I defied early predictions of my demise and was soon being wheeled around the town in my black, high-sided perambulator by a proud and relieved mother. This early brush with death was probably a strong motivating force in my later life. I heard the story many times and it became ingrained in my thinking that we are only here for a short time. I felt that I'd been given some form of second chance and had to do my best with whatever time span I was granted.

But my place of birth gives little information about where I came from and the influences that shaped my life as a youngster growing up in rural County Cork. These influences still exert influence on me today; I am the product of the ultimate form of mixed marriage: a Kerry father and a Cork mother. Thus I've always felt at home in both counties and able to support Kerry in football and Cork in hurling.

My parents were similar in that both came from farming backgrounds and grew up in rural areas. My mother's family were better off and had a more sheltered life on the richer lowlands, while my father came from tougher, mountainy stock.

My parents were Daniel Dowling and Helena Cashman. My father was born in Kerry in 1895. His family lived in Glenmore townland between Camp and Annascaul, off the main Tralee to Dingle road, and in the civil parish of Kilgobban. His parents, Denis and Julia, had a small holding. Farming was difficult and, as a boy, he must have done his share of tough, manual work. The land was poor and this was an isolated place in the early twentieth century, but it had outstanding natural beauty in its mountains, lakes and ocean views.

Daniel Dowling.

The roadside hedges were resplendent with fuchsia bushes while soft mists rolled over the peninsula from the surrounding Atlantic. As a boy, Daniel grew up hearing Irish spoken around him and his family spoke both Irish and English. This was, and still is, a place rich in folklore, myths and stories. He would have heard of the adventures of the Fianna and the journeys of Diarmuid and Gráinne through the surrounding countryside, and these myths were treated as being as real as the current terrible tales of far off warring nations.

There was music, both natural and man-made, in Glenmore. This is still a place with a vibrant music tradition and the young Daniel must have heard great fiddle playing, singing and piping in his own home and the houses and halls around where he lived. Indeed, one of his nephews later became a master fiddle player. Radio had yet to arrive and there were few motor cars, except those belonging to the gentry, or lorries carrying the Black and Tans - irregular British forces. His was the last generation of Irish people to live and be content with natural silence. He was close to nature and heard, too, a natural music from the wind, waves and the plaintive calls of the curlews on the bog and the rasp of the corncrakes among the crops.

It is hard to imagine what life was like for my young father and, sadly, I was never to hear it directly from him; parts though can be imagined easily. While there was music and sport then as distractions, life itself was hard. The Great Famine was still a living memory for some; its ghost in the shape of ruined, deserted cottages haunted the countryside. Parishes nearby are recorded as losing up to thirty per cent of their families in the ten years from 1841 to '51 and a great many more fled in the years afterwards. The Famine was an unspoken presence and those remaining often felt a strong survivor's guilt that penetrated deep into their psyches.

The Famine was the past; my father came of age during the time of the Great War, our own War of Independence and the subsequent Civil War. The last was divisive, splitting families and friendships and laying down a legacy of bitterness and rancour for decades after. It's easy to understand why a young man such as himself would search for a new and different path, seeking an alternative to the division of the past and becoming part of the building of a new tomorrow.

Daniel was the youngest of thirteen children. While he stayed in Ireland, most of his siblings emigrated to Britain or the United States;

an older brother eventually inherited the farm. Emigration was the safety valve for young Irish people then as they fled a grim reality for the promise of a new beginning in a foreign land. I presume my father went to school locally, in the national school in either Camp or Annascaul. The latter was the home village of the great explorer Tom Crean, who would have been setting out on his great Antarctic adventures when Daniel was a youngster. My father may have been captivated by romantic tales of exploration in distant lands as these men faced danger at every turn.

I know relatively little of my uncles and aunts from Glenmore. I've met cousins since in Kerry and the United States. They have filled me in a little on my father's family. In truth it would have been hard to maintain contact with those abroad given the great distances separating them and the paucity of communications available. In addition, there may have been a slight coolness for a time between my father and the rest of his family for he never visited his parental home and rarely spoke of it as far as I can remember. The reason for this apparent estrangement remains a mystery to this day. It was not a great division though, for my father used to send a plug of tobacco to his mother, an avid pipe smoker, practically every week.

When it came to his turn to leave home, my father chose a hard route by staying in Ireland and playing a role in the creation of our fledgling State. He joined An Garda Síochána, the newly-created police force. He had relatives who had been members of the Royal Irish Constabulary (RIC) and this may have influenced his choice. The Gardaí replaced the RIC in 1922 and absorbed some former RIC members at the founding of the State.

He trained in Dublin before moving to Cork city, Buttevant and then being assigned to Cloyne in East Cork. That town's population was mixed between Catholics and Protestants, and indeed, it was the seat of bishoprics from both persuasions. The Civil War was ended but its legacy lingered. Brothers had fought brothers and firm friends had become hardened enemies. Keeping the peace was a difficult business and called as much upon the art of diplomacy as the imposition of law.

It was love rather than rancour that marked my father's time in that country town. For it was there that he met the young woman who was to become my mother.

The Cashmans were what was then termed "county people." They were relatively well off farmers. My mother was the youngest of five children of Maurice and Catherine. They lived in Ballyshane, a cluster of eleven homes by the sea in the parish of Aghada, about six miles south of Cloyne itself. This was a wondrous place and I spent many childhood summers there. It was a land of neat fields, mixed farming and carefully observed rituals and social norms.

I gather that my mother's family weren't too pleased when their daughter started doing a line with a young guard, something perceived as being a step down from themselves. By then my mother worked in the town as a book-keeper and so was away from the farm and the watchful eyes of her parents and family. My mother was a beautiful redhead and turned many a young man's head in the town. Love flourished and Daniel Dowling and Helena Cashman were married in Cloyne in 1931.

I know little about my parents' marriage celebration other than it happened and it caused a significant relocation for the young couple. Gardaí were discouraged from serving in a district where they had family and so my father, having now acquired family connections in the area, was promptly transferred to Doneraile, fifty miles to the north-west. Here he was to join four other Gardaí and took on the duties of the town's truant officer.

Doneraile is a pleasant, rural town now and was then, too. It is surrounded by green, fertile, rolling countryside. The river Awbeg, a tributary of the Blackwater, flows through the top of the town and close to the Protestant church. Arthur Young, a nineteenth-century travel writer, describes it as a "neat village" although J. Crofton Croker was less complimentary, describing it as an "unpicturesque and miserable town."

The ground rises from the river and the gentle incline climbs to a small hill. The town takes its name from "Dún ar Aill" or the fort of the hill.

Despite its name's Irish origin, it was a highly anglicised settlement. It had a concentration of British nobility with retired British soldiers working for the landed gentry.

It was a post and market town, built for the estate's needs with a full complement of shops, craftsmen and artisans. There were cobblers, bakers, butchers, dressmakers, hardware and grocery stores, public houses, churches, a pharmacy, doctors, midwives and undertakers. I'm not sure if there was a candlestick maker but there was certainly a demand for candles as rural electrification hadn't reached Doneraile when my parents arrived and candles were essential to supplement oil lamps in the home.

I remember that there was a wide main street, lined with two- and three-storey buildings. Most of the shops and other commercial premises had living quarters on the upper floors. Shopkeepers usually lived above their premises. I recall a lively and bustling town, having more than enough to occupy the time and imagination of a young boy.

Doneraile was my first home and even at the distance of seventy years it fascinates me still. It was here that I was first introduced to the magic of storytelling. I learnt that a person's value could come as easily from the stories they told as from the wealth they owned.

First Class, Doneraile CBS, 1940.

We lived in a small house on Convent Road. An elderly woman, who, though no relation, I called 'Granny', helped my mother mind us three children. I was the first-born of three. My sisters, Mary and Kitty, were born not too long after me. It was Granny who was the great, protean influence upon my childhood. Her proper name was Mrs Minnie Deloury. If there is anyone who could be described as the source of inspiration for *Highways and Byways*, it is herself. To her I owe more than I can ever repay. She taught me to love my past, my place and my traditions with all the warmth and affection of which she was capable. She introduced me to the golden lore of "the Court", the oul' Lord, the Canon, the good people, the evil eye and to Peggy's Legs (a kind of hard sweet) which she produced from the deep, cavernous folds of her long black skirts.

Fact in Doneraile was often stranger than fiction, and if it wasn't, it certainly gave it a good run for its money. The reservoir of the bizarre was filled mainly with tales of the gentry and their doings. The St. Legers were Lords of the Manor in Doneraile Court. The family name lives on in the horserace named after Major General Anthony St. Leger, the St. Leger being the oldest of Britain's five classic races. The Major General was the nephew of the first Viscount of Doneraile. The race was first run on the 24th of September 1776. It was for three-year-old fillies and colts, and it has become a part of the classic racing programme worldwide.

Horses featured in many of the stories I heard as a child. I was told how the first ever steeplechase was held in 1752. Edmund Blake raced Cornelius O'Callaghan from Buttevant church along the banks of Awbeg River, jumping walls, ditches, and fences in a hair-raising dash to the steeple at our church in Doneraile.

The St. Leger women were also the subjects of legend. Elizabeth St. Leger was known as "the lady freemason." The first Viscount of Doneraile was a freemason and the father of Elizabeth. Legend has it that Elizabeth was one day reading in the library which adjoined the meeting room. Part of the wall had been removed and so she inadvertently overheard the masonic proceedings within. She had no way of exiting the library other than out through the meeting room, and the door was at the far end of that room. She managed to slip undetected past the meeting but as she opened the door, she was confronted by the butler, Tyler, with sword drawn. Her scream alerted the meeting to her presence. She was detained while the Lodge discussed what to do. Finally, they decided to initiate her into the Brotherhood. So she went through the same ceremony that she surreptitiously witnessed earlier.

The St. Legers were one of a number of Anglo families that lived or had lived in Doneraile's environs. Other gentry achieved literary fame. Edmund Spenser, the poet and author of *The Faerie Queene*, lived less than five miles away in his castle in Kilcolman. It appears that he wrote a good part of this famous work while living in Ireland. He had estates near Doneraile as well as further south in the county. He was a beneficiary of the Munster plantation along with his friend, adventurer and fellow land-grabber, Sir Walter Raleigh. Spenser had a jaundiced view of Ireland and the Irish. He described the country as a "diseased portion of the State". He believed the people descended from barbarian hordes that swept across Europe on horseback and settled in this country. He advocated a scorched-earth policy as a remedy for the Irish problem. It is ironic that the great Hugh O' Neill drove him from his lands and set his castle alight during the Nine

Years' War in the late 1500s. His luck continued to fail him after his flight from Doneraile. He returned to London where he soon died at the relatively young age of forty-six. His bad luck would appear to have lived on after his death, too, as his son had his throat slit by his own wife in Mallow.

We lived close to the gentry, their land abutted onto the end of our garden where the demesne marked the end of our world and the beginning of theirs. My earliest memories are of pigeons, pigeons that from early morning till late at night, called out their monotonous message, "Buy two cows, Davy. Buy two cows, Davy," as they vied with the always-present crows for better positions in the tall trees, the tops of which brushed the sky above the wall.

Personally, I knew little about the St. Legers, except that I often paid the rent for my mother.

Early equestrian pursuits in Doneraile, with sister Kitty, 1942.

Their agent lived in sarcastic and powerful immunity down by the river near the saw mills. I knew, too, that you had to get a 'permit', if you please, to cross the Park. You weren't allowed to pick the daffodils, the Bainne Bó Bleacht, or the bluebells. Indeed, we natives weren't allowed to tarry inside the great gates at all. The river teemed with fish that had such a lovely taste. Deer, too – there were hundreds of them, always in the distance, looking up with antlered surprise and then sweeping away across the North Park, like a brown wave in the purple dusk. The St. Legers owned it all; they owned the town, and there was cap-tugging servility then for those who came in from their estates. I knew even as a child that wrongs were sweating and hurting somewhere under the urbane skin of this place.

I remember well one day after a local point to point, hearing an old lady, a friend who often shared a boiled egg with me – I had a mysterious habit of turning up at tea-time – reciting with great gusto:

> *"Alas, how dismal is my tale,*
> *I lost my watch in Doneraile,*
> *My Dublin watch, my chain and seal*
> *Pilfered at once in Doneraile.*
> *May Beef or Mutton, Lamb or Veal,*
> *Be never found in Doneraile;*
> *May heaven a chosen curse entail*
> *On rigid, rotten Doneraile,*
> *Oh! May my couplets never fail*
> *To find new curse in Doneraile."*

She paused to tell me that Doneraile was a great place for characters, the understatement of the year, and that the man who wrote what she called *The Curse of Doneraile,* and which went on for a year, was a travelling bard named O'Kelly, who sampled well, if not wisely, of the local brew, and who ended up minus his Dublin watch.

'However,' she said, with great relish, '"th' oul' Lord" (no one ever referred to the "young lord", if you said "Our Lord" you were merely blasphemous), "th' oul' Lord" or his good Lady bought another watch for the poet and, like the weather, he changed and wrote':

> *"How vastly pleasing is my tale,*
> *I found my watch at Doneraile,*
> *My Dublin watch, my chain and seal*
> *Were all restored at Doneraile*
> *May Beef and Mutton, lamb and Veal*
> *Plenty create at Doneraile;*
> *May Heaven each chosen bliss entail*
> *On honest, friendly Doneraile;*
> *And may its Lady never fail*
> *To find new joys in Doneraile."*

Later, of course, I learnt that O'Kelly while on a visit to Dublin met King George III of happy and insane memory who said:

> 'I see, Mr O'Kelly, like your two great contemporaries, Scott and Byron, you are lame!'

To which observation, O'Kelly replied, with typical modesty:

> *"If God one member has oppressed*
> *He made more perfect all the rest."*

And then, at George's request, he composed, extempore naturally, a memorable quatrain:

> *"Three poets of three different nations born*
> *The United Kingdom, at this age adorn –*
> *Byron of England, Scott of Scotia's blood,*
> *And Erin's pride, O'Kelly, great and good"*

The St. Legers actually bought, took or robbed, whichever word you prefer, the lands around Doneraile from one of the Spenser family. Indeed, the demesne of Doneraile Court, with its looping carriage drives, its bamboo groves, its soporific lime walk, its clotted lily ponds, and its gently whispering river, was dear to several of the great Elizabethans: Spenser, Raleigh, smoking the first pipe seen in Doneraile, and Sir Philip Sidney strolled in the green alders' cooling shade.

Sir William St. Leger was the first to arrive and the family shadow, in varying degrees of substance, lies across Doneraile.

Doneraile Court, once the focal point of a large and thriving local society, now stands forlorn, shuttered, deserted, and empty. The house, built in 1725, looks across the great grassy sweep where carriages, flunkies, lords and ladies, poets and beggars once mingled, where the red deer gathered around the house before a Lord's death and where music from the great ballroom echoes wistfully on ghostly nights across the nodding daffodils, or mingles with the scent of newly-mown hay in long Doneraile dusks.

Character, in that house, seemed to be imprinted on every hour, every face, on the stone of crumbling walls. It was an archetypal mansion like something from an eighteenth-century print. It was a place where upstairs' life was lived to its brutal and joyful satiety and where downstairs, those who served from without the high walls did so with sullen, resentful, soul-destroying servility.

One of the St. Legers had a pet fox and was in the habit of driving with the animal perched beside him on the carriage through the demesne and town on fine days. This particular day, whether 'twas fine or wet makes little difference, the fox bit the Lord and here's what the good people of Doneraile insert as a moral into the tale: Reynard also bit the coachman. Now, the latter wore leather gloves and was unmarked. The Lord, as befitted a man of his high station, wore only the best of fine silk gloves. The fox bit him to the bone. His blood, whether royal blue or common red, flowed and when he saw it, he went stark raving mad and had to be restrained in a room at the top of the house. An old man told me in a fearful whisper:

> *"They had to smother him you know... that's it... put him down... they had to smother him between two ticks; the coachman, he lived to be an old man; the fox... well the people of Doneraile thought that he was a lovely animal. People living in the town have reported that on certain nights, the Lord, the fox and the coachman roam abroad on their carriage pulled by headless horses. When you look at this ghostly vision closely you'll see that the Lord's right glove is blood-stained, a sight that would make your flesh creep."*

Incidentally, you can still see the stone that the Lord kept the fox under. And you can see where the chains holding the fox have chafed the stone.

I first crossed Doneraile Court's threshold in the mid-sixties. It was high summer when Viscountess Doneraile – she always signed her letters *"Mary Doneraile"* – sat me down to the tea and cucumber sandwiches, inevitably trimmed of crust. I was, as ever, researching another radio programme about this place that still holds a deep fascination for me. She was polite, gentle, well-bred and hailed from New Zealand - different from those who preceded her. Of course, she had married into the family rather than being a blood St. Leger. So she has no connection with the time when the Droit de Seigneur was common-place there. Then local young bucks had the first rights in the bed of any local woman getting married. When Tally women were well-fed, ravished and rejected with monotony, when local gentry would have a hunt with a difference , they'd take a few of the most winsome local girls, coat them in aniseed and then follow with horse and hound in a macabre and revolting chase. The girls were physically unharmed, by the dogs that is, but the Lord or buck had "bed rights" over any girl run to ground.

So Lady Doneraile and I talked as her dog snored peacefully and, when tea was over, we trod carefully between the bric-a-brac of many centuries of St. Legers who looked down from the walls, the ladies' somewhat bulbous of eye; the gentlemen's faces snuggled into beards, their eyes now glazed into an artist's moment of concentration. She recounted tales and legends directly from the source about the former residents. I felt that I would be among the last to hear these tales and that they were already gathering cobwebs and dust and would soon be consigned to the furthest recesses of memory.

The St. Legers were the dominant nobility in the area when I was growing up. They weren't the only ones nor was their arrogant behaviour emulated by all of the others. One family whose path I crossed many times and who had a great influence on me, were the Bowens of Bowen Court. That family arrived in the wake of Oliver Cromwell, hardly the most propitious time to come to Ireland. Indeed, Elizabeth Bowen, the writer, once told me that her Welsh ancestors had no real desire to settle uncomfortably among the warlike natives of North Cork but that Colonel Owen, a Welsh man, had in some way incurred the wrath of Cromwell and was told to remove himself, bag and baggage, to Ireland to be out of sight and mind. It was a sort of to-hell-or-to-Munster gesture.

To soften the blow, Cromwell suggested that the family could have whatever land lay within his pet hawk's flight for a day. The hawk, being a mightily intelligent bird, as well as possessing admirable taste, flew over North Cork coursing the lands of Farahy, nodding benignly towards the Ballyhoura Hills, gazing fleetingly at Spenser's Kilcolman area and then coming to a quivering, well-satisfied rest where Bowen's Court was to be. The Bowens, as usual with the Anglo-Irish, set about stabilising their position, building a house and, of course, the usual demesne walls. Bowens' Court, completed in 1776, was to be the last Bowen landmark in North Cork. A severe-looking Italianate many-windowed house, it stood at the foot of the Ballyhoura hills facing South-South East.

The first time I met Elizabeth Bowen, I was startled by a strange sense of déjà vu, a feeling that we had met somewhere before and, when I began to think about it, I realised that of course, we had! She was straight out of her own novels. She was the perfect Anglo-Irish prototype, a classical example of what Seán Ó Faoláin has called "a resident alien". She explained to me that when she began to write seriously in the early twenties, she, in her own words, hoped to make "an uncorrupted attempt to say something not said before." She discovered that she had little in common with other Anglo-Irish and, apart from a somewhat unlikely sympathy for her Irish neighbours, there was nothing for her in Ireland. So she left for England.

She has left us, what I think is, a fair reflection of the Ireland in which she grew up; an Ireland in which her people really had, indeed, still have, a meaningful place if they choose to look for it. Writing of her family, she says:

> *"My family got their position and drew their power from a situation that shows an inherent wrong. In the grip of that situation, England and Ireland each turned on the other a close, harsh, distorted face."*

Given that Elizabeth Bowen spent a good deal of her life in Ireland, Doneraile, North Cork had entered deeply into her heart and mind; Bowens Court, was never too far away. Indeed, standing on any North Cork road on a summer evening, one can feel the glow of her writing as it spills over from the written page and mingles, miraculously with the life around you: Take *Summer Night*:

> *"As the sun set its light slowly melted the landscape, 'till everything was made of fire and glass. The haycocks now seemed to glow in the after grass; their freshness penetrated the air. In the not far distance, hills with woods up their flanks lay in light like hills in another world. Against those*

hills, the burning red rambler roses in cottage gardens along the roadside looked earthy."

The conclusion is effectively unsurprising: *"The road was in Ireland."*

I first visited Elizabeth Bowen's old home in early spring 1962. I wrote then, somewhat romantically, in a little diary:

> *"This is a magical place. It is forlorn. It's deserted yet in an April dusk it seems alive with the past. Through its shuttered windows and securely fastened doors, one peeps at desiccation and dust; still, it seems that a certain kind of life goes on. The house, no matter what may happen to it in the future, can never forget what it has been. One feels strange here, as if entered by the past; feeling that whatever happened here once still goes on, in one form or another. History seeps forward..."*

The next time I went back, Bowen's Court was gone. Elizabeth Bowen was with me, as were several school children from Doneraile. It was a wet October day, rain misting down between us. It would soon be dusk. There was about the scene an air of stylised melancholy, perhaps for Elizabeth Bowen, indeed, certainly for her. There were echoes hidden from us. Warm summer sun on the upper tennis court, a party on the lawn, a sense of possession, of belonging, the noise of rooks in the evening, laughter in the orchard, the rumble of wheels on well-kept gravel walks and the trees, always the trees. Early childhood, days and nights always tinged with summer. Now it was autumn, the last lights were gone out, the leaves were folding their wings, and a few pitiful tree-stumps looked amputated in the twilight.

I remember a child asking Elizabeth Bowen, 'Why did you leave?' 'A matter of money, my dear' 'Why didn't you ask the neighbours to help?' 'That, my dear, is the story of Ireland.' She turned her face away from the weeping hills, away from the churchyard at Farahy where her husband lay, where all the Bowens lie, including herself now, away from the past. No one spoke. The children understood. Her face was wet. Her own writing alone had voice:

> *"This was a day of October size. How long this autumn had felt. This was the peace of the moment in which one sees the world for a moment innocent of oneself. A rapture of strength could be felt in the rising tree trunks, rooted, gripping the slope and there travelled through the layered, light shaded thinning and crossing foliage, and was deflected downwards on the laurels, a breathless glory."*

The gentry were only one rich source of legend. We, the native Irish, had our own stories, too. Granny regaled us with tales of banshees cutting through carriages' forks and curses cast on farmers who dug up fairy forts. We heard of the power that holy wells had to cure ailments, from warts to paralysis. We learnt to check for evidence of cloven hooves should an unusual stranger arrive in the town – especially if it was a dark winter's night.

What strikes me now is the seamless way in which these tales wove fact, history, myth and legend together to create a new, mystical truth. These stories formed and informed us. They gave us a sense of place and connection with previous generations and the community, our neighbours and friends. Doneraile was in that sense a typical Irish town.

I garnered these stories as a child, storing them away for use later. I played in the Protestant graveyard and traced out the names and dates of the dead generations carved on the tombstones and mausoleums of the local grand families. I came across the St. Leger motto carved in stone there too: "Haut et Bon." They may have been high and good in their lifetimes but they were laid low by the time I came across them there.

The ghosts sometimes yielded physical gifts. Lord Castletown's wife grew lovely peaches, apples and grapes during her lifetime, and the Lord believed that she would still want these in the afterlife. So every night, he left fruit on her grave and, sure enough, by morning it was gone. We youngsters did our best to support the Lord's belief in his wife's eternal appetite through early morning feasts.

"...whenever one looks twice, there is some mystery," so wrote Elizabeth Bowen. Starting school deepened my local knowledge and the opportunity to look twice and more times at life around me. It was then, and is now, full of mystery and magic. I began my education in the junior school of the Presentation Convent. It was the beginning of a long association with the sisters and they played a significant role in my later education and career. I have never claimed to be a diligent scholar and I demonstrated this on my first day at school. I was either four or five when I

A note from Elizabeth Cameron, neé Bowen.

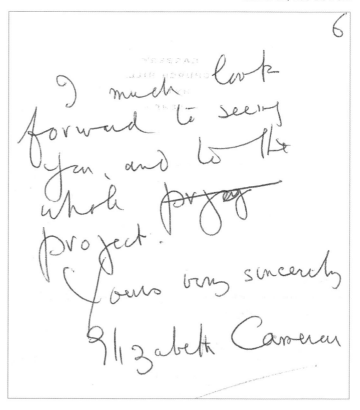

went to the good sisters. At lunchtime on the first day, I decided that I'd had enough, slipped out and skedaddled home. It was only a short distance down the road. My father cycled home daily for his lunch and he promptly marched me back up the hill to Sister Coleman's class. It was a cause of some embarrassment for him, the truancy officer.

On graduation from high infants, I moved to the Christian Brothers' national school. The school was close to the river Awbeg, one of the many distractions for us boys as we dawdled to class. It was

At the front carrying the Cross at the Charleville Corpus Christi Procession 1945.

around this time that I was trained and inducted into the ranks of those be-surpliced and soutaned young boys: the altar servers.

I have been back to the church of the Nativity of the Blessed Virgin Mary many times. It is curious that the Church seems to me to be bigger than it was when I was a boy there. The baptismal font is now inside the altar rails, but everything else has remained the same. Standing at the back still manages to give me a nasty feeling as I remember lighting candles around coffins in the pitch black early winter morning before serving Canon O'Connell's early Mass.

This was the time of Missions when the Redemptorists and the Vincentians would arrive and frighten the hell, literally, out of all of our local sinners. The missionaries rained down fire and brimstone from the pulpit, promising damnation without much hope of elevation to the other place. They used to ring the church bell for all sinners. We'd stop our bicycle riding to look carefully, and hopefully, up and down the main street. We never saw a sinner brought to redemption. I suspect that they were all at the Mission.

These were happy, simple, uncomplicated days bounded by the Church, school, holidays, fishing for pinkeens and collies in the Awbeg, hunting for bees – "Bumblers" – "Red Asses" and the occasional wasp, only to release them again in the evening when we felt it was time for them to go about their business.

The Church filled the vacuum left by the nobility; the priests expected people to doff their caps, bend their knees and step aside to make way for them, just as the Lords of big house had done before. I remember vividly when a cinema opened in the town. It almost caused a schism in our local community. The Canon railed against this new-fangled abomination from the altar. He promised that with the cinema, "sin" was arriving in Doneraile. The congregation was anxious to sample this lascivious temptation, but on the other hand, no one wanted to offend the Canon. The unfortunate proprietor of the hall had a dreadful few days. Still, it was alright in the end. We all went to the pictures, three nights running, and a new medium, if not a message, had arrived in Doneraile.

No one in Doneraile ever spoke of: "Canon Patrick Augustine Sheehan, the novelist lived here." They didn't have to. "The Canon" was quite sufficient to describe one of our town's celebrities. Everyone knew of him and held him in great affection.

The Canon's output was prodigious. During his two decades in the town, he published ten novels, two books of essays, a book of poems and numerous short stories. He opened up Doneraile to a great many people in far-flung places and they saw the place through his perceptive and friendly eyes: "Poetising and dreaming" as he described it himself. In a very true sense, he captured and moulded the memories that I have of my own place.

There is a monument in the chapel yard that represents him with pen in hand. This is how he is best remembered by the many who begged, 'Please put me in your next book, Canon.' Local memory too recalls an Aeríocht (an open-air concert) in 1910 where the Canon and Lord Castletown presided. Old people remember the Canon recited Seán Ó Duibhir's A *Ghleanna*, which he gives in his novel, *Glenanaar*:

> *"Here's a health to your and my King*
> *The sovereign of our liking;*
> *And to Sarsfield, underneath whose flag*
> *We cast once more a chance;*
> *For the morning's dawn will wing us*
> *Across the seas, and bring us*
> *To take our stand and wield a brand*
> *Among the Sons of France*
> *And though we part in sorrow*
> *Still, Seán Ó Duibhir, a chara,*
> *Our prayer is: "God save Ireland!*
> *And pour blessings on her name!*
> *May her sons be true when needed*
> *May they never feel as we did*
> *For, Seán Ó Duibhir a' ghleanna*
> *We're worsted in the game."*

The Canon, curiously, is the fourth of a great quartet of Doneraile parish priests. The first was an tAthair Eoghan Ó Caoimh, a poet and scribe who lies buried in Old Court. Second was an tAthair Peadar Ó Laoghaire, who mentions Doneraile in a not too complimentary way in *Mo Scéal Féin*. He describes the Awbeg as a small dirty river. And the third and probably most famous parish priest, the great Archbishop Croke himself also served here as he rose through the clerical ranks to his later elevation as archbishop, first in Auckland, New Zealand and later Cashel, and most famously as the patron of the GAA. He lent his name to the Gaelic Athletic Association's Mecca, "Croke Park" in Dublin. And thereby hangs a tale. Doneraile hurlers were always known as the "Doctor Crokes" in my time and even to the present day, local boys play hurling and football in "Croke Park" in Doneraile, a humble pitch named after the former parish priest. There is no doubt but that the local connection to this eminence of our national sport was one of the influences that stoked my passion for our native games, although I myself was destined to be an audience member rather than a leading performer.

For a boy such as me, the greats of hurling and football were akin to the mythical warriors of the Fianna whose achievements were beyond the ken of mere mortals. Canon Sheehan captured for me the joys and magic of hurling in two of his books, the first, *Paregra,* where he says: *"it is a glorious and exhilarating sight."* And like the little boy who, when the school inspector asked him to give an example by way of explanation rather than define the word "splendid," promptly answered: "a fight." So, too, will I, if asked to illustrate the words "glorious and inspiring," promptly reply: "a Gaelic tournament."

In the second, the Canon captured the spirit of local combat that infused my love of the clash of the camáin in *Glenanaar.*

The novel is based in Doneraile and describes events around conspiracy trials that took place there. In it, an apparent outsider, a Yank, a dark and mysterious stranger, steps forward to lead the town's team to victory in a local derby in a struggle of Homeric proportions. That sight and sound of two teams striving for victory with every sinew are part of my earliest memories of Doneraile. The matches that I see now in my mind's eye are akin to that described in the great Canon's work. Here, he captures a scene in fiction that I have witnessed in reality a great many times:

> *"At three o'clock the teams were called to their places by their respective captains. There was a brief consultation with the referee, a coin was flung into the air, sides were taken, the winners turning their backs to the wind, and in a moment, one could only see that ball tossed hither and thither in the struggle, and a confused mass of men and camáns, as they fought fiercely for victory and the tide of the battle rolled uncertain here and there across the field. And the combatants were curiously silent. This, too, is a modern characteristic, and a wholesome one. Instead of the whoops and yells of olden times, the words of fierce encouragement or expostulation, the cry of victory, and the curse of defeat, one only saw the set faces and the flying figures, the victory snatched out of the hands of one, the defeat of the other retrieved, and the swift, tumultuous passion that swayed these young athletes as they strained every nerve in the all-important struggle for victory."*

Warm summer days, when the river croaked rather than murmured, was when bare legs were spattered with cleansing fluid as anxious

sheep were pummelled and washed in the sheep-dip by the river and then let run free again up the hill. We scurried from watching this contest of man, beast and a Jeyes fluid-smelling dip, drawn by the sound of ash on ash and the roar of the crowd beckoning us latecomers to hurry up. These were the sights and sounds of my early years – an idyllic youth, perhaps, never forgotten but faded somewhat now, a dream within a dream.

Yes! The Canon embodied our Ireland, our parish, our town and our sense of ourselves. He charted many a course. His own youth, with his memories of the funeral of the great Fenian Peter O'Neill, never left him and his message was always a simple one, belief in ourselves.

He dominated our lives in lots of ways. At school, the kindly Presentation sisters were forever reminding us of the Canon and his twice daily visits to the school and his almost legendary love of children.

I'm sad to admit that he never influenced me as regards schooling in the least. Indeed, the more I thought about school, the less I liked it. Not all the sweets, nor all of the moulding of marla (plasticine) could persuade me that bright sunny mornings were to be spent in the chalk-smelling indoors. On one occasion I banged my big toe so badly in my rush towards the door that I was limping and crying for days after. We went barefoot in summer and this state of pedal undress provides memories of trying to walk on aftergrass in the fields around town.

Another day, the poor nun, her patience exhausted, told me that Holy God wouldn't like me. Like the good queen, I was not amused and bolted, only to run headlong into a rather small matronly sister, a happening, which, for reasons of delicacy, I won't elaborate upon, made me realise that women, or at least nuns, are different from men.

Another morning comes to mind when we had lessons in the open air. The weather was fine and we were all relaxed, delighted and delighting in the company of blackbirds, thrushes and robins. The nun teaching us allowed me to sit in a chair she said belonged to the Canon. 'Maybe, you'll be a writer,' she said, with more hope than conviction. Maybe I haven't turned out in the way she hoped but I like to think that through my broadcasting I have been, and am, a spinner of dreams, with words as my yarn, and a painter of memories with those same words as my paint.

The Canon's grave was always a favourite visiting place for us young children. We coveted the glass wreath with its delicate white birds and flowers. We knew the words on his gravestone by heart:

"Where dwellest thou, Rabbi?

And Jesus said, Come and see"
We wondered and we wondered...

Convent Road where we lived also hosted Duffy's Circus in Jones's Field. There were more regular attractions. On Thursday evenings, a man driving his horse and cart came up the road shouting "fresh herrs, fresh herrs," not by way of a tribute to Germany but as a shorthand for selling fresh herring. He also sold ling which was as stiff as the clothes on a line on frosty nights.

One particular day, Granny's son, Dinny, loaded all of us children onto his donkey and cart and drove us to Annakisha Races. This was the greatest day in the year. Even if we never saw a race, and I, certainly can remember none, we saw what our children, even with multi-channel colour TV, will never see: strong men balancing iron wheels on finger-tips; knacky men eating, or at least swallowing, rats and razor-blades; thin men lying on nails; fat ladies telling fortunes, and so much more. And then, finally sated and sleepy, we jolted our way homewards with songs and sweets and memories to last beyond forever.

There were others, too, who strode colossal in their knowledge and dark suits on Mass morning, Sunday. There was, above all others, Pat Pigott, the tailor, who lived at the foot of Convent Road. He lived there with his wife, who wore dark clothes, his daughter, Maureen, and a little dog called Flossie. Pat was the first to enthuse me with stories of "The Canon". I can still remember the childhood fascination of watching his deft fingers snip, sew and stitch on Saturdays when we had no school and then, when I had my tea with the Pigotts, the lamp would be lit and he'd continue, 'I remember well,' he'd say, 'we brought the Canon to the tournament in the Horse Close in 1895 and after it, he went home, sat down, and wrote *Glenanaar.'* Perhaps he did. At all events there is no doubting that Canon Sheehan had a great enthusiasm for hurling.

Often too, in the summer evenings (they were always summer evenings), Pat, the Tailor, Flossie, the dog and others of us among his disciples, would listen to the Angelus on the tinkling convent bell and he would solemnly consult his pocket-watch and remark, rather astutely, how extraordinary it was that the Presentation Nuns who were enclosed, managed to know everything that went on in Doneraile.

Other names flit across the moonlight of memory. There was Walter A. Jones, the antiquarian and pharmacist for whom John B. Keane worked when "Jones Scour Specific" was a nationwide brand;

Jim Titteridge's shop where we bought ice cream, *The Beano, The Dandy* and *Ireland's Own*; Paul Mannix's bakery where the smell of warm fresh buns was only equalled by their eating. Then there was "Tommo's," that most lovable of pubs where gentle and simple people met on equal terms with the lords and ladies of Doneraile. Here, the Duhallow Hunt would gather to sip genteel stirrup-cups on autumn mornings. These were childhood autumns when frost rimmed the windows and horses snickered and danced, their flanks steaming like laundries, mornings when breaths like grey whistles thrust against the blue of the sky, the hounds leaping and enthusiastic forecasts of a quick or slow demise of a fox. Soon the riders and hounds clattered and padded towards Caherduggan or Saffron Hill or Byblox in pursuit of their wily quarry.

Serving Mass was my first public function. It was my introduction to performing in front of an audience and I relished the opportunity. We learnt to whisper in the dark, incense-smelling sacristy under the watchful eye of Mrs Kearney. We learnt to whisper and giggle in moderation as Fr O'Keeffe, a robust and cheerful curate, led the Rosary and Benediction at a rare old huntsman's gallop. There was too, a young curate, Fr Andrew Barry who often said second Mass on Sunday and then brought me with him to serve in Heatherside which then housed unfortunates who suffered from the curse of the time, TB or "consumption". I was told that the disease was catching and while I loved serving Mass, drinking the Matron's tea afterwards was a major complication. While visiting there, I drank from the left side of the cup as I figured that most people being right-handed would drink from the other side and the left side would be less likely to be infected. I never contracted TB so I must have been right.

I remember serving station Masses and even a death Mass where I saw a corpse for the first time. The memories of his eyes held shut by two English pennies remained with me for a long time. Another time I served Mass in a farmer's house where the daughters seemed very grown up and after the breakfast sang, *Drink to me only with Thine Eyes*. I never found out how Ben Johnson found his way to a Doneraile farmer's station Mass.

Another time I served Mass in a big house. It was Catholic, obviously. I was given breakfast afterwards in a cold, dank basement. Canon O'Connell, the Parish Priest, kind man that he was, insisted that I join him upstairs in the parlour for the tea and hard-boiled eggs. He was not impressed at the attempt to banish me to a lesser place. His description of the family as "Castle Catholics" was the first time I had heard that particular expression. We drove back to Doneraile in the calm dignity of Billy Finn's hackney car which had a blind back window. It wasn't the attempt to segregate me that upset me during that journey; it was the more prosaic fact that I didn't get a copper for my pains.

Canon O'Connell was parish priest of Doneraile for most of my time as an altar boy there. He had a reputation for stiffness and parishioners felt him aloof. I never found him either. The locals explained his remoteness by the fact that he had been a chaplain during the First World War and was shell-shocked. I often observed him twitching as he celebrated the first Mass of the morning. I can still hear the muted whisper of his *Introibo ad altare Dei* of some seventy-five years ago when the guttering candles lit his pale face and threw flickering shadows across a boy's first efforts to serve water and wine, and where wax spluttered in a cold stillness only broken by the Canon's classic Latin and the click of Mrs. Kearney's rosary beads.

He often invited me to his house, where his housekeeper, Miss Murphy, presided with a kind of distanced dignity and served only the best apple tarts. The garden was my special place. It was here that I often sat in Canon Sheehan's chair in the little arbour. Indeed, Canon O'Connell often reminded me of this distinguished predecessor and told me that the household had an atmosphere and that Canon Sheehan had left his mark.

It was years later that I would read the Canon's description of a fictional garden in *Under the Cedar and the Stars,* which bore strong resemblance to the one I recall from those far off days:

> *"It is a hortus conclusus et disseptus* (enclosed and protected garden). *It is a secluded spot, and in one particular angle, at the western end is walled in by high trees and shrubs, and you see only leafage and grasses, and the eye of God looking through the interminable azure. The monks' gardens bound it on the northern side; and here, in the long summer evenings, I hear the brothers chanting in alternate strophes the Rosary of Mary."*

This then was my garden, where my child's wonder evoked miracles all around me.

Home life in Doneraile was happy and I look back on my early childhood years with great fondness and a touch of wistfulness. My father features prominently in my recollections. And just as I can clearly conjure up the Canon's garden, so I recall vividly our own in Doneraile. My father loved to garden. It was his sanctuary in the evenings to plant, tend and then deliver the produce to us for eating.

He grew vegetables as staples for our dinner: cabbage and spuds to go with the bacon, but he also cultivated roses and cared for them as if they were children themselves. He was a quiet, contented man and the garden gave him an opportunity to enjoy the peace and tranquillity. When I describe him as quiet though, he wasn't totally so. He whistled and had an eerie knack of imitating bird calls and used to do so while digging and planting.

Family life was homely and warm. My father listened to the radio, a Philips set, in the morning as he shaved. My mother baked bread and apple tarts filling the house with rich smells that stimulated the digestive juices. A whiff of baking from a neighbour's house now transports me back through the years to those happy childhood times, just as the taste of madeleine's brought Marcel Proust back to memories of his childhood.

All children love treats and ours were cones and wafers bought in Titteridge's, Doneraile's ice-cream parlour. Miss O'Connell sold sweets and this was where we indulged our sweet tooths. In most cases though, life's little extra pleasures came from jam on well-buttered fresh bread or drinks of cool milk on a hot summer's day.

My father was a caring soul. He made and left sandwiches on the windowsill when we were out playing. We could come and graze on these as we wished. Life was simple enough but enjoyable. He would take me on his crossbar to matches in Buttervant and Mallow and these expeditions were to strengthen the foundations of a great love of Gaelic games.

Horses were one of my father's passions. He didn't gamble but he knew a good horse and handled them adeptly. He was skilled in breaking them and I've never fathomed where he garnered this very special ability. He was comfortable around horses and others valued his expertise. He bought a pony one time on behalf of his in-laws in Ballyshane. It was a black filly named "Molly" and we children took a great shine to her. He gathered all of his gear together and set out one morning and rode Molly all of the way to East Cork. It was a Don Quixote sort of adventure that brought him fifty miles south through east Cork. The journey home was a more prosaic bus ride.

Drama came in several forms. There were the touring groups, the fit-ups; Anew McMaster's was perhaps the most famous of these. The group arrived and over a few evenings held the town spellbound with performances of classics and contemporary favourites. Amateur performances, whether concerts, variety or dramatics, filled the long winter evenings and gave all of us the chance of a moment of local celebrity. These productions introduced me to the magic of the great playwrights and the storytelling power of acting.

My first stage performance took place shortly after I had mastered the basics of walking and talking. One of my cousins, Kitty, brought me to a performance from one of the fit-up companies that had trundled into town. I was there, not as an audience member but simply because if she hadn't taken me along, then she would have missed the show. There was a talent contest during the interval, a common enough occurrence during these shows. My cousin wasn't paying me the sort of attention that you need to give a wiry five-year-old. Suddenly, out of nowhere she saw me march onto the stage and perform what was probably the best, and only, rendition of *Baa Baa Black Sheep* that had ever been performed in that hall. I got a long and loud burst of applause that may have sparked a love of the public performance deep within me that has attempted to shine through since. It was one of my regrets that I never headed off with one of the fit-up companies and toured the towns and villages with them. Perhaps that yearning re-emerged in my charity walks through the highways and byways.

2 CHANGED UTTERLY

My father was taken ill towards the end
of 1946. It was sufficiently serious for
him to be confined to bed for an extended
time – something which was most unusual
for him as he had been a strong, healthy,
hardworking man ...

Confirmation Day, 1946.

AND THEN ALL OF a sudden the idyll that was Doneraile came to an end. It was December and I was ten years old. My father was told that he was being transferred to Charleville some 12 miles away. The move was swift and immediate. I don't believe that there was any special reason behind the move other than some bureaucratic decision made in some far off office that was to impose major change on one family's life.

We moved just before Christmas. I remember it well. Everything we owned was piled high on a truck. We followed behind in a taxi. Our friends and neighbours lined the street, some weeping, others in silence, waving to us as if we were setting out on a voyage to the furthest corner of the earth. Our taxi driver was Jacky Roche. He told us to watch for the two spires that signalled our approach to Charleville. In doing so, our taxi driver was echoing Marcel Proust's remembrance of the twin steeples of Martinville *"on which the setting sun was playing..."* For him it was a special pleasure; alas for us it was no such thing. It was deep in December and we had been plucked from the home we loved to the beginning of what was to prove a new and very different life.

We arrived at our first home in that town sometime in the evening of the 13th of December 1943. We had a flat over a bakery and I remember the smells of cooking bread and confectioneries rising up the stairs and through the very floorboards it seemed. The flat was small and I remember it being particularly cold when we arrived. This was during 'The Emergency,' as World War II was referred to, and a great many staples, including fuel, were in short supply. We had three rooms and large, draughty windows facing onto the main street. In my father's absence, it seemed a lonely and forlorn place. We did not complain though as we knew that there were millions of families worse off than us across blacked-out Europe.

My parents set to try and make the place more homely for Christmas. I remember that we didn't have a Christmas tree that year. My father put lighted candles in each of the tall windows and took us out onto the street to see them lit up, blurred by the condensation on the panes. That Christmas stands out for me for one other reason: I received as my Christmas present, Canon Sheehan's *Glenanaar*. For me it was more than a novel, it was a connection with the town I remembered and which I am still proud to call my home place.

Charleville church had the biggest crib that I had ever seen and on the outside was a statue of a camel. For me this was one of the most exotic things I had ever seen and most of all I wanted to ride it. And as any child with the capacity to turn a fantasy into reality, I climbed on board and started my imaginary journey across the deserts of Egypt. A cuff from the broad hand of the parish priest brought me back to earth in the cold, dark of Ireland. It brought me to his attention and he recruited me into his service as an altar boy.

We had to start rebuilding our lives over that winter of 1943-44. My father had to report for duty straight away suggesting that his transfer was the result of a shortage in Charleville barracks at the time. He had been a duty officer in the barracks in Doneraile while in the bigger town of Charleville, he had the typical duties of any guard. The barracks here was larger with two more guards and a wider range of duties to perform.

The New Year marked my return to school and the transition was made easier by the fact that I continued under the tutelage of the Christian Brothers. The Brothers decided that I should join third class, taught by a lay teacher by the name of Davy O'Riordan. His wife, Statia, had a pub across the road from our flat. This was a school of some eminence as it counted both Éamon de Valera and Archbishop Mannix of Melbourne as past pupils. Mr de Valera will re-enter my story later but it is worth saying something of Archbishop Daniel Mannix now.

He became the most prominent Australian cleric in the twentieth century. He was a complex character. While president of Maynooth College, he pushed for its acceptance as a constituent college of the newly-formed National University of Ireland. He discouraged students from taking notes and encouraged discussion of social issues such as temperance, co-operatives and social housing.

As someone who enjoyed learning by heart, or perhaps for the love of it, rather than from notes, his approach had a certain appeal to me. He greatly enhanced prospective priests' educational attainment and ensured that all achieved degree status. At the same time he could be extraordinarily strict and sent Kevin O'Higgins down for smoking. Indeed, over ninety per cent of students were teetotallers on graduation.

It was his political naivety though that was to be his undoing and resulted in his achieving ecclesiastical greatness far from these shores.

He welcomed Kings Edward VII and George V to Maynooth. Pádraig Pearse saw him as a "Castle Catholic" and questioned whether he was a friend of Irish nationalism. He was appointed bishop of Melbourne in 1912 and remained there for the rest of his life.

His beliefs were contradictory: he could support the declaration of World War I while strenuously opposing conscription. He was liberal in his views on a number of social issues but traditional and doctrinaire on others. He died in his ninety-ninth year in 1963. He was active and involved to the end and in his late years was to express his regret that he hadn't been more like Pope John XXIII. There is one thing more than any other that I take great consolation from and that is that both of these famous pupils, Éamon de Valera and Archbishop Daniel Mannix, lived to be happy and healthy nonagenarians – something that gives me hope.

I had developed a great interest in sport during my early years in Croke Park, Doneraile. My poor eyesight prevented me from actually playing and I'd been demoted to the side lines to mingle with the supporters, town pundits and those whose hurling was of the on-the-ditch variety. It is, perhaps, the gift of short-sightedness that from an early age I was filling in the action I couldn't see from comments snatched from others in the throes of a game. It developed my inner sporting eye and drew me to radio commentaries, dependant as they were on the ability of the commentator to transmit pictures through the wireless.

The Riordans, as I mentioned, lived and traded directly across the main street from our flat. And the Riordans had a wireless. They invited me into their house to listen to match broadcasts with the commentary by the even then well-established Micheál O'Hehir. It was from him that I learnt the magic of radio and its ability to transport listeners to a different place and paint intricate pictures in their minds. I could never have imagined then that I would one day end up working with this broadcasting icon in RTÉ.

We had a radio ourselves at the time but I cannot recall why I didn't listen to it at home with my father. I have memories of him listening to Lord Haw Haw, the Nazi propagandist's, broadcasts while he shaved before heading off to the barracks in the morning. I can only surmise that for some period our radio suffered valve failure or there wasn't a sufficient aerial to receive the match broadcasts. Regardless, I fostered my love of the broadcast match in Riordans and was treated to minerals and other such wonders a pub environment offered a young boy in those far away times.

It may seem strange that my father listened to German propaganda during World War II. He was not alone in so doing as I often heard the men of the town discussing Haw Haw's latest pronouncements in the shops or on the street corners. Radio Éireann offered a very limited service and it was severely censored and so we cruised the dial to supplement our listening and keep ourselves up to date with world events. For my part, I listened to the BBC Light service and owe it a deep debt of gratitude as it instilled in me a great recognition of what quality State broadcasting could offer.

During The Emergency, we knew that none of the protagonists was giving unbiased information about the progress of the war. As a nation we had only just emerged from a vicious War of Independence followed by a short-lived but equally cruel Civil War. We had suffered under the burden of a six-year trade war with Britain which had imposed severe social and economic pressure on farmers and manufacturers doing business with the North or the island of Britain. This had barely ended before the declaration of the Second World War and so Irish people looked on this external horror with trepidation. There were rumours of threats or actual invasions which, together with the bombings of Dublin, Belfast and to a much lesser degree but much closer to home, in Campile, Co.Wexford, reminded us all that there was a real and ever present danger.

There is a strange irony though that we should have ended up listening to William Joyce who became better known as Lord Haw Haw. His broadcasts were sprinkled with specific Irish references to place names, music or historical events. Even as children, we were surprised by this and local knowledge made the broadcasts all the more credible. There were mixed feelings about the war and people rejoiced when we heard that the British suffered losses on the battlefield or the high seas. Britain was still perceived as the enemy and memories of the Black-and-Tan atrocities encouraged the view that England's enemy was Ireland's friend.

The reality, though, was that the Irish government weighed up the threats more judiciously and as a neutral country, we were more neutral on the side of the Allies, especially after the Americans joined the war. Joyce though was a queer fish. Like our then Taoiseach, Éamon de Valera, he was born in the States but raised in Ireland. There the similarities end. Joyce's Irish home was in Galway and as a teenager he developed a great knowledge of the local terrain something that he put to fatal effect when he acted as an informer – giving information on Old IRA Volunteer movements to the British Army and the Black and Tans during the War of Independence.

The war impinged upon us in much more prosaic and mundane ways through rationing and restrictions of movement caused by fuel shortages. I stress though that as a young garsún growing up in

County Cork, my parents and the broader community protected us from hearing the worst of the horrors that befell our continent.

It was Davy O'Riordan, my teacher, who first whetted my appetite for poetry. He had a love of language and sought to imbue us with the same. We learnt, along with John Kells Ingrams, not to fear to speak of "Ninety-eight"; with Douglas Hyde, to voyage with Colmcille; to bid adieu to Belashanney and the winding banks of Erne with William Allingham; or experience the little waves of Breffney tumbling through our souls as Eva Gore Booth described. William Rooney, James Clarence Mangan, Aubrey de Vere and Thomas Moore became our ghostly classmates, guiding us on a journey of discovery around our own country, and through the trials and tribulations of our history. Our literary education spanned more than the Irish poetic canon, we studied the great bard, Shakespeare, himself, and from him, gained eyes upon the wider world of kings, courts and conspiracies as well as that all elusive emotion, love. Hearing these poems may well have inspired my own wanderlust that expressed itself in my future charity walks.

We boys knew little of our teacher's experience of love or romance. We learnt quickly, however, that he enjoyed the farmers' dances held, I think, on a Wednesday evening in the town. We knew that he had been dancing when, on the following morning, he came in and with barely a glance at the assembled fresh-faced boys, he told us to work on our own on spellings or some other simple tasks. He propped himself comfortably in his chair and napped until he felt able to face the rigours of the teaching day.

There was alcohol served at the farmers' dance – something that wasn't allowed at the Saturday one. I don't make any connection between our teacher's tired state and this additional information other than to provide as complete a picture as possible. I made good use of that and any other time we had for studying. I had a gift for learning poetry and I crammed my head with poems and plays as easily as I read comics. I find these stanzas surfacing suddenly, sparked by some familiar word or reminiscence, as if they were trapped in the attic of my mind like actors awaiting a cue.

There was a second teacher in that school who influenced me greatly and whose gift is still with me. It is something that has spanned nearly sixty years and conceivably opened up the possibility of the career that I now follow. Brother Ryan taught Irish while also training the school hurling team. This brother had a particular fondness for the language, he had a depth of knowledge about it and ensured that we boys spoke and wrote it correctly. He wasn't concerned only with grammar and structure but with Irish as a living language that spoke from the soul of the Irish people. Now I find that it's all mixed up, the different declensions, tenses and spelling. The language has now become a melange. At school, I enjoyed conjugating Irish verbs and using the correct form in sentences and essays.

The Confirmation Class of 1946 at Charleville CBS.

Brother Ryan's other role was as coach of the hurling team. I denied my short-sightedness sufficiently to put myself forward as right half back for our team. My boyish hurling focus was on leading the county team to victory in Croke Park in Dublin, delivering a fluent, moving and modest victory speech in both languages and holding supporters and opponents spellbound with my skill and panache on the field as well as off.

Unfortunately, my focus on success was more than over-balanced by my lack of focus without my glasses on the park. It was during a match in Kilmallock that this imbalance became all too obvious. In the thrill of the hunt for the sliotar, I inadvertently, in the words of Christy Mahon in Synge's *The Playboy of the Western World*, "*hit a blow on the ridge of his skull, laid him stretched out...,*" that is I floored another player with my flailing hurl. Compounding this offence was the fact that it was our own full-back that I stretched. Dangerous play perpetrated against an opponent commonly results in the referee applying a sanction against the offending player, it is much rarer that a referee is forced to put off a player for hitting one of his own team. I was ordered off but refused to go but eventually had to.

I remained obstinate though and refused to travel back to Charleville with the team in the back of a truck. Instead, I chose a more stylish form of transport and returned in Davey Ryan's hearse – eating ice-cream as we went. There is much that can be mined from this small incident. It showed that as a youngster I was willing to try and beat the odds even when they were stacked profoundly against me. What I recognise now in that young boy was a sense of justice and a challenging of authority – something that would recur at different stages in my life.

I would love to say that I was a great and dedicated scholar but I wasn't. Although I could learn by rote easily enough and I enjoyed the music of poetry and our own Irish language, I found the classroom confining and always yearned for the outside and the freedom that it promised. Teachers I remember still, such as Brothers McGee, Conway and Kennedy, were constantly correcting me for staring out the window where I found the intermittent pigeon flypast of greater interest than whatever was being taught to us at the time.

All of our play then was outdoors; there was no television to tempt us inside. We'd spend our times messing about at the river – fishing for sticklebacks, called "collies" locally, or anything else that we could catch. We built dams and imagined creating great lakes or water courses. Hides, too, were a never-ending attraction, building or finding some place that was secret and ours alone.

We had other diversions as we grew a little older and a great deal bolder. Young love continued to blossom in the springs and summers in Charleville and the courting couples were literal and metaphorical targets for our horseplay. We scoured the local countryside as meticulously as redcoats searching for fleeing rebels, seeking out couples locked in passionate and, in those days, illicit embraces. Depending on their passion and how oblivious they were to their surroundings, we'd sneak up on our prey and launch a sod at them. Very little passion will endure the belt of a wet sod on the side of the face. There then followed the chase as the young man vented his spleen at us while we ran chanting that we'd "tell his Ma."

And later, when we met these ardent young men on the way to Mass, or for a return assignation, we couldn't resist the chance to yell "Nobber" at them – this being the local slang for a young lover. But sometimes the sod rebounds and smacks you back in the face, even if it is in a metaphorical way. Some thirty years later, I was taking to the stage in Hunter College, New York, where I was due to compere a concert when I was assailed by the heckle "Nobber!" from the back of the auditorium. We two alone, the heckler and the heckled, knew the provenance and meaning of the insult. We settled our differences with reminiscences and a pint afterwards.

Religion played an important part in the life of the community as well as in our family. We were Catholic and brought up to be proud of our faith and public in its practice. There was no rancour between different faiths though. Indeed, some young Protestant boys attended our Catholic school without any difference emerging. The only annoyance was that they were free to play and sport outside our classroom window while we, of the 'true faith', applied ourselves to learning our catechism by rote.

The church helped my transition from Doneraile to Charleville. It was through the fraternity of the altar boys that I made new friends and gained playmates for the remaining years of childhood. I was introduced to young lads then, many of whom I still meet from time to time. I recall people like Kevin Owens, whose father and uncle worked with the Oriel Press. A lad named Mickey Flynn and myself used to make wooden revolvers together to add some authenticity to our re-enactments of cowboy gunfights, the storylines for which were gleaned from the local picture shows. One of our number then, Dan O'Mahony, went on to hurl for Cork – a truly great hurler, sadly no longer with us.

One young lad who was most influential was Noel Tarrant. His family had a gramophone and we became close through playing his family record collection. We'd listen to the great tenors of the time, people like Mario Lanza or more locally John Count McCormack or Josef Locke, who was a great favourite although we only came to his recordings after the war. This stimulated my interest in singing and music – something that has stayed with me ever since. Michael O'Duffy, the Derry tenor, was gaining a reputation for himself at that time and we enjoyed his beautiful version of the Thomas Moore ballad, *Love Thee Dearest*. Funnily enough, I wasn't too interested in the traditional Irish music at that time as my main musical influences came from the Light station on the BBC. Concerts in the local hall had tenors topping the bill, making them the celebrities of our time.

Serving as an altar boy introduced me to more than friends though.

Interviewing school friend, and gramophone owner, the late Noel Tarrant, co-author of the *Charleville Review*, at the Deerpark Hotel in the mid-1970s.

It was also my first introduction to the reality of death and all of the ritual that surrounds a passing. As we lived close to the church, I was asked to light the candles around the coffin before the ceremonies began. I was on my own with nothing but a vivid young boy's imagination and the countless ghosts that it would summon until others arrived to break the spell. Canon Burke was the parish priest at the time and had a reputation for being severe. He was nonetheless a pious man. We had moved into a proper house by this stage, into "The Turrets", close to the church and presbytery and we could hear the Canon late at night pacing the garden while reciting the Rosary aloud.

I recall I was assigned communion-plate duty during one Sunday Mass. The Canon was distributing the communion wafers and my job was to hold the communion plate beneath the chin of the person receiving the sacrament to ensure that no crumbs of the sacred host fell on the ground. A woman approached with her lips rouged with lipstick and wearing slacks. The Canon was incensed. 'Madam,' he intoned, 'Take off that stuff from your lips and take off your trousers – we'll have no women wearing those in the house of the Lord.' The poor woman fled in a state of deep mortification.

We were somewhat elevated altar boys in Charleville as we wore red soutanes while serving Mass on days other than those of fasting and abstinence. We owed our superior garb to the fact that one of the priests, Dr Browne, was a doctor of divinity and thus entitled to this additional honour. He was a man with an interesting past. He had served as a chaplain in World War I and was yet another sufferer of post-traumatic stress disorder, although we didn't know it as such, while he ministered in our parish. This demonstrated itself in a number of ways. He disliked men kneeling on one knee behind the pillars or at the back of the church and he'd call out to them: 'Come out ye one-eyed gunners.'

He may well have been referring to Cornelius Healy, a fellow Cork man, who had lost an eye. After de Valera declared the ceasefire that ended the Civil War, Con Healy decided to carry the war on alone. He shouldered a sub-machine gun and avoided capture for a further five years until his house, near Cork, was surrounded and he was captured. Doubtless the men perched on one knee reminded him of the snipers he faced in the trenches. Dr Browne's brother was the famous Fr Frank Browne, the photographer whose pictures captured life in Ireland in the early part of the twentieth century. He is best remembered for his images of the RMS Titanic, taken on board before his disembarkation from the ill-fated liner on her last port of call, Queenstown, now Cobh.

Politics also came to Charleville. In 1944, the government of the day fell following the defeat of a vote on the Transport Bill, necessitating a general election. Éamon de Valera was the Taoiseach and in his prime. He came to Charleville campaigning. In those days, the political rally was key to energising support and were events in themselves. There was usually a procession through the main street, with the banners, flags, pipers – all lit by burning barrels of tar. Dev addressed the crowd without the aid of a megaphone. His platform was the back of a truck on the main street. Small as I was, I managed to squirm my way to the front of the throng and climbed onto the truck.

I was close enough to shake hands with Seán Moylan and even asked for his autograph but was curtly dismissed and told to have some sense. I then rode my luck a little further and shook the great man's hand. I didn't have the opportunity to address him before a burly guard collared me and brought me unceremoniously to earth. As ill-luck would have it, the guard was my own father, and I was sent home with a flea in my ear. As a guard's son, I was expected to be, like Caesar's wife, above suspicion. It wasn't until I read Robert Grave's great book, *I, Claudius,* that I realised that as a child I was more like Livia, the wife of Caesar Augustus, whose deviousness knew few bounds. I realised that if you couldn't be good, then you had to make sure that you were never caught!

Life in Charleville improved for us as the years progressed. The war ended and previously rationed goods began to return to the shop shelves. Our house in The Turrets was, and remains, one of a pleasant terrace of two-storey houses with a central front door with windows on either side. Ours was a friendly terrace. Miss Spillane, a national school teacher, lived next door. Mr and Mrs Horan lived there too – she had been housekeeper to Bishop O'Brien, the famous nationalist Bishop of Limerick. The Burkes lived a few doors down from us and it was in their kitchen that I listened to their radio and heard Éamon de Valera's famous riposte to Winston Churchill's post-World War II address.

There were shortages but we negotiated these as best we could. There was a national fuel shortage during and immediately after the war. My father met our fuel needs by buying a tree from one of the local farmers. He then felled it and chopped it into logs. Some of his friends locally brought the wood home to us with a pony and butts. A tree kept us warm for a year.

Life in the '40s and '50s is often painted as grey and dismal. It wasn't so for young people like me growing up in a rural town in Cork. We had less spare time as we had school on Saturday and household duties, religious practices and getting from A to B ate into our spare time. Radio was the main source of outside entertainment at home and I personally developed a great fondness for the BBC Light station programmes, *Music while you work* and *Grand Hotel* - the latter specialising in Palm Court music – the light, lyrical melodies that gained prominence in the '20s and '30s before the war.

The '40s and '50s were part of Cinema's golden era and, despite occasional objections, Hollywood came to Charleville in the form of actors such as Gary Cooper, Bing Crosby, Betty Grable and our own Maureen O'Hara. The weekly "flicks" fired our imaginations and created a hunger to experience the wide world beyond the parish boundary. Live entertainment was more common and easier to access then. Amateur dramatics took off in Ireland following the War of Independence and local communities enthusiastically performed plays and held variety concerts throughout the winter evenings.

These performances were punctuated by visits from the professional performers and fit-ups. These were high-quality, professional productions that brought us magic and brilliance in the dark of a rural winter. Their repertoire included everything from Shakespeare's tragedies to Lennox Robinson's farces. Some of the great names of the time visited either in fit-ups or variety troupes. I remember well Jimmy O'Dea, Hal Roche and Maureen Potter in variety performances and actors such as Milo O'Shea, John Cowley, Barry Cassin and Moira Deady.

And then my life changed utterly. My father was taken ill towards the end of 1946. It was sufficiently serious for him to be confined to bed for an extended time – something which was most unusual for him as he had been a strong, healthy, hardworking man. He rallied early in 1947, his recovery coinciding with one of the worst winters in living memory and, indeed, one of the worst I have experienced since. We were aware of changes that symptomized an underlying malaise. He no longer cycled and his breathing had become heavy and laboured.

Yet, as I remember, he was in good humour. I recall him reading a news report to us about the running aground and sinking of the SS Irish Plane off the Ballyshane coast. The ship suffered engine problems during a severe storm and, despite the crew's best efforts, drifted towards the shore and ran aground. For some time she stood upright on the rocks beside the cliffs. The local rescue services were able to string a line from the cliff top to the ship and the crew used this to cross to safety.

The sinking led to many tales, one notable one being an account given by one of the sailors of the terrible event. He was wakened from his sleep by an almighty jolt as the boat hit the rocks. He described the incident thus: 'I jumped out of my bunk and looked out of the porthole and when I saw a cow staring in at me, I knew that there was something wrong.'

This was a memorable event made more so by our having local knowledge; it was our mother's family's home, and so I was able to embellish the tale with local detail when retelling it in school. Some of the detail was true but there were additional "facts", such as my knowing the captain well, which were pure make-believe. The event is firmly fixed in our extended family memory as the salvage crew brought considerable business to the local economy buying all of their provisions such as potatoes, cabbage and eggs from the locals. My uncle's pigs benefitted too as they dined on the leftovers.

I still have a vivid recollection of my father reading because it is one of the last memories I have of him as a more or less healthy, contented man, at peace with his family and the world. My father's remission was short and, within a few months, he was confined to his bed again. The local doctor, Dr Magner, attended him and made it clear that he didn't expect him to pull through his illness. My father declined rapidly and finally slipped away.

He died in the evening of what had been a sunny, bright 22nd of May. His breathing had been heavy and laboured and the quiet of his room was broken only by the quietly murmured prayers of a good nun, Mother Francis, who had kept a vigil beside his bed. This nun was to prove to be a great practical help to me a few years later. I was beside him as he passed away and knew when I touched his hand without any response that his time had come. His was an untimely death: he was only 51. I miss him to this day and even now as I write these lines I can recall the terrible sense of loss, loneliness and deep, deep sorrow that I felt then. I find consolation in the words of Alfred Lord Tennyson in his evocative poem, *Crossing the Bar:*

> *"Sunset and evening star,*
> *And one clear call for me!*
> *And may there be no moaning of the bar,*
> *When I put out to sea,*
>
> *"But such a tide as moving seems asleep,*
> *Too full for sound and foam,*
> *When that which drew from out the boundless deep*
> *Turns again for home.*
>
> *"Twilight and evening bell,*
> *And after that the dark!*

And may there be no sadness of farewell,
When I embark;

"For tho' from out our bourne of Time and Place
The flood may bear me far,
I hope to see my Pilot face to face
When I have crossed the bar".

Yet as I grow older and thus closer to my own crossing, I still have no idea of what awaits us on the other side.

While his passing was gentle and dignified, I was not prepared for the wave of change that would follow so swiftly. Some of my father's people had travelled from Kerry before his final hours and more followed on his death. I did not know these people well and, in many cases, not at all. So, in addition to dealing with my loss, I had to cope with an influx of strangers. They brought with them different customs, one being the use of the Kerry Caoine in lamenting my father. This was a chilling, arresting sound that reverberated around our sad house. It was the one and only time I've heard this form of lamentation and its sound has stuck with me.

We bade farewell to our father in a stiff and formal way with a short kiss on his cold lips and a brief touch of his hands. I recall vividly the terror I felt as a black cowl was brought over my father's head covering his face. My mother clung to his hand as long as she could until eventually she, too, was led away from his side.

The funeral was a large affair with a big turnout from the Gardaí and the community generally. The top brass was represented and I remember there was someone down from Dublin for the ceremony. My father was well liked, even loved I'd say, in the community and it was these people rather than the figures of authority from the Gardaí that helped us through that terrible time.

The events immediately after the funeral remain in my memory most vividly and still cause feelings of pain and anger. The first ignoble act was one of my relatives from Kerry insisting on taking my father's bicycle and bringing it home with him. It was a petty act that still rankles as he had no claim to it, nor could it have had any particular sentimental value as we'd had little or no contact with these people until then. Indeed, we had little to do with them thereafter.

Perhaps the greater offence was caused by the Gardaí themselves. A guard arrived at our house very shortly after the funeral. We didn't know him and he was officious and unempathetic. He took my father's uniform from the wardrobe, gathering up some extra buttons from the dressing table as he did so. Then, without ceremony, he took my mother's most valued keepsake of my father, his notebook. Any other small items from my father's time as a member of An Garda Síochána were taken, leaving us without one single tangible memento of that time.

My father's death left us in a perilous state. My mother wept frequently and was lost without her rock. She wore black mourning clothes while we children wore a small black armband. The house was silenced and a black veil put over the radio which remained quiet for a year. It was a lonely place and permeated with a fear of hard times and poverty.

My mother was entitled to a paltry pension but actually getting it took perseverance and bowing and scraping before the Force's bureaucracy. A solicitor acted as the superintendent in Mallow. This was common then and all of his legal peculiarities had to be placated before money was released. I was aware that I was now the eldest child and as such, was frequently told to be "the man of the house" or to "look after your mother." Others conveyed the same meaning but in a more subtle form when they commented, "you're a great comfort and support to your mother."

I felt pressurised as I believed I was doing little to fulfil this new role that had suddenly fallen upon my teenage shoulders. I knew, too, that it cost my mother a lot to feed, clothe and educate us and, although no one hinted at this, least of all my mother or sisters, I felt myself to be a burden. A solution magically presented itself in the form of a possible vocation to the religious life.

A local man had spoken to a brother recruiting on behalf of the Presentation Brothers and indicated that I had the qualities needed to become a brother. It was also apparent that this was an offer that my family was unlikely to refuse. The brother who acted as recruiting officer painted a picture of an idyllic life with swimming pools, sports, and hikes through the fields to the seaside. Coupled with this was the possibility, when the time came, of taking the cloth and becoming a great teacher or missionary, depending on where God chose to call me to. I would be fed as befitted a future soldier of Christ and live a joyous communal life with my classmates.

The proposition had great appeal for my mother, too. It meant that she would have one less child to feed, clothe and look after. There was an attraction, too, in the safety that the seminary life offered. It was going to be hard for her to bring up a teenager on her own without my father's support and guidance. The brothers appeared to offer a practical alternative. The arguments strongly favoured committing to the Brothers and so I signed up for a life of religion away from home.

This was the summer of 1947, a few short months after my father's passing. I believed I was doing what he would have wanted and this apparent blessing gave me strength to carry on. My new station in life required a new wardrobe and I was bought, among other things, a hurley, a red football jersey, two clerical black suits and a daily Roman missal. I gathered these and my other possessions into a battered suitcase and took the bus to Passage West, leaving my mother and sisters weeping at home. It was only a short journey from Charleville to St Teresa's, the juniorate, but it was sufficient to mark the end of one life and the beginning of a dramatically different one.

Loneliness characterised my first few months in the juniorate. I recall crying myself to sleep in the dormitories where the only other sound was the muffled sobs of the other boys. It was tough but with the kindness and help of the Brothers, especially Brother de Sales, I settled into the daily and weekly routine that was to define our lives while we were scholars there.

As would be expected in a Catholic religious institution, Sunday Mass was a pivotal event in our week. We walked in a crocodile formation to the parish church in Passage. On the fourteenth Sunday after Pentecost, we heard Fr Seamus O'Flynn preach for the first time. He was no ordinary preacher. Unknown to us boys, Fr O'Flynn was a social innovator. He believed that Shakespeare offered children a route to connect with their emotions and gain insights into their true selves.

He set up a cross between a youth club and a theatre in an old hay loft over a small sweet factory in Shandon in Cork City. He called it "The Loft" and in it he used the performance of The Bard's plays, speeches and sonnets to build the confidence and self-belief of poor young children from his parish. He is reputed to have helped people overcome problems caused by stammering, shyness and poor diction. He schooled many of the actors who graced Cork's stages, professionals and amateurs, including Joe Lynch. Gus (AA) Healy was a prominent dentist and Fianna Fáil TD for Cork who attributed his success to Fr O'Flynn's help in overcoming a disability that resulted from a childhood accident.

Fr O'Flynn's delivery was spellbinding and dramatic. He lived his sermons and I found myself caught up in them as if watching a film or a play. He linked the words of the New Testament with the congregation and contrasted the simple needs of the birds of the air and the egregious demands of some of the parishioners seated below him.

I was mesmerised by his preaching and his ability to hold the attention of the usually fidgety mass goers. Shortly afterwards, following Confession, I got chatting to him and he enquired where

I was from. On hearing I was a Charleville man, he began reciting verses by the great Irish poet, Seán Clárach MacDomhnaill. He was once regarded as the greatest of the River Maigue poets and that circle of poets met occasionally in his home in Charleville. Fr O'Flynn followed his recitation by asking if I liked the works of William Shakespeare. I said I did and he then decided that he would call upon me and the other boys in St Teresa's the following week.

I struggled with Euclidean geometry and it was as Greek to me as was the man himself. Brother Aenghus was charged with teaching us mathematics and I dreaded his Monday morning classes in particular. I had told Fr O'Flynn that we were studying *Henry IV, Part One* and he was keen to give us the benefit of his extensive knowledge of, and insights into, this masterpiece.

I contrived that he would so do on Monday mornings and so the great Shakespearean scholar entered our classroom through the French doors, proclaiming the opening lines of *Henry IV Part One* enthralling us boys while irritating Br. Aenghus greatly. Fr O'Flynn was to visit us regularly and opened up to us the wonder of Shakespeare's writing. He brought the play to life and showed us how the characters developed and grew. He showed us how Shakespeare's

Playing guitar on stage at the Parochial Hall, Charleville, with Mrs Connelly, accompanist, Kevin Owen and Tom McAuliffe.

text was still relevant and drew lessons about people's behaviour that resonated with a class of 15-year-old boys.

I learnt much from that great priest, especially an appreciation of Shakespeare and drama generally. It came as no surprise to me that he was featured in a BBC television documentary, *It Happened to Me*. RTÉ chose Fr O'Flynn as one of the people of the Millennium 2000.

While I may not have learnt much algebra or geometry, I did recognise the importance of bartering. I found writing easy and enjoyable and frequently wrote four compositions on the same topic in exchange for others doing those exercises I found more difficult. We spoke Irish throughout and grew to love its richness and poetic beauty. We studied the writings of many of our great scholars and leaders in our native tongue and developed a special appreciation of its worth. I'm still moved by the beauty of one of the final paragraphs in Pádraig Pearse's short story, *Eoghainín na* nÉan describing how the young boy, dying from consumption, wants to migrate with the swallows that have been his companions during his illness.

> *"'A mháthair,' arsa Eoghainín, 'tá siad ag glaoch orm.' 'Tar uait go dtí an tír a mbíonn an ghrian ag soilsiú i gcónaí ann—tar uait, a Eoghainín, thar na farraigíbh fraochda go dtí tír an tsolais—tar uait, a Eoghainín na nÉan!'*
>
> *'Ní fhéadaim iad a eiteach. Beannacht agat, a mháithrín—mo mhíle míle beannacht agat, a mháithrín mo chroí. Táim ag imeacht uait . . . thar na farraigíbh fraochda . . . go dtí an tír ina mbíonn sé ina shamhradh i gcónaí.'*
>
> *Lig sé a cheann siar ar ghualainn a mháthar agus chuir sé osna as. Cluineadh gol mná san áit uaignigh úd—gol máthar ag caoineadh a páiste.*
>
> *Bhí Eoghainín imithe i bhfochair na bhfáinleog'."*

> *"'Mother,' said Eoghainín, 'they are calling to me.' 'Come away with us to a country where the sun is always shining – come with us Eoghainín, across the wild seas to that sunny land – come with us, little Eoghan of the birds!'*
>
> *'I cannot deny them. Bless you dear mother – my thousand, thousand blessings to you dear mother of my heart. I am going with them ...over the wild sea... to the land where it is summer always.'*
>
> *He put his head on his mother's shoulder and let forth a sigh. There was heard a woman crying in that lonely place – the tears of a mother mourning her child.*
>
> *Eoghainín was gone with the swallows."*

This story moved me at the time and reminded me of my own bereavement less than a year before. I found consolation in the intensity of the shared emotion and recognised the great power of a well-told tale.

On passing the Intermediate Certificate, I was transferred to the Presentation Brothers' Novitiate, Mount St Joseph, at the top of Blarney Street in Cork. This is an imposing red-brick building somewhat removed from the street, with heavy wrought-iron gates and solid granite walls. This was a more austere world with an emphasis on the spiritual rather than the physical world. Bedtime was 9.00p.m. and we drifted off to sleep in summer time to the sound of children laughing and calling to each other outside the walls. We washed in cold water in the morning - we rose early, at 5.30 – and then filed to Mass.

We were warned to avoid all occasions of sin even when we had no idea what these meant. We were alerted constantly to the dangers of "particular friendships" and the need to maintain "custody of the eyes." We were taught how to shake hands modestly with young women. Unfortunately, this was theoretical rather than practical as I never had the opportunity to put this skill into practice while I was in the Novitiate. Our reading was strictly controlled and restricted in the main to the lives of the saints, although we did manage to steal an occasional glance at *The Cork Examiner* on Mondays for the sports results.

I gradually became disillusioned with life in the Novitiate. There was no one reason and much of my time there was made as pleasant as it could be by the brothers, particularly the older ones. Old Brother Martin stands out in my memory as an unworldly saintly man who devoted much of his time to prayer in the chapel. I had spent a great deal of time with the Presentation Brothers but realised that their life wasn't for me and, despite my best efforts, I couldn't find a vocation to the religious life within me.

And so, I made an appointment with Brother Benignus who was master of the novices and told him that I wanted to leave. Our conversation was brief. I told him that I wasn't cut out for the religious life. He asked only one question: 'What will your mother say?' I said I didn't really care at this stage and that I was sure that she would come around to the idea. Once certain that my decision was final, he shook my hand and bade me a speedy farewell.

My parting was accomplished with little ceremony. The brothers packed my possessions into my case and brought me to the bus station where they gave me a £5 note and sent me home to Charleville and a warm welcome from my family. There were no spoken recriminations but perhaps there were subtle ones: I was made wear my two bible-black suits until they were well and truly worn out.

Charleville was much the same on my return as when I had left it. We now lived in 45, Holy Cross Place. My mother struggled to survive on her paltry income and tried to supplement it in whatever way she could. At one stage she opened a small shop operating through the front window of the house. She sold smaller items, like cigarettes, in demand locally. There was insufficient business and so she had to give up that idea.

I felt the financial pressure in the house. The comments that I was the man of the house struck home and I wanted to live up to that responsibility. I felt, too, that I owed something to my family as, by not staying in the Novitiate, I had added an extra mouth to feed and body to clothe and keep warm and well. I determined that I should get a job and pay my way as best I could.

Summer

Ballyshane was my second, or holiday, childhood home. It was not the same as the holiday homes that pepper the countryside now, many of which have their origins in the splurges and excesses of the Celtic Tiger. No, this was the traditional holiday base of the young townie that was sent, in my case willingly, to spend a greater proportion of the summer out from under their mother's feet at the rural ancestral farm where there was space to play and an infinity of work to be helped with. My mother's family, the Cashman's, had a decent farm with a good mix of crops and livestock. It yielded an adequate living.

Charleville and Ballyshane are linked inextricably in my memories, one a sometimes winter and the other a perpetual summer of boyhood and early manhood. The former symbolised school and work days while the latter remains a patchwork of sun-flecked and sea-splashed summer memories. Ballyshane was my golden age when I came as close to true freedom as I ever had.

The holidays always began in more or less the same way in my childhood days. They started with a bus trip to Cork city and at Grand Parade I mingled with other travellers, messenger boys and bus conductors and inspectors enunciating the names of familiar and far-off places, a litany of the known and the tantalising: "Whitegate, stopping at Carrigtwohill, Midleton and any other stops deemed necessary." We rushed to our bus. The conductor helped those putting bikes and bags on the roof while Paddy O'Connor, the driver, waited until we were all on board.

We made our way through the traffic of the South Mall passing on our left the famed Arcadia Ballroom, across from the railway station with its puffing steam engines and shrieking whistles. We stopped in Carrigtwohill, well known for the quality of its hurlers. Then we proceeded down the opulent main street of Midleton, bearing right for Ballinacurra, passing on the way the convent where my mother went to school. My heart pounded as the bus neared Whitewell Cross where I alighted to be greeted by my cousins, waiting in the pony and trap ready to bring me the rest of the road.

'Sit up now,' my cousin instructed as we reached the first hill and we sat forward in the trap to make it easier for the climbing pony. I watched the familiar landmarks slip by. The scent of newly-scythed hay joined other summer smells to fill my nostrils and stimulate comforting memories. Uninterested cattle chewed the cud and watched our passing. Dogs barked us onwards and from behind Curtins' gate, the grey and white gander stretched his neck in silent hiss – standing sentinel as many of his species had done in Roman times.

And then, as if by magic, I had my first glimpse of the sea reflecting the summer evening light. This then was Ballyshane and, with a sharp turn right at Croisairín, the pony, who seemed to know she was now home, trotted purposefully in the boreen, the middle of which was summer green and we were in the yard for the annual warm welcome and the sense that everything was just as I had left it the year before.

This was a home from home. Here, my stash of well-thumbed, much-loved books was once again delved into. The blue cover of *The Lights of Leaca Bán* faded and ragged, the bulky *Percy the Schoolboy Baronet,* a copy of *Blackcock's Feather,* like the one I had in Charleville and old editions of *Masterman Ready* and *Mr Midshipman Easy* sat silently side by side.

I always brought *Flowers from Many Gardens* with me, an anthology of poetry published by the Christian Brothers. It bore the names of previous owners, a testimony to book recycling, "James Lysaght, Main Street, Doneraile, Co. Cork," "Harry O'Grady, Mallow Road, Doneraile," those of my two cousins, Kitty and Maurice Duhig, and, of course, my own name written and dated no fewer than eleven times from 12.9.1946 up to 23.10.1957 and a grand address that terminated on "The World" and the "Universe" – no crisis of identity possible there.

The house was long, single-storeyed and thatched, its gable end facing the road. The hall door, not often opened, faced the garden. The back door, fronted by a portico, faced onto the farmyard. I describe it as single-storeyed, but there was a loft, approached by a narrow stairs leading to two small rooms that were above the kitchen. The kitchen was the domain of my two aunts, my cousin's mother, Maggie, and her unmarried sister, Jo, either of whom would trim the oil lamp on the wall near the only window in the room. I mention this only because soon after my epic day travelling, and after darkness drifted across the land, rest was invited to the soundtrack of sticks crackling on an open fire and the murmur of Hail Marys from the nightly Rosary. My uncle Jim, my favourite person but not my real uncle, married to my aunt Maggie, would soon leave the kitchen and retire to what I called the middle-room.

Beyond this and up a little hallway was the parlour, dark and unused, filled with the faded, desiccated opulence of a dark-coloured chiffonier, a round table and a large sofa. Ancestors' photographs stared down severely on the younger ones who ventured the occasional, fearful, upward glance. The fire was only lit for breakfast for the parish priest at the station Mass. You went through this unlived place to the upper room where my Aunt Jo slept in spinster isolation.

The hallway linking the two ends of the house housed a long-dead resident: an ageless stuffed pheasant in a glass case standing on a table. Above him an old framed print showed a cavalry regiment from the British Army charging on to inevitable and timeless glory. The pheasant shook eerily each time you tapped his glass casket.

The garden was a haven where I hid under currant bushes and ate the crop above, like some bird that gorged itself until it could no longer move. This garden was where, long ago now, my Aunt Jo first heard the banshee. 'She cried all the way into the garden from as far away as the Croisairín. She was like a woman in great sadness, her wail rising and falling and it all happened in the middle of the day.' Our father died not long afterwards.

It was in this house that many of my ancestors died, many before their time, in an era when consumption "had no pity on blue eyes and golden hair."

There were pictures of a gentle-looking young man, my Uncle Thomas, called "Sonny," who died in his youth and who seemed to gaze wistfully towards a future that never was. My grandmother, Catherine, was also there, dead long before her time and leaving her husband and young family desolate. She had, however, gained a reprieve before. My grandfather, beside himself with grief, sent for a local curate who came on horseback from Aghada to pray over her. As my mother once told me, he was thought to be a man of great spiritual powers and prayed for a long time. My grandmother's days were briefly extended but at a price. She recovered, but a valuable young colt died in the stables and, as my brother said, 'The Lord gave and the Lord took away.'

My mother, youngest of the Cashman family in Ballyshane, remembered a barbaric and cruel custom, that of removing young children from the environs of the dying. When my grandmother subsequently died, her little family was removed to the cold yard in their night-clothes. Her journey from this life to the next was undisturbed. Then the clocks were stopped, the mirrors were covered. Time and place were out of joint and this time no one was born to set it right.

There was a strange, grim story of the death of my Uncle Jamesy. He was buried with all due propriety in the family graveyard in Inch. As my mother told it, there was a custom that they, the spirits of the dead, would come back to their home on the first Saturday night after their death.

Anyway, they were all kneeling, saying the Rosary around the fire on the first Saturday night after uncle Jamesy's death when they heard the sound of horses and a carriage coming into the yard. 'We were all silent, there was a step, the latch of the kitchen door was lifted, dropped and then the steps retreated and the carriage, or whatever it was, left and headed towards Croisairín. No one said a word!' I'm not surprised and have no comment one way or another. Be all this as it may, that house had its mysteries and could be a chilling place and I spent many a sleepless night listening to the ticking of the kitchen clock and my heart beating in time.

One experience I had is related but yet removed from Ballyshane. It occurred when another of my aunts, who had been a nurse in Dublin, became ill at the beginning of 1946 and my father, not so well himself, went to Dublin. On the night before her death we - my sisters, Kitty and Mary, and myself - were all in bed in my mother's room in Charleville. The Rosary was being said when I heard a most dreadful crying around the house which went on for a seemingly long time. My mother blessed herself and said, 'Your aunt is dead,' and she was. Later on, nothing would persuade my mother that anything other than the banshee had come to warn us. That all happened in late February 1946 and I have never forgotten it.

These weren't gloomy and sinister holidays though; there were sports days when young men strove with might and main to win cycle races, donkey derbies, pillow fights and a long-distance run from Ballinrostig Church to the sports field. I saw one young man spit blood as he won, while Cuck Maguire, a local character and noted reciter, stood on the ditch and without invitation incanted:

> *"Did they dare to slay Hugh O'Neill?*
> *Yes, they slew with poison him they feared to meet with steel."*

These lines are taken from Thomas Davis's lament for the *Death of Eoghan Ruadh O'Neill*. I also recall when a neighbour of ours, Pad Garde, wept openly as he recited with great vehemence *The Drunkard's Dream*.

Ballyshane introduced me to life's realities. We were called on to help out with the work around the garden and the farm. The house had a vegetable garden that produced the vegetables and potatoes we ate for dinner. I remember a pig being slaughtered in the yard... the squeals, the blood and guts. I don't recall objecting to the bacon that formed the central part of our dinner sometime later. We ate everything – head, ears, the lot! My aunts churned butter and we drew water from the well in the yard. This was a proper well with a bucket and pulley for drawing water. The toilet was an outside one. We washed in old enamel tubs on the occasions when washing was essential.

The glad and sad commingled in those summers of the 1940s and the 1950s. We children knew our place and addressed adults as Mr, Mrs or Miss, as appropriate, and the old order seemed written in stone. My aunt employed a servant boy and I noted that he had to eat his meals separately from the family.

This was the end of the era of the travelling man or woman. Never beggars, they walked the roads of east Cork from town to town, village to village and were generally welcomed wherever they went. I suppose they were like oral newspapers bearing with them the local news from parish to parish. Gerry Mullane was one such man. The dogs didn't even bark when he came into the yard with news of cousins in Ballymacoda or haymaking in Churchtown South. He spent many a summer evening by the hob listening to Vincent Kelly telling stories or my Uncle Batt playing the accordion or the Jew's harp.

Night was spent in a shakedown in the barn and before he left after a hearty breakfast, he was urged to, 'Call again' and, 'Tell our cousins in Warren we were asking for them and the old sow produced a great litter.' Later, if and when any traveller became old and infirm, they were visited in the local hospital in Midleton and they were never buried without being remembered.

Other callers were of a more worldly nature. These, like the "Jew man", arrived in due season bearing with them ladies' cross-over aprons, straw hats, blouses, trousers, artificial flowers, statues of the Child of Prague, mouse-traps and other sundry supplies for farmers' wives. They were welcomed in a business-like way, laying their wares on the kitchen table or opening large suitcases on the kitchen floor.

Sunday Mass in Ballinrostig when we sat in the Cashman family seat was much cherished by the older generation. The adults travelled in the pony and trap while we generally walked across the fields and on the roads, joining in with young Kellys and others on our way. The church boasted three aisles. We sat sideways to the altar in the seat our grandfather paid for, while across from us the Kellys from Ballyshane sat in their seat. Miss Kelly, with chin on hand, gazed haughtily across the altar. Mr Eugene, so known, wore a summer blazer and slacks.

My Uncle Jim sat on the outside of his seat, looking spruce and clean-shaven although often bearing a little plaster on the cuts from his weekly shave. The priest was usually brisk and sharp in his sermon. I remember the odd Holy Hour, somnolent and warm after a summer day, when the candles, the dusk and the sleepy crows were gentle accompaniments for incense, Rosaries, blessings and hymns. These hymns remain still in my mind, the *O Salutaris*, the *Tantum Ergo* and, above all else, the closing hymn, *Nearer my God to Thee*.

The hymns were always led in style by Dan McCarthy, the organist who came from Aghada. His marvellous baritone voice rang round the holiday church, eclipsing even the harmonium's occasional wheezing. Somewhat later in life, I listened every Sunday morning to a BBC radio programme called *The Chapel in the Valley*. The singer, Mr Edwards, reminded me of Dan.

A great social and commercial event that lives on in my memory reflects long summer nights and early dawns driving cattle more than ten miles to the fair in Midleton. This was an occasion when cattle and youngsters were united in fear of the dark and in haste to get a "good spot at the fair." We usually left Ballyshane at about 1.00 a.m. and I dreaded having to run along in front as, not only was I on my own but I was a target for cranky sheepdogs. I had to "block" side roads from the cattle and then run on ahead.

Midleton was a relief but standing around if you did not sell the cattle quickly was painful; no worse though than suffering the blandishments of "tanglers" or "jobbers" as they thrust advice, mostly insincere, at you, endless hand slappings and cautions of the "don't break your word" calibre. A neighbour said of one such tangler, 'that's a man for you; he's as sincere as a whore's kiss.' Probably true, though I didn't know what he meant.

As always, there was breakfast at Miss McSweeney's Emporium, a few shillings for lemonade and, if you were lucky, a lift home when your uncle, now cheerfully glowing, might ask you to recite *The Wreck of the Hesperus* or the more sentimental tale of the Ormonde peasant's daughter with *Blue Eyes and Golden Hair*.

My summer days in Ballyshane moulded me into being a true country boy. My usual life was one of a small town but these summer interludes gave me an insight into and a love of rural life that was to influence programmes I made, and shaped how I viewed the people that I would later interview and share reminiscences with.

3 ONWARDS AND UPWARDS

... I am nothing if not persistent. Once I set myself a target, I'll work flat out to achieve it. It was so with studying for the matriculation exam. I turned to the Mercy nuns for help ...

Starring in a one-act play in the Parochial Hall, Charleville.

I ENTERED THE WORLD OF work at the age of 16. This is young by today's standards but it was normal for all but the privileged few then to leave school early, often as young as 14.

I was lucky to be offered and accept an apprenticeship as a dental technician with our local dentist, Paddy O'Riordan. He was a gentle, kind man and I was fortunate to find work with someone such as him.

He had a dental technician already, John Morrison, and I learned my craft from him. John was kind but somewhat distant and self-contained. My pay was agreed at five shillings a week, to rise to ten shillings after six months' probation, which it did. Dentistry was relatively primitive at this time. I helped fix and repair false teeth and carried out other general mundane tasks.

We worked next door to the room where the dentist operated and could hear, at close quarters, the suffering of the unfortunate patients. Dental anaesthetics were also primitive and laughing gas was frequently used to put a patient under. The dentist's main practice was in Charleville but he practised in Kilmallock on Tuesdays and in Kilfinane on Fridays. Our busiest day was Fair day as farmers from the surrounding countryside arrived for their appointments. Overall though, it wasn't too arduous a job and I settled in quickly and soon began to pick up the skills that I would need to pursue a career as a dental technician.

We worked a six-day week and I had a half day on Thursdays. The little I earned gave me some independence. In addition, I no longer had homework to complete and so had more time in the evenings to take part in the town's sporting, social and cultural activities. The summer was generally devoted to outdoor pursuits and, together with Bill Gilligan, a good friend and our neighbour in Holy Cross, I'd cycle to Mallow to watch hurling games there.

Bill was a great companion and a gifted player. Off the field he was warm and gentle but when on the field, was a match for anyone. He played on into his forties. His hurling genes carried on as his son and grandson were accomplished players also. North Cork was and is a great hurling stronghold and much of daily conversation was taken up with chat about matches, players and prospects.

I often used my half day to cycle back to Doneraile. I retained a great fondness for the village and enjoyed meeting those I had known in my childhood and gazing down into the Awbeg River, contemplating Canon Sheehan's *Glenanaar* and how little the town had changed.

It seemed that my studying days were at an end but I still loved reading, writing, drama and music. I was also blessed with a strong foundation in the Irish language and so I could explore these arts through either Irish or English. My employer, Paddy O'Riordan, loved reading and had built up an extensive and eclectic, library, and very kindly agreed to me using it.

I read voraciously from a wide selection of writers. There were plenty of current novelists included in his collection and I read everything from thrillers to great classics. Agatha Christie and Edgar Wallace were two of the former while Dickens was one of the great classic writers I recall reading then. In addition to sharing his books, Paddy also gave us the daily paper, the *Irish Press* and the monthly *Reader's Digest*. He used the *Digest* page, 'It pays to Increase Your Word power,' as a way of expanding my vocabulary and instilling the importance of precision in meaning when using words – a skill which I hope I still use in my broadcasting and writing. Paddy was a caring employer in other ways, too. I recollect him carrying down his own radio to our workshop on Saturdays in March so that we could listen to the commentary on the Irish rugby internationals.

Soccer came into my life around this time. Noel Tarrant, my friend with the gramophone, whose record collection I listened to avidly, used to get a copy of the programme from Manchester United's home games sent to him every second week. It sparked an interest and whenever we had the money and opportunity, we'd watch Cork Athletic playing in the Mardyke.

They were one of the great teams of their era. They won the 1949 league of Ireland and won the double of FAI Cup and the league in the following year. I was privileged to watch great players such as Florrie Burke, an incisive centre half, and Paddy O'Leary who was brilliant with his head around the box. Noel Cantwell also played for Athletic. He later went on to huge success with West Ham and Manchester United and as an Irish international, before pursuing a career as a club manager in England and the States. Noel was an all-round sportsman and used to both bat and bowl for Cork Bohemian Cricket Club.

Letter writing was the normal means of communicating with someone at a distance. Telephones were unreliable and prohibitively expensive. You also ran the risk that the local postmistress or exchange operator might listen in and your most private business would become

Winner of an interclub billiards'
tournament at the Parochial
Hall, Charleville, in the mid-50s.
On right, Big John O'Toole,
runner-up. At back Paddy
Sheridan and Tim McCarthy.

town gossip. I was a prodigious letter writer and wrote regularly to
my heroes of the time. In those days, celebrities replied to fan mail
and I received back letters and autographed photos from the likes of
Jo Staffford, the traditional and popular singer and actress, Donald
Peers, who sang of *A Shady Nook by a Babbling Brook,* and Tommy
Moroney who played midfield for West Ham and played for Ireland

when they beat England 2-0 at Goodison Park in 1949 – the first time that England had been beaten on home soil by a non-UK team. Tommy was also gifted at rugby and played for Cork Constitution and Munster in his early days. He never had the opportunity to be capped for Ireland in rugby as the Five Nations Championship was suspended during WWII when he was eligible.

I started a correspondence with Peter Desmond, a Cork man from Evergreen Street in the city. Having served in the army, he played for Shelbourne before being headhunted to England. He was capped four times for Ireland and had played in the famous Goodison Park game and had won the penalty that was converted into a goal. He was with Middleborough when we started exchanging letters and, generous man that he was, he sent programmes and other small mementos from the club. I met him only once when his train stopped in Charleville. We shook hands and said hello and good-bye and that was the only time I ever saw him, and to this day I'm proud to have done so.

My love for the Irish language had flourished during my time with the Presentation Brothers. It was our lingua franca and I enjoyed being able to speak my native tongue fluently and with some grace. Mainchín Seoighe came from Bruree and gave talks about Irish culture and the language. As a consequence, I became a committed member of Conradh na Gaeilge, the Gaelic League. The league promoted a Gaelic revival and encouraged speaking Irish and activities that promoted an Irish culture. Its ideals were in tune with my own. For my own part, I organised a drama group and also helped to stage concerts, using Irish. We staged events in the Parochial Hall and brought our productions to nearby villages. I began to see myself as a future Micheál Mac Líammóir. We performed an early play by Bryan McMahon in the first North Cork Drama Festival where McMahon was the adjudicator. The playwright was surprised, if not startled, to be re-introduced to one of his early works but, alas, didn't declare us winners on the night.

We also ran variety concerts in the Parochial Hall and I persuaded my employer, Paddy O'Riordan to act as the compere. He did so with some panache. He wore a dress suit and had as excellent a line of patter on stage as he did when treating the teeth of Charleville's citizens in private.

My involvement in the League expanded to include the Parochial Hall. This ran as a social-cum-youth club. Membership was £1 for the year. The hall had two top-quality billiards tables. Members also used it for card games and listening to the radio. I became a member of the committee and then secretary. Paddy O'Riordan chaired it and Fr Linehan was the President. We organised a celebrity concert, an idea

```
        COIR  CHUMANN  NA  HOILSCOIL


   T H E   C H O R A L   S O C I E T Y

           Presents


   T H E   B E G G A R ' S   O P E R A


           Words By Gay

        Music Arranged By:-

           Pepusch - Dent.




                           Price 3d.
```

```
                    C A S T
              ( In Order of Appearance)

BEGGAR          ...        ...    JOE MORRISSEY
PLAYER          ...        ...    D. TOWNSEND
PEACHUM (a "fence")        ...    DONAILL P. FARMER
FILCH           ...        ...    CHRISTY O'DONOVAN
MRS. PEACHUM    ...        ...    ELIZABETH McENIRY
POLLY PEACHUM   ...        ...    MARY CULLINANE
MACHEATH        ...        ...    FRED SOUTH
MATT O'THE MINT ...        ...    DENIS DOWLING
DRAWER          ...        ...    JOHN CULLINANE
BETTY DOXY      ...        ...    C. O'DOHERTY
SUKY TAWDRY     ...        ...    MAURA MAHER
MOLLY BRAZEN    ...        ...    PHIL DEASY
MRS. VIXEN      ...        ...    MARY McCARTHY
JENNY DIVER     ...        ...    ELIZABETH McENIRY
CONSTABLES      ...        ...    JOE McCARTHY
                                  DENIS O'SULLIVAN
LOCKIT (Jailor) ...        ...    GERARD WRIXON
LUCY LOCKIT     ...        ...    MARIE BUTLER
MRS. TRAPES     ...        ...    MARY COLLINS
TURNKEY         ...        ...    JOHN CONNOLLY
              LADIES OF THE TOWN
E. Rodgers, H. Foster, E. O'Neill, M. Flavin, M. Foley, M. Fraher,
P. Deasy. M. Maher, W. McCarthy, K. Ryan, M. McCarthy, F. O'Connell,
J. Barrett, F. Kelleher, I. Nagle.
              HIGHWAYMEN
J. Cullinane, P. Meade, M. O'Riordan, D. Green, K. Brennan, J. Connell,
R. Fitzgibbon, M. Greehy, W. Moore, N. Buckley.
```

which was then coming into vogue, held in the Parochial Hall on St Valentine's Day in 1954.

Two singers from Cobh, Michael Murphy and Terry Cashman, sang for us that night and I was so impressed I determined that I would get my voice trained. The two singers recommended a teacher, Ms Kate O'Connor. She listened to me and felt that I had potential and so every week, on my afternoon off, I headed for Cork with hopes that this might one day provide a path that would lead to stardom.

There was plenty of music in my life at this stage. The radio particularly the *Light* programme on the BBC and Radio Éireann's sponsored programmes gave access to what was new and interesting in post-war music. The Presentation nuns organised the choir for the church and I had sung with them until my voice broke and, after a suitable interval, as an adult choir member. I also helped organise céilithe with popular céilí bands such as The Vincent Lowe Trio. Their accordionist was the young Dermot O'Brien. We held these in the Pavilion Cinema. We held eight-o'clock-to-midnight dances in the Parochial Hall with music from bands like the "The Tostal Céilí Band." My taste in music was, I suppose, eclectic; I was open to every type, tradition and form. This Catholic musical appetite was to stand me in good stead in my later broadcasting career.

I had not neglected my spiritual well-being at this time. Earlier, following my return from the seminary, I had signed up to the Legion of Mary. I cannot say that I was the most enthusiastic legionary to have enrolled in this institution, but I joined nevertheless. The Legion is a Catholic organisation that promotes devotion to the Blessed Virgin. It encourages prayer and good acts among its members.

We met weekly, at first in the Christian Brothers' school, then later in the parish church sacristy. I attempted to spread my enthusiasm for the Irish language into the spiritual world by having the meetings conducted through Irish. The older members had difficulty understanding what was going on so English became our operating language. We prayed at each meeting and also decided on what work we should carry out to promote devotion to Our Lady. I was a dedicated member; it's fair to say that when I decide to do something, I devote myself fully to it. As a result, I was promoted and became a member of the senior Praesidium.

We met weekly under the chairmanship of Jim Burke, the station master. Regular attenders were Tom Daly, Pat Gray, TJ McCurtain and my friend and mentor, Michael McGrath. Michael and I joined

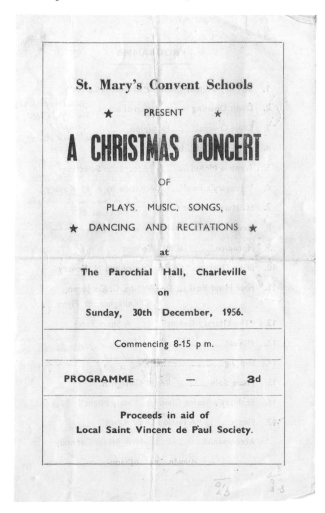

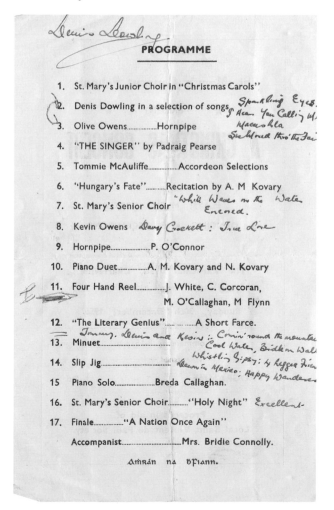

together on Legion work each week. We visited homes and gave out small religious booklets to the families. We'd return a few weeks later to discuss the booklet's contents with the household. Michael was the postman, known and liked by everyone. As a consequence, we were always invited in for a cup of tea and a chat. Michael was a kind and gentle man who knew not to pressurise or embarrass people. He'd ask in a general way if they had enjoyed the book and this usually elicited an equally vague positive response that they had. These preliminaries completed, we then moved on to conversation about the more secular aspects of life. I often spotted the most recent pamphlet tucked behind the radio or the mantelpiece clock, along with all of the other booklets we had delivered.

The Praesidium met on Monday evenings and we reported on the progress of our visitations. We were able to report that the booklets were received with gratitude and had been read with interest in the town's homes. The Canon was delighted with our good works and stressed that a good book is always worth reading more than once. TJ McCurtain chimed in with a comment to the effect that a cup of tea is always nice in the middle of the day.

We had something of an evangelical experience during my times in the Legion. We had a visit from a young legionary from Dublin. His aim was to spread God's word and he certainly did this with enthusiasm. I was assigned to be his companion – a sort of Tonto to his Lone Ranger. I had little enthusiasm for this task as it required me to accompany him on Thursday afternoon, my treasured half-day. Normally, I'd have spent the time cycling across to Doneraile or devoted to jobs such as cleaning the late poet Seán Clárach MacDomhnaill's headstone, in our local graveyard.

Instead, my companion and I headed to the village of Newtownshandrum. I was somewhat disingenuous in my choice of this village as I had figured there wouldn't be anyone around in the middle of the afternoon. We arrived to find a cluster of the younger men gathered on the street corner. My fellow legionary leapt off his bike and approached them, intent on their spiritual reawakening.

We were greeted with: 'How's it goin', Cove? What's the crack?' This was the standard greeting between young men and was usually followed by an equally anodyne response. They were not expecting what followed from my fellow traveller, 'Do you know Jesus?' I received a hard glare from the young men and a direct question, 'What sort of lunatics have we here?'

The Dublin legionary led me immediately to the church where he proceeded to pray aloud – something I had never done without a priest being present. And halfway through a decade of the Rosary, one burst in, wondering what we were up to and telling us in no uncertain terms to get back to where we came from.

We skedaddled. Almost immediately upon our return, I was summoned to an audience with Canon Burke in the Parochial Hall. There I was told that explanations weren't necessary and that our Dublin guest was going to catch the evening train back to the city. The matter was closed.

My memories of those times in Charleville are suffused with Munster finals between my own Cork and our neighbours and arch rivals, Tipperary. These events impressed me deeply and their memory has stayed with me until now.

My mother's home place in Ballyshane, near Cloyne, my childhood holiday home, was often my starting point for my pilgrimage to the final and there was no more fitting place to begin as it was near the home place of the legendary Christy Ring. The build-up to the match was filled with stories, anecdotes, insider information and fantastic celebration, as if we believed that if we hoped hard enough and believed firmly enough, the day was certain to be ours.

Weather was always a concern approaching final day. We watched the sky for days before, looking for signs of a settled spell of fine weather. The day before, we wondered would good weather hold or break before the ball was thrown in.

And so preparations for the epic journey began. I remember my first final well. It began with our saying the Rosary, extended with lengthy "trimmings", the additional prayers said after the five decades themselves. These included prayers seeking the intercession of saints to guide our journey, protect our purity and guide Cork to a great victory. Prayers completed, we turned our attention to discussing provisions for the trip and the allocation of the farming duties while we were away. My aunt made sandwiches of ham and chicken and added bottles of lemonade, water and stout. We passed a restive night before an early start after milking.

Our journey was a two-day affair. We were to travel in a small Ford, washed and polished for the occasion. We pushed it out of the barn and coaxed it to life with rigorous turns of the starting handle. We stowed our belongings in the boot, sandwiches, drinks, overcoats and a dozen fresh eggs for my mother and my sisters; Charleville was to be our overnight stopping point. My uncle Jim took the backseat while I acted as co-pilot in the front passenger seat beside my cousin, Maurice. I was promoted to this position on account of my superior knowledge of the route from Ballyshane to Charleville.

We broke our journey for lunch in Fermoy where the weather remained fair and my uncle quenched his thirst with a pint. All of the talk in the car was of the heroes of the past and the might of the present-day team. We reached Charleville in the late afternoon with all our doubts banished and Cork's victory certain.

Charleville was in festive mood I remember that evening. One of our own, John 'Danno' Mahony was selected for Cork. My uncle stressed the degree of his closeness to Christy Ring as he sat in Davy Ryan's pub supping a pint, and regaled the locals with his stories. Afterwards, it was back to our house in Holy Cross for tea, followed by the Rosary, with more extra prayers for a Cork victory.

Canon Burke officiated at first Mass and he had a large and fidgety congregation waiting for the final prayers so that they could begin their journey to Limerick. The Canon added to the agony with the delivery of a 15-minute-long sermon before we were blessed and dismissed with an "Ita, Missa est, Deo gratias" to venture forth on our journey.

We arrived in Limerick early and parked the car on the outskirts, with its nose pointing homewards. We then walked down O'Connell Street in the baking sunshine. We made the final part of the journey by jaunting car. The crowd that day was estimated to be forty-two thousand, but to me it seemed as if the population of the entire two counties was there. There were ballad singers and musicians singing and playing outside the ground. I met Brother Ryan who told me that I had grown into a fine young man.

The atmosphere was electric. We struggled towards the gates and I rushed to the side lines searching for Micheál O'Hehir, to see him if I couldn't hear him as usual on the radio. I didn't manage to see him and it tainted my experience slightly. The game was one of the great matches between our two counties. Christy Ring played the game of his life and my memories of it are edged in gold. The only blight on the whole day was that Tipp won!!!

The voyage home was a silent one, with some tears and sad faces. There would be other days, great days. I had just to wait for them.

Life continued in Charleville much as ever. My love of the Irish language grew as did my interest in republican politics. I became a street seller of a magazine called Rosc. I found that few of the town's denizens had any interest in our language or republican politics – certainly not enough to invest in an issue. I had friends in the town with the same interests. Diarmuid Ó Donncha who worked in the post office lent me books in Irish and these expanded my horizons further.

I met Seán South who was active in the Gaelic League, the Legion of Mary and the Knights of Columbanus. He was also an important member of Sinn Féin and was shot dead while taking part in a raid on an RUC barracks in Co. Fermanagh a few years later. I corresponded with Sinn Féin and got my copy of *The United Irishman* regularly through the post. Reading this prompted me to take the leap from observer to active service and join the IRA.

I headed for Cork on the bus and went to the address that I had for the IRA. The woman I found in their rooms seemed unimpressed with my ambitions to bring about a United Ireland. 'They're gone home for their tea,' she told me, 'Come back tomorrow.'

'I'm from the country,' I told her.

'Too bad.'

And so my attempt to become a revolutionary fighter fell at the first fence and I returned to my law-abiding life in Charleville.

My settled routine was suddenly disrupted by a young lady who walked up our street to catch a bus every day. I noticed her heading off each morning and soon began to make it my business to be hanging around in the evening to watch for her return. The local wags soon noticed my interest in bus movements and I was the subject of a few good-natured jibes. Vera Galvin was the name of the young lady in question; she was a beautiful brunette with a poise and sophistication. She was a teacher in Ballyhea and this was the reason for her daily bus trips.

With Vera at a College dance in the early 1960s.

I made my first move some time afterwards at a St Patrick's Day dance in the Parochial Hall. The dancehall was packed as on stage for the night was Jim Cameron's Scottish Band. They were one of the big bands of the time and their recordings are still widely available. I asked Vera to dance and the band struck up *Under the Bridges of Paris* and this was later to become "our tune." It was an old-time waltz. The next dance was a ladies' choice and I was in luck; Vera came over and asked me again. And so began our relationship which has lasted through thick and thin.

Vera and I shared a lot in common. We both loved music and she encouraged my own interest in things musical. She had had an excellent musical education and this added an extra dimension to our blossoming relationship. Vera came from close to where my mother's family lived (although strangely the two families didn't know each other) and this was, of course, a place that I knew and loved. While her beauty drew me to her, it was her intelligence and insight that bound me further. She had tremendous faith in me and my potential – something which I hadn't acknowledged myself but which she spoke to me about openly. Our relationship developed and deepened and we soon became soul mates and she became my guide and advisor.

Up to this time, I had let life happen to me. My father's death had been a major blow and I did not realise or acknowledge how deeply the scars ran. After his passing, I had followed whatever path presented itself without really thinking what I wanted for myself. Perhaps, joining the fit-ups or becoming a singer were the closest I allowed myself to get to dreams or ambitions.

I was also comfortable, if confined, then and I suppose I was afraid of doing anything that could cause another major upset. But at some deep, subconscious level, I knew that I wanted to achieve more. Vera was the first to really recognise this and say it to me. 'You're much better than this,' she told me. She then advised me to sit the matriculation examination for entry into University College, Cork (UCC) something that I had never even contemplated or believed I could possibly achieve. University was something for a small number of the privileged – not for the lowly son of a Guard's widow living in a rural Cork town. But Vera gave me the confidence to pursue the dream.

I am nothing if not persistent. Once I set myself a target, I'll work flat out to achieve it. It was so with studying for the matriculation exam. I turned to the Mercy nuns for help. Sister Berchmans was the leader of our choir practice and a kindly and understanding individual. She took me under her wing, as did her sisters in the convent. They applied themselves to sourcing the books I needed – calling in favours and begging or cajoling others to provide them. They lent me these books and guided me on how to prepare for the different subjects.

It was difficult to knuckle down to study again; I hadn't done so for four years. It was something I enjoyed, though, and I soon got back my capability and set to with relish. My employer was also very supportive. He was surprised by my intentions when I told him first, but he told me that he'd help in whatever way he could. His library had sustained my appetite for reading and the range of material had stimulated my curiosity and kept me mentally agile.

My matriculation was not without panic. The letter informing me

Michael McGrath, Donncha and Sister Berchmans, UCC, on the Bibi Baskin Show.

of the examination, its location and time only arrived on the morning of the exam. I dashed into Cork and arrived late, without a pen or any other implements. The custodian of the door took pity on the sweaty youth before him and not only let me enter but lent me a pen too! I sat down and started writing.

Not long afterwards, I received a letter informing me that I had matriculated. Once again my life had changed.

4 ACADEMIA AND EXPLORATIONS

... An undergraduate education is as much about social life as it is about studying. I studied hard and had to devote half days and Saturdays to earning enough to meet my daily needs, but I did enjoy the student life ...

Mr Denis Dowling BA (Hons) 1960.

AUTUMN BROUGHT REGISTRATION IN UCC. I was excited and apprehensive turning up on, what I remember as, a fine autumn day. It was all very strange to me. I had only received about one-and-a-half years' secondary school education and so studying at a more senior level was an unknown experience for me. Besides, university attendance was for those privileged few.

Privilege came in three forms: inherited, from recent riches, or from education. Children of wealthy landowners, whether from the landlord or farming classes, were the inheritors. Children of the merchant class, professionals and bank managers, comprised the recently rich. While the educated were those bright people from poorer backgrounds that someone, usually a religious order, sponsored or helped to complete their Leaving Certificate and possibly win one of the small number of scholarships for people with insufficient means. I was an anomaly in that I did not belong to any of the above. I was there off my own bat.

I opted for Arts as I didn't have the money, or prospects of it, to allow me pursue studies in dentistry which might have seemed the obvious option. In retrospect, it was fortunate that necessity drove me into Arts as that was where I found my true interests and passion lay.

I adapted quickly and easily to my student life. Necessity meant that I had to earn some extra money while I was studying. Here my former employer, Paddy O'Riordan, helped out in a very practical way. He gave me an introduction and, more importantly, a recommendation to another dentist, A. A., better known as Gus Healy. He had a dental laboratory on Grand Parade at the heart of the city.

Gus was a generous man with an excellent practice. He was well-known locally and an active member of Fianna Fáil. He was a TD and would later serve as city Mayor. Gus gave me a part-time job that ensured that I had some financial fluidity during term time. Once again, I worked with the smell of wax and plaster.

As was common at the time, I lived in digs. I had one room in a house belonging to Mrs Keane in Buxton Hill, Sunday's Well. It was close enough to the college which meant that I could economise on bus fares and walk to and from my lectures. My walk to Grand Parade for my dental work was longer and felt even more so as I was generally there in the evenings or at weekends. I quickly developed a routine and didn't find it too onerous to both work and study in that first year. I believe I benefitted from my time in full-time employment which had instilled a work discipline which my fellow students had to learn for themselves.

I chose to study Irish, English, Irish and European history and Latin. I took the first three at honours level and Latin at pass. Irish was an easy choice to make. I loved the language and was fluent in it. I had also read widely and presumed, mistakenly as it transpired, that authors such as Pádraig Pearse would form an important part of our studies.

In choosing history, I hoped to build upon my own attempts at educating myself in the progress of the Irish and European nations and gaining some insight into how we came to be as we are. English was the easiest choice to make. English literature was the most accessible as far as I was concerned. The head of the department was Professor B.G. McCarthy who was also an established author and playwright. I was familiar with her play, *The Whip Hand*, a comedy about life in rural Ireland. This gave me the false impression that she looked sympathetically on the type of place from where I hailed.

The receipt for the fee of £8-0-0 for Bachelor of Arts degree examinations.

I should have read her more academic *The Female Pen* to get a greater appreciation of what she was about. She was a Pre-feminist writer and her work was cited in the same breath as Virginia Woolf's *A Room of One's Own,* a seminal critique of the development of women's literature. She may not have had as much time for a young lad from Charleville as I had originally hoped. Indeed, she induced fear in many of those she taught.

I remember her first lecture when she swept imperiously into the theatre to face the begowned, notebook-clutching freshmen and began, 'This is a class for pass and honours students.' She then asked the pass students to rise and her following comment set the tone for the year, 'Ah, the poor will always be with us.'

Things were as challenging and eccentric in our Irish lectures. Risteard A. Breathnach was the professor and had a very low opinion of our grasp of our native language. He questioned the degree to which we were intellectually committed and decided that we should only be lectured in English. This was a strange and demotivating approach to studying a language. His approach and lecturing style may explain why few chose to pursue honours in his class.

I had an additional difficulty studying Irish. The powers that be had changed the language dramatically since I studied it in school. The traditional letters and symbols were replaced by the Roman alphabets and 'h' was used to replace the *séimhiú* that I had grown up using. It was one more challenge that I had to meet and overcome.

The old-school professors were counterbalanced by some of the younger lecturers. One of these was Seán Ó Tuama, who led our Saturday Irish literature class as well as his modern Irish one. These were the highlights of my week. These lectures introduced me to a whole range of modern writers like Liam O'Flaherty and Séamus Ó Ceileachair. O'Flaherty had a well-established reputation internationally as the author of *The Informer* which John Ford made into a highly successful film.

Seán Ó Tuama confirmed my belief that poetry is best read aloud and he demonstrated this by getting us to read aloud, among other poems, *Caoineadh Airt Uí Laoghaire*, written by the subject's wife, Eibhlín Dhubh Ní Chonnaill. This poem laments the shooting of her husband, Airt, on May 4th 1773, while fleeing the forces of the Crown. He had refused to sell his horse for £5 which was the legal value of a horse owned by a Catholic. Airt's horse had just beaten the High Sheriff of Cork's horse in a race.

The poem is a passionate tale of love and loss composed over the corpse of her husband. It chronicles their life together and describes his killing, the bloodied horse's return home, she finding the body under bushes and her subsequent woe. I can still recall and recite much of it. The first verse captures its strength and beauty:

> *"Mo ghrá go daingeann tú!*
> *Lá dá bhfeaca thú*
> *Ag ceann tí an mhargaidh*
> *Thug mo shúl aire dhuit*
> *Thug mo chroí, taitneamh duit*
> *D'éalaíos óm athair leat*
> *I bhfad ó bhaile leat"*

I've translated it as follows:

> *"My love you are forever!*
> *The day that I saw you*
> *At the gable of the market-house*

My eye took notice of you
My heart gave joy for you
I fled from my father with you
Far away from home with you"

This is a beautiful lament and I can still hear Seán Ó Tuama's voice declaiming it in his soft Cork accent. He demonstrated to us students that to understand the language properly we must express our inner selves, our passions and our desires through it. This explains why he once asked the class if we ever made love through Irish. It was not a question that any, other than the nuns sitting in the front row, were willing to answer.

It did make us realise that poetry was not some dry-as-bones assemblage of words but an expression of love, life and passion. The music of the words flowed over us and the accent and the sound of Munster certainly awoke in me a whole new composition of thinking and feelings. Not a syllable was lost, not a note was dropped as we supped deep at the well of our culture.

History brought delights of a different kind. Séamus Pender was our professor for Irish history and he quietly but firmly brought us through eighteenth-century Ireland before leading us through the Act of Union and its subsequent impact. European history proved to be more flamboyant. Kennedy F. Roche was a larger than life personality with well-manicured fingers and a love of his subject matter. We were soon immersed in the world of the sun king, Louis XVI, and his beautiful queen, Marie-Antoinette. We walked the streets of Paris with Roche and could almost smell the blood and cordite or hear the swish of the dropping guillotine as he led us through those turbulent times.

Kennedy F. Roche was my idea of the ideal lecturer. He had little interest in Napoleon and his only real interest in the great emperor was in his horse "Marengo" which, local folklore claimed, was bought in Buttevant. More reliable sources suggest that the horse was, in fact, an Arabian and captured during the emperor's campaign in Egypt. Anyway, who cares? I didn't!

Latin was my weak subject and here Messrs Treston and Fogarty did their best to instil a basic understanding of the fundamentals of that ancient language. They were fighting a losing battle as I found it hard to reconcile people throwing themselves at Caesar's feet, *Caesari ad pedes se proiecerunt*, with day-to-day life in Sunday's Well where there was a distinct lack of Caesars and an even greater want of people willing to throw themselves at their feet – even if it demonstrated the correct use of the dative case in connection with parts of the body! I passed without distinction or leaving a lasting mark on the Classics department.

An undergraduate education is as much about social life as it is about studying. I studied hard and had to devote half days and Saturdays to earning enough to meet my daily needs, but I did enjoy the student life, too. I was fortunate that Vera changed her job and moved from teaching in Ballyhea to St. Vincent's in Shandon in the city. Vera lived close to my digs, allowing us to be in close contact when we were free.

We both enjoyed walking, in a sense making a virtue out of necessity as it was often the only mode of transport open to us. I recall having to put newspapers into my old shoes to stop the rainwater coming in through the holes in them.

Friendship is easier in college than in most other walks of life and I made some great and lasting friendships while at UCC. People like Liz McEniry, Vera Jones, Michael Riordan, Charlie Corkery and Frankie Hickey became an essential part of my student life. These were the people with whom I discussed and debated issues that were important, be it our studies, politics or sport. They helped me form the beliefs that were to guide me in later life. The college was alive with societies and clubs. I was not much of a 'joiner' unless I saw an opportunity to be a leader within whatever I joined. My lack of sporting prowess meant that the sports and athletics clubs were closed to me and so I gravitated towards the literary and dramatic side of college life.

Seán Ó Tuama put on some of his plays in college and I had a small part in one of them, *Ar Aghaidh Leat a Longadáin*. Ó Tuama and his wife, Betty, hosted a party at the end of the run for the cast and all of those who had helped with the production. It was an all-night affair and I have distinct memories of meeting Aindrias Ó Gallachoir and John O'Sullivan, two well-known Radió Éireann presenters based in Cork. There was a special beauty to the sound of their voices and that music rests in my memory still, despite the passing of nearly six decades.

I used Sunday walks to explore the city and learn how it ticked. I was a country boy but I used my separateness to gain an understanding of that great conurbation and its people. We walked along the River Lee and looked northwards at the large, well-tended gardens of Sunday's Wells' well-to-do. The river had a majesty to it, lent in part by the swans serenely gliding on its surface. The odd electric blue flash of a kingfisher diving added to the poetry of the scene. The air was scented with smoke on those autumn, winter and spring days and evenings.

We attended the occasional concert in the winter evenings and now and then I went to a game of soccer in the Mardyke where Cork

Athletic was the club representing the city at the time. There were the occasional shows, such as *Othello* with Anew McMaster playing the lead role. And, of course, we went to the pictures where we watched black-and-white films through clouds of cigarette smoke. Listening to the radio was my special treat at the end of the week. Seán Ó Ceallacháin reported on Gaelic games and I also listened to the Audrey Park Ensemble.

Time passed quickly and I soon found myself in the final term. I studied hard and spent much of the time on my own. The exams came and went. In those days, the results were posted on a notice board and you had to look them up in the full view of everyone else. My luck held and I passed all four subjects. While it was important that I passed the honours subjects, Irish, English and History, my greatest relief was in passing Latin; I would never have to study it ever again.

My celebrations were short lived. Success in my exams meant that I now had to earn enough to support myself for the next year. So on the day after we had seen the results posted on the notice board, I headed to England to find summer work. There was little prospect of my getting work here in the Ireland of the fifties. Jobs were scarce and poverty haunted the city's streets and lanes.

With Vera, Graduation Day 1960.

Together with a classmate from First Arts, Séamus Byrne, and a young man called Rupert Swann, I boarded the Inisfallen with a third-class ticket to sail from Cork to Fishguard. Our journey was not unique; many young Irish men made a similar trek from small towns and villages to the factories and ghettos of English cities to try and earn a living. Dónall Mac Amhlaigh was later to describe the plight of these unfortunates in his masterpiece of that misfortune *Dialann Deoraí*.

Later, through my radio programmes, I was to hear regularly from, and meet occasionally, people from all over Britain who were forced to take the boat to our neighbouring isle in search of work. Séamus, Rupert and I were lucky in comparison. Our stay was limited and our ticket was a return one.

BA (Hons) Irish class graduation, University College, Cork, 1960 - standing l-r: Pádraig Ó Riain, Denis Dowling, Seán Ó Sé, Cathal Ó Corcora and Eamon Draper. Seated: Joan Kelly, Professor of Irish, Risteárd A. Breátnach, Professor of Old Irish, Eoin Caomhánach, and Sister Joseph.

It is hard to explain the excitement and sense of adventure I felt making that journey. It was my first time outside of Ireland and everything seemed different and interesting. The post and telephone boxes were painted red; the shops had strange and interesting names; the English spoken around me was heavily accented and sometimes hard to understand for someone reared on a quiet Cork blas.

Séamus had organised both work and accommodation for us in Aylesbury in Buckinghamshire. We were employed as ward orderlies in the Stoke Mandeville Hospital. Our charges were mainly paralysed men who were veterans of WWII. This was not a sought-after post and we were the only English-speaking orderlies there. The matron made it clear we'd be fine if we had strong backs and stomachs. While we may have had the back strength, the work was difficult to stomach. We had to help the paralysed patients with all of their needs. These were quiet, stoic men who had suffered greatly winning the war and continued to suffer while living the peace. They didn't seek pity and kept their dignity despite the dreadfulness of their condition.

I was not suited to this kind of work and the matron saw that this was the case. After the less-than-successful completion of other duties, I was assigned the role of sluice officer and glove cleaner. I quit shortly after; I believe I had only lasted four days and it is an experience I remember vividly. Séamus and Rupert followed me shortly afterwards.

Aylesbury was a quiet rural English town. It was in the midst of the "green and pleasant land" and had all of the appearances of being so. Work was plentiful and I got a job as a waiter in a restaurant called the "The Old Beams" in Market Square in the centre of town. The clientele was generally farmers and farm workers. The food was traditional, wholesome, solid and definitely English. The tables were laid properly with carefully folded napkins, referred to as serviettes. I became partial to Banbury cakes that were delivered fresh every day from the town of Banbury, about forty miles North West of Aylesbury.

Mr and Mrs Hempsel were the proprietors and I got on well with them as I did with all of the staff. George, the head waiter, taught me never to react to customers who clicked their fingers or whistled for attention – that behaviour was for calling dogs not waiters. The chef, Ray, was fiery. His anger was quickly aroused when a coachload of tourists arrived. Invariably, they were all served fish and chips regardless of what they had ordered. I found the Cockneys the friendliest and they were the people I liked best. There was, though, one strange old fellow there, a porter. He mentioned one day that he had worked in Ireland for some time. He told me that the people in Ireland had a nickname for him then, "Black and Tan."

My time in the "The Old Beams" was made much easier when Vera came across to work there, too. The fact that she was a teacher impressed the Hempsels and she was given an office job, keeping their books.

I returned to UCC in the autumn and started studying my three remaining subjects, Irish, English and History in greater depth and intensity. I relished this harder, but much more rewarding, work. May Conroy led us through Chaucer's *Canterbury Tales* and showed that, despite the passage of centuries, people were very much the same. I enjoyed trying to find the modern-day equivalent of the characters described, their foibles and their dreams. Social life continued, too, and I played a small part in a college production of Gay's satirical piece *The Beggar's Opera*. The examinations rolled around quickly, and soon I was once again seeking summer work to fund my final college year.

I landed a job as a night porter at the Southern Lake Hotel in Waterville, on the Iveragh Peninsula in Co. Kerry. I owed my getting this position to Jack O'Connor, the accountant there. Kerry at that time of the year was beautiful and Waterville particularly so. It is a small town on a narrow strip of land that runs between Lough Currane and Ballinskelligs Bay. I joined a happy and contented staff whose accent and quiet demeanour echoed that of my late father, who came from the neighbouring peninsula. The work was straightforward and not too strenuous. Most of the time was spent polishing shoes, stoking the furnace and delivering room service during the night.

One delivery I can recall was being asked to take tea and toast to a room at 3.30 a.m. and being surprised to find the couple naked. It was a shock to my system, such that it almost, but didn't, put me off my breakfast of lobster which I ate just before knocking off duty in the early morn. The staff was as well fed as the customers in that hotel. I enjoyed myself and my role in the Southern Lake Hotel, but at times couldn't help but feel that I was living the role of 'Michael The Boots' in Lennox Robinson's play *Drama at Inish*.

The countryside was extraordinarily wild and beautiful. The roadside was lined with fuchsia bushes, waiting for their flowers of dancing pink and purple ladies to add an almost Mediterranean touch when the buds blossomed in July. I cycled these roads and lanes absorbing the scent and colour of the place. Most afternoons, I visited Seán Ó Donghaile who spoke to me in Irish and recounted tales of Eoghan Rua and Aogán Ó Rathaille, two great poets from Sliabh Luachra. I felt empathy with Ó Rathaille whose father had died while he was a young boy and who carried the burden of this for the rest of his life.

The Irish poets weren't the only ones who exercised my mind in those Kerry days. I had brought TS Eliot's poems and also the works of Gerard Manley Hopkins with me and I was struggling to gain a proper understanding of both of these great poets. The Hopkins was easier to comprehend, his poem, *Inversnaid* readily evoking the countryside that I walked and cycled through:

> *"This darksome burn, horseback brown*
> *His rollrock highroad roaring down,*
> *In coop and in comb the fleece of his foam*
> *Flutes and low to the lake falls home."*

I fell asleep one night reading TS Eliot and during a frenzied dream, tore one of the pages of the book. The fragment I found in the morning, from Part III of *Burnt Norton*:

> *"Here is a place of disaffection*
> *Time before and time after*
> *In a dim light..."*

This summed up his writing for me then, if not now.

I wasn't in a place of disaffection but I was dissatisfied with one key aspect of my life as 'The Boots' and that was the pay. I received £4 a week which was insufficient to allow me to save enough for the following year's fees. Reluctantly, I quit my post as a night porter and took the night boat to England and London.

1958 was a year of change in London. A new young generation was coming of age and they weren't happy to live the sort of life that their parents had endured. London had become a melting pot with different races, political perspectives, beliefs, outlooks and lifestyles. It was the year of the Aldermaston marches, protests against the H bomb, the Notting Hill riots, and visits from up-and-coming State-side acts such as Elvis Presley and Buddy Holly. London was on the cusp of the swinging sixties and everything that it was to bring.

I arrived this time without any arrangements made, without a job and a lack of clear direction. I was wandering across Clapham Common when I spotted three or four lads pucking a sliotar around the park. I engaged them in conversation and they gave me the practical support I needed in the form of an invitation to stay with them in their flat until I found work. I soon found a position as a sandwich maker and grill hand at Fortes, 75, The Strand. It's still a food emporium but now under a different name, Zizzi, and selling pizzas.

My work day started at 8.00 a.m. with a break at 4.00 p.m. and then carried on until 11.00 p.m. I made sandwiches in my first shift and then worked in the grill for the evening. There was a more cosmopolitan mix in Fortes than the Southern Lake. Here I worked alongside Cockneys, West Indians and, of course, Irish. Outside, a diminutive Viennese woman worked in a kiosk and she welcomed the occasional cup of coffee I brought to her. In return, she delighted me with stories of her time in her native city. Vienna is a time-honoured centre of musical excellence and she shared her memories of concerts given by the great Richard Tauber.

The Strand bustled with traffic and life. A poem published four or five years before by R.P. Lister, *Buses on the Strand,* captures this life in its first two verses:

"The Strand is beautiful with buses
Fat and majestical in form,
Red like tomatoes in their trusses
In August, when the sun was warm.
"They cluster in the builded chasm
Corpulent fruit, a hundred strong,
And now and then a secret spasm
Spurs them a yard or two along."

Indeed, the sun was warm that summer I spent in Fortes. The café attracted actors and show people working in theatres nearby. The musical, *Salad Days*, was playing in the Adelphi Theatre across the road from us. Further up the Strand, *A Raisin in the Sun,* was running in the Vaudeville Theatre. I was drawn to the theatrical people – perhaps harking back to my earlier yearnings to run off with the fit-ups. One of those I met was John Slator, star of film and stage. He invited me to tea and gave me tickets to a box for *The Ring of Truth*, a play by Wynyard Browne, which was running in The Savoy. He played a sergeant in the play about the loss of a wedding ring, with other stars including David Tomlinson and Irene Browne.

I took one weekend off to hit some of the great shows running in London. An early lunch in The Embankment gardens allowed me to enjoy the Welsh Guards' brass band open-air concert that included a selection of Percy French melodies. I started my theatre-going with a matinée performance of *My Fair Lady* in the wonderful Theatre Royal in Drury Lane. This was a star-studded cast in which Alec Clunes, father of Martin, now famous on television and film, played Professor Higgins, while Stanley Holloway and Robert Coote also played starring roles. That evening, I went to the Queen's Theatre on Shaftesbury Avenue and there saw Michael Redgrave play HJ in his own adaptation of Henry James's novella, *The Aspern Papers*. Flora Robson played Miss Tina.

I had hoped to attend an open-air production of *A Midsummer Night's Dream* on the Sunday of my cultural weekend but unfortunately rain prevented me from doing so. I was a bit dejected returning but a chance encounter with Bob Hope and Audrey Hepburn changed my day and I was grateful to get their autographs. London was a much safer place and famous people were less security conscious in those days and it was possible to encounter well-known personalities in the streets. One Sunday, I recall seeing President Eisenhower being driven down The Strand without fuss or security. Events in November 1963 were to render such an occurrence unthinkable.

London offered temptations other than cultural. Soho was the established red-light district and, for a young man from Cork, it offered something that definitely wasn't to be found off Grand Parade or around Sunday's Well. I wandered the streets taking in the seedy outsides and occasionally ventured inside one or two to look rather than to partake.

I parted from London in good financial standing, as the manager in Fortes had kept the greater part of my wages in the office safe so that I wasn't tempted to spend it foolishly. He offered me a permanent job there, too, which was gratifying. I did spend some of my funds:

I bought a briefcase from the British Rail Lost Property Office and books from the myriad bookshops along Charing Cross Road.

My final undergraduate year was dedicated to hard work with little time left for other activities. I did, however, make time for a production of William Saroyan's *The Beautiful People* in which I played the part of a parish priest with a strong fondness for drink. I might have even won a best supporting acting award had Hilton Edwards, the adjudicator in Limerick, not taken my artistic pauses and lulls when I was delivering my lines, as forgetfulness and waiting for prompts.

The workload in that final year was unrelenting. My digs were now in Summerhill and I walked to and from college in a new pair of hard-wearing shoes – walking about ten miles a day. In the library and back in my digs, I ploughed through *Paradise Lost* and *Regained*, seven of Shakespeare's plays and TS Eliot's *The Wasteland*, Eliot going on to play a major part in my final examinations. I wrote an essay on his impact on my life and piled in every word that I had ever read of his. I succeeded in these examinations but I do remember B.G. McCarthy later remarking that, as Arnold Bennett wrote of Eliot himself, I was, "*sometimes walking near the limits of coherency.*"

At last, I had graduated. And, of course, I had to decide what to do next with my life. I had little idea of what I wanted to do but knew that it was in a direction other than teaching – the profession that absorbed a great many Arts' graduates at that time. I recognised that I had taken a great risk in pursuing a third-level education and I wanted to use it to open up new and different opportunities from those that might have come to me if I had stayed in Charleville, or as a novitiate with the Presentation Brothers. I determined that I'd try and carry on in academia and complete a Master's degree. My chosen subject area was English literature and so I made an appointment to visit Professor McCarthy in her home in Wilton Road, Cork.

I wasn't sure if the professor had noticed me or if she considered me to be a worthy candidate. I was caught off-guard by her quick acceptance to be my supervisor. I was keen to study Canon Sheehan of Doneraile and explore his work in greater depth; it was virgin territory academically and something in which I had a great interest. Failing that, I would have enjoyed working further on TS Eliot's poetry – something which had come to mean a great deal to me. However, I found that this wasn't an option and instead she told me that she thought Elizabeth Bowen would be a suitable subject. I confess that I had never heard of the woman up to then and the professor prescribed *The Death of the Heart* as the place to begin my studies. It was an introduction to a wonderful writer whom I would meet and interview later, but it also opened my mind to Irish women writers generally, who were often ignored or little studied or appreciated. From then on, I felt I was an advocate for their cause and I pursued this espousal whenever the opportunity presented itself.

The professor also intimated that I should join the English Literature Society in the University which I duly did and became auditor for three most enjoyable years. The society met fortnightly and read plays and writings of the greats such as Chekhov, Sartre, Shaw, O'Casey, Joyce and Synge. While I often read the male leads, the professor read the narrator or sometimes the lead female parts. It was a marvellous experience and a very pleasant introduction to the work and thinking of the major writers of the nineteenth and twentieth centuries.

We also organised literary tours to the surrounding countryside. One occasion stands out in my mind as I led the society on a tour of the literary sites of north Cork. It was a wild day and I remember Professor McCarthy being none too pleased when we couldn't get any boiled water for a cup of tea in Doneraile Court. We ventured onwards to Edmund Spenser's castle and there met Lizzie Roche. After I had given a short lecture to the assembled scholars on the significance of the monument, I asked Lizzie about the many great figures that had travelled the busy road past the castle. Lizzie's reply was down to earth and brought me down a peg or two, ''Tis indeed, Sir,' she replied, 'This surely is a busy road, especially on Sunday nights when the world seems to be out on it on the way to Bingo in Charleville.'

We invited speakers to address our gatherings, too. Many attended but two who got away but were gracious in their refusals were veteran Irish film star, Cyril Cusack and *Lord of the Rings* creator, JRR Tolkien. Cusack was touring at the time and didn't feel that he would have the energy to address us while so doing. Tolkien's health wouldn't allow him to make the journey to address us.

I was working steadily on my Master's at the same time. It was tough as I found it hard to work my way into Bowen's thinking and approach. I found the subject dry and it taxed me intellectually. It is true though that persistence brings its reward and eventually I found that I had gained an understanding of her perspective and approach and developed a love of her literary style and expression. Her life had great difficulties and challenges and she used these to add richness and empathy with her characters. Her father's mental illness, her mother's early death, her sexless marriage and extra-marital affairs, including one with Seán Ó Faoláin, all took their toll on her life and her own response to these was reflected in her novels and short stories.

I visited Bowen's Court which was deserted, but I did make contact with the woman who had been the Bowen's housekeeper, Molly O'Brien; we were to become great friends. When I eventually met Elizabeth Bowen, while she was on a visit to Kinsale, she was astounded to find out that someone was writing a thesis about her. She was most friendly and agreeable. It was striking, though, that someone who had such a tremendous ability with the written word suffered from such a terrible stammer. On consideration, it was perhaps the reason that she preferred to express herself through writing.

I was ever on the watch out for some additional cash. I was fortunate to get some work as a part-time teacher with the Presentation Brothers in their college on the Western Road, Cork – close to the university. It was an upper-class school, unlike those I had attended myself. I was back in a familiar atmosphere with my former teachers and mentors. I received £4 a week for this – not a king's ransom but a little extra to tide me over. My duties weren't too onerous, teaching English and Irish, and I was asked to take the first years for rugby training, too.

I knew little of the game other than what I had picked up from listening to radio commentaries of the internationals when I worked with Paddy O'Riordan in Charleville. I was careful to carry a little book of rules with me when I ventured forth with my charges and was happy to take a non-interventionist role in the day's activities.

I was keen to share my learning with the boys and brought Joyce's *Ulysses* into the class to read to them. I was taken aside quietly by one of the brothers who suggested that it wasn't the best choice of text and I had better leave it for the present.

5

FROM DOWLING TO Ó DÚLAING

... I received a telephone call at the office
in Ford's from Ms. Ní Bhriain telling me
that I had been successful but saying that
there was one more hurdle to overcome - a
microphone test to assess the suitability of
my voice for broadcast. ...

In the Control Room in the RTÉ
studio in Cork with Liam Devally
and Lord Mayor, Pearse Wyse TD
during the recording of On Stage
in Cork.

IRELAND WAS CHANGING IN the early sixties. Seán Lemass was Taoiseach and endeavouring to modernise Ireland and the Irish economy. The First Programme for Economic Expansion was in place and driving change across the land. Work opportunities were beginning to open up as, to quote Lemass's favoured phrase, 'a rising tide lifts all boats.' While agreeing with the sentiment, I shunned the "boats" and sought to elevate myself by means of the motor car. I had been perusing the noticeboard in college and noted that Henry Ford and Sons of Cork were recruiting graduate trainees. Fords was a major employer in Cork at the time.

Henry Ford had established his plant there in 1917, first to produce tractors but then moving into car production. If you'll excuse the mixed metaphors, it was the Rolls Royce of jobs and the place where every upwardly mobile Cork mother wanted her son to work and daughter to marry into – at management level, of course! The workforce was strictly divided between those who clocked in and built the cars and those who managed them and didn't clock in. I aspired to the latter group. I arranged an interview with Tommy Brennan and soon received a job offer starting at £10 a week. I accepted with alacrity.

I saw Ford's as my first proper employment. I had always known that my time as dental technician was a stopgap while I worked out what I wanted to do. My temporary and part-time jobs were aimed only at providing the finances for my studies. Now, I had embarked upon a career and I could see a life stretching before me of training, management and perhaps even an executive role. This was something I had never contemplated when younger and now it seemed a potential reality.

My life in Ford's began with an interview with Mr Jim Butler, Company Secretary. This meeting helped establish the different organisational levels for me. One only entered his office on invitation, waited until he looked up or addressed you, and one spoke only when spoken to. I had never before been addressed simply as "Dowling" and I never really liked it, even coming from so august a person as the company secretary. I was sent to work in each of the organisation's departments and report back to him after each of these assignments. I was also assigned two mentors who were to guide my progress through the company maze. They were the Kerry footballer, Paudie Sheehy from Tralee, son of John Joe a county footballing legend, and Finbar Ambrose. They worked for the internal audit function and I was dispatched from here to each of my postings. It was inevitable, therefore, that I was regarded as a company spy working undercover.

The offices looked out over the River Lee. I loved watching the cargo ships from Dagenham berth and unload their boxes of car parts onto the quays. There was a rough beauty to this process and I enjoyed the mechanical dance of the stevedores and the cranes. The boxes containing the parts were solid and well made. They were prized trophies as the bases for furniture, hen houses and dog kennels.

Life was regimented in the company. It was paternalistic and, as I recall, unions weren't recognised. There was strict discrimination between grades, best expressed in the eating arrangements, ranging from a factory canteen to a plush executive dining room. There was an executive toilet too but, try as I might, I failed to find out just what made this so special.

When I had completed my training programme in Cork, I was sent to Dagenham, Ford's plant in east London, to join a graduate trainee class made up of people from Ford's operations all around the world. This was a very different journey from those that I had made when travelling to find summer work to pay my fees. This time I flew from Dublin – an era when flying was an enviable luxury rather than the chore it has since become. I began my time in Dagenham as I intended to continue. The training executive met me on the first day and asked, 'Where do you dine in Cork? Executive, I suppose?' I didn't disabuse him and dined regally for my two-week sojourn there.

There was a certain romance to the motor trade in those days that The Beatles later captured in their song *She's Leaving Home* that talks of a young girl running away to meet "*a man from the motor trade.*" It was something exciting and a bit shady.

I enjoyed watching the cars move along the production line, hearing the banging and whirring as they moved from one section to the next. I remember buying my first car, a sleek two-tone turquoise and black Anglia 105E, and watching its progress along the assembly line until it came to the end and into my waiting arms. Car models had much more individual design and gave a sense of personality back then. My Anglia had rear -light wings that gave it a sporty feel and I felt that I had arrived.

Once trained, I took a proper job in the purchasing department, a critical area in terms of cost management and control. An important part of my work was to take part in the annual stock audit of steel which was held in Springs Ltd in Wexford. We carried out this count manually on the premises. Tom O'Keeffe was the assistant purchasing manager and he was responsible for the audit. Together with Marcus Hurley, who was an operative and the person who actually counted the steel, we travelled to Wexford.

Ford's Training course at Langley, Berkshire, 1961.

This trip exemplifies aspects of the class divisions that infested institutions such as Ford's in those days. Tom was supplied with a company car for the journey and, as we quit the city, we cast aside our collars and ties – something that would have been unheard of in the offices. It's just as well people can't see how I'm dressed for my broadcasts on Saturday nights now! One striking example of the divisions between layers in business was the fact that Tom O'Keeffe gave us permission to use his first name for the duration of the trip. Our accommodation was also determined by our position in the hierarchy. Tom and I stayed in the Talbot Hotel in Wexford town while Marcus made do with a guest house. The trip gave me a chance to learn more about Tom and his background. He came from Cobh and told stories of playing tennis, wearing "whites" for weekend games. This was the reason I had never played tennis in Charleville, I couldn't afford the clothes which were mandatory in clubs and which, of course, emphasised divisions within society.

Cork society was highly stratified then. There was a small minority of the better-off who controlled much of life for the majority. Privilege expressed itself in the place one lived, the school one attended, ones sports and pastimes and ones expectations of life. I found that I straddled the divide, my college education having allowed me leave my rural past to get a foothold on the lower rungs of Cork's social ladder.

I also learnt on that trip that individual enterprise was thriving alongside Ford's corporate success. Towards the end of our Wexford trip, Marcus made a somewhat startling statement when he offered a special service to Tom. He quickly clarified that what he meant was that he cut his hair and offered to cut mine too. He had brought his clippers, combs and scissors with him and, "afterhours, of course" , he gave both of us the standard, unfashionable short back and sides. I learnt afterwards that he was barber to lots of the men in the plant.

What made the trip revealing was the way in which we automatically resumed our allocated positions in life and Ford's on the return leg. We put on our doffed collars and ties and Tom became Mr O'Keeffe again and the casual, informal conversation became formal and constrained once more.

I devoted much of my free time at evenings and weekends to my thesis. It took a lot of effort and concentration to return to my books after a hard day's or week's work in Ford's. My opus did cause some interest in my employment and it led to a story that spread widely through the management in the works. One manager, from personnel, who aspired to a loftier station in life than he then possessed, claimed that he was a personal friend of Dowling's professor whose name was Bowen! Such a faux pas quickly became embellished as it travelled through the plant. I completed the thesis and Mary Murphy, who worked in Ford's, typed it. Professor McCarthy decorated the manuscript with pencils' worth of blue lines and margin notes. She granted me a good pass while believing that I was worth more.

I was glad to have it finished and to end what I now recognise was a major turning point in my life. My time in college had made my Ford's experience possible and was to provide the foundation for the rest of my career. I had two women to thank for my academic career: Vera who suggested that it was a possibility, and Professor McCarthy who moulded me into a scholar and a graduate. I never felt fully

Champion Pancake tosser -
Jury's Hotel Shrove Tuesday,
1982.

satisfied with my thesis. I would have preferred to have followed my own instinct which was, as I mentioned, to study the works of Canon Sheehan but that was not to be. I have had the opportunity to return to both the Canon and Ms Bowen in my broadcasting career, so perhaps I've had the best of a number of worlds. I never attended my graduation ceremony for my Masters. I had moved on and left my student days behind me.

Ford's gave me security and, having completed my Masters, the chance to get on with other aspects of my life that were left on hold. Vera and I married on the 14th of February in 1961. It was a Tuesday and that most romantic of days, St Valentine's, was made even more propitious by being Shrove or Pancake Tuesday, the day before Lent begins. In those days weddings weren't allowed in Catholic churches during Lent, so Shrove Tuesday was the last opportunity for forty days to get married.

Vera and I had lived quite a distance from each other prior to our wedding. She lived in Sunday's Well while I was in digs in Summerhill. Our meetings required my making a bus journey on the single decker, number 14. I got to know the conductor well. The night before the wedding, I was travelling with my wedding clothes carefully bundled beside me. Johnny, the conductor, sat beside me and as I was leaving, he shook my hand and from his top pocket he took out a ten shilling note and put it in my top pocket. He wished me a happy day for the morrow. There were tears in my eyes as I alighted at my stop. Such kindness from one who wasn't the most cheerful of men normally, touched me deeply and it is a memory that I carry with me still.

Vera and Donncha with, from left, Vera's brother, Lieutenant Colonel Tim Galvin, Vera's mother, Mrs M. Galvin, and Donncha's mother, Mrs H. Dowling.

Fittingly, our wedding took place in the Collegiate Chapel of St Finbarr in UCC. We had three priests officiate. Fr Dan O Callaghan from Aghada parish was the chief celebrant while Fr Andrew Barry from Doneraile and an tAthair Tadhg Ó Murchú assisted. I travelled to the church flanked by Cathal O'Corcora, my best man, and Michael Riordan, my groomsman. My sisters, Kitty and Mary, were Vera's bridesmaids. Most of my classmates were there. Another Vera, Vera Jones, a good friend from Croom in Co. Limerick, played the organ, accompanying Denis Leahy, an excellent tenor from Kanturk. Weddings were morning affairs then and our wedding Mass was at 11 o'clock. Afterwards, Liam Kennedy took some pictures and then we proceeded like royalty in a limousine to our wedding breakfast in the Metropole Hotel. I remember that meal fondly, the food, toasts and speeches followed by a dramatic rush to Kent station to catch the Dublin train for our honeymoon night in the old Jury's Hotel in College Green.

Our honeymoon destination was Paris, a city that both of us dearly wanted to visit. We took the Aer Lingus Paris flight from Dublin the next morning. The flight was particularly memorable as there were two nuns sitting in the seats directly in front of us who prayed constantly for the flight's duration. We weren't seasoned fliers by any

Hotel wedding breakfast bill and receipt.

Arc de Triomphe
Vera & Sunshine in the Louvre →

Champs Elysées. Vera looking 'knowing' studies a street Picasso.

"Meditation" in the Louvre
"he Unknown Warrior"
mean where the flowers are laid!

Place De La Concorde & Vera.

PARIS

Vera, bag and all at A. de Triomphe

The Man Himself. Did he ever leave the Wife says "Arc De Triomphe"!!!

"Rond Point, Champs Elysées + Vera
"The Obelisk," lovely hieroglyphics!
N.B. That is Vera at the Corner! →

Mona Lisa escaping from the Tuileries Gardens, or to be mundane Unknown model being photographed.

Arc De Triomphe in the Shade of Denis. X marks the spot.
Not the fat man on Right!
For information on Pigalle
etc. etc. please ring ......

You guessed!
Vera at the A. de Triomphe.
N.B. the "Raymond Kenna in Paris" gaze or is it daze!

means and the appeals for divine intercession did little to calm our nerves. Our honeymoon time was limited; each of us had been given a week's leave.

We decided to spend most of this in Paris, staying at the Hotel Phénix on the Rue du Général Lanrezac. This was close to Place de l'Étoile at the end of the Avenue des Champs Elysées. We were a short walk from the Metro station and had Paris at our feet. We walked everywhere and saw the sights and enjoyed Paris in the springtime. We had first danced together to the tune *Under the Bridges of Paris* and now, as man and wife, we were able to see and walk across them. Thomas Jefferson once said, 'A walk about Paris will provide lessons in history, beauty, and the point of life.' We took this lesson to heart. In our breaks from the buildings and galleries, we gorged on croissants, rolls and cups of strong aromatic coffee. That time in Paris was too brief but we have returned since to refresh our memories and lay down new ones. It is our favourite city and as Humphrey Bogart told Ingrid Bergman in *Casablanca*, 'We'll always have Paris.'

We took the train and boat from Paris to London as I wanted to meet my old friends from the Strand and introduce them to my new wife. I also wanted to enjoy, if only briefly, that city in its smoggy dirtiness.

Back in Cork, we settled into married life. We had an apartment that we gradually made our own. Indeed, on our first night back we found that our bed hadn't been delivered and so our first night together in Cork was spent sleeping on the floor.

Life felt good then and every day dawned with promise. Work in Ford's was rewarding and I enjoyed being with and dealing with those of the motor world. There was a certainty and perhaps a lack of adventure, though, that gnawed inside me. Perhaps, I was afraid that like Eliot's Prufrock, I, too, was quickly growing old and my thoughts might soon be worried about wearing the bottoms of my trousers rolled. Thus I began to cast about for a new, different challenge. I knew that I had to use my degree quickly before it lost its lustre. I realised that my preference was to work in the world of the arts rather than commerce. I must have conveyed my restlessness to others as a colleague in Ford's, Tom O'Donohue, drew my attention to an advertisement in *The Cork Examiner*.

Perhaps he saw an embryonic broadcaster in my nature but it was sufficient to fire my imagination. Radió Éireann was looking for a Programme Assistant to work in Union Quay in Cork. The duties included broadcasting in Irish and English and co-operating with the Regional Officer. I decided to throw my hat into the ring. My letter of application covered every aspect of my life to date that might in some way prepare me for a radio career. I was gratified to receive an application form a short time later. This I completed and waited for further developments. I wasn't overly optimistic as I had no contact in Radio Éireann.

Early in 1964, I received an invitation to attend for interview at the studios in Union Quay. The letter acted like a starting gun for my intensive preparations. My first step was to buy a reel-to-reel Grundig tape recorder to practise speaking into a microphone. I was shocked by what I heard. My accent was flat and identifiable not just to Cork but to a few

RADIO ÉIREANN

G.P.O. Dublin 1, Ireland. Tel. 42981

17th December, 1963.

COMPETITION FOR POST AS PROGRAMME ASSISTANT (CORK)

Dear Mr. Denis P. Dowling

With reference to your application in connection with the above you are invited to attend for interview at Radio Éireann, G.P.O. Dublin (1st Door, Henry Street)/Broadcasting Studios, School of Music, Union Quay, Cork, at 4.45 p.m. on 7th January, '64. You should bring this notification with you.

Applicants will be required to defray their own travelling etc. expenses.

Please reply by the 2nd January, 1964 stating whether or not you propose to attend.

Yours faithfully,

S. Ó Murchadha
Personnel Office

towns and villages in the north of the county. In those days there was a huge emphasis on pronunciation and a lack of accent. The BBC had a big influence in this regard; they required the broadcaster-preferred 'received pronunciation,' that is speaking in the way that the upper-class spoke in the English southern counties. Radio Éireann had its own version of this, a type of 'Hiberno-received' pronunciation. There were regional and local accents heard on the national broadcaster but these were a more refined version of what I heard day-to-day. My confidence took a further knock when I met a classmate from UCC who told me that he had also applied and that he knew two people who worked there and they assured him that he was a dead cert for the post. I was crestfallen but I'm not one to give up easily and attended for interview, determined but without too much expectation.

I had very little interview experience in my time. In reality, Ford's had been my only proper one. I waited in the foyer to be called by Síle Ní Bhriain, Radio Éireann's Regional Officer. I felt real empathy with anyone who had faced a firing squad – waiting is a terrible thing. The interview with Ms Ní Bhriain and two colleagues, Mr Kevin Roche and Mr Gerry McLoughlin, stuttered and stopped in parts, but otherwise went well. A letter from my former Professor impressed, as did my fluency in Irish. I left with hopes not too high, buoyed up only by a comment from the man at reception that I had lasted longer than the others. I was surprised then when a week later I received a telephone call at the office in Ford's from Ms. Ní Bhriain telling me that I had been successful but saying that there was one more hurdle to overcome - a microphone test to assess the suitability of my voice for broadcast.

The test involved reading a script describing a walking holiday in Greece. This was an alien and unsettling experience. It resembles the first time you are X-rayed. You're prepared and then the technician leaves and takes up a position behind a glass window and you are there alone. A red light comes on and you know that the rest of your life could depend on a favourable outcome. Ms. Ní Bhriain wished me good luck and I set to reading the text. There were unscheduled pauses, sharp intakes of breath coupled with my leaving out of the, to me, unpronounceable Greek names, but I muddled through and at the end heard through my headphones that I was in.

The first problem presented to me was the issue of my name. I always had been "Denis Dowling." Ms Ní Bhriain said that everyone there used the Irish version of their name and she asked pointedly what I intended to do. I had no second thought; I was now Donncha Ó Dúlaing. This was a permanent and pensionable position and so I also had to undergo a medical examination. I went through the usual tests and in the end, the doctor asked me if I had ever spent time in hospital. Thinking that this question was an indirect reference to the scourge of TB that had ravaged families in Ireland up until this time, I answered, 'Never.' Without missing a breath, he asked, 'Did you take out your own tonsils then?' I apologised and told him I had forgotten about that event. He gave me a clean bill of health and I was into RTÉ.

My early days were spent familiarising myself with the way things were done there. I had grown used to the Ford's way of working and broadcasting was very different. Like any neophyte, I had to learn where everything was and what everybody did. Every organisation has its own culture and set of unwritten rules and RTÉ was no different. I had bought a sheepskin coat in the belief that it was the type of fashion accessory worn by a broadcaster. I hung my new possession on the closest free coat hanger but was soon informed that I had usurped the Regional Officer's peg.

The first people I met in the Radio Centre in Union Quay stay fixed in my memory. They were the ones who provided advice and quiet guidance that has stood me in good stead down through the years. Joe Gibbons, the sound technical superintendent; Paddy O'Connor and Oliver O'Brien, both sound in self and in occupation; Douglas Gunne, the Balance Control Officer – for sound; Ettie O'Mahony, the secretarial assistant; Mrs Brady, the tea maker; Paddy O'Keeffe, who manned reception; Paddy Corcoran, who cleaned, wooed pigeons on the roof and yodelled; and Máire Ní Mhurchú, my fellow programme assistant. Uinsionn MacGruairc joined us at a later stage.

Radio broadcasting in the sixties differed significantly from what we know it to be today. Television was in its infancy in Ireland. Not everyone had a TV set as they were expensive to buy and were often hired for a weekly charge. RTÉ television was the only station that most people, living away from the East Coast and the North, could receive. It depended a lot upon imported programmes from the US and there was only a limited number of home-grown programmes.

Radió Éireann was only on air for part of the day. Recording was primitive and time-consuming relative to today and sound mixing was an art rather than the computerised science that it is now. Our influences were more local – we looked to the BBC for information on the latest thinking in technology or content rather than across the Atlantic to the States. We were aware, too, of the tremendous responsibility that we bore to inform and, to an extent, to educate. Most of us had a commitment to foster and promote Irish culture and, wherever possible, the use of the language. There was a little of the missionary zeal about us but tempered by our belief in the importance of avoiding bias and the promotion of personal agendas. We produced programmes such as *A Munster Journal, Annso's Ansúd sa Mumhain, Late but Light* and *A Woman's World.* My co-assistant, Máire, compiled and presented a range of children's programmes.

I began broadcasting at the bottom rung of the ladder. I started by introducing a programme entitled, *Conversations with Missionaries* which, as its name suggested, featured Síle Ní Bhriain in conversation with members of the clergy who had spent their lives working in the developing world. I gradually moved from a basic continuity role to presenting programmes. My first programmes were the weekly *A Munster Journal,* which covered news and items of interest for people living in the province and its sister programme in Irish, *Anso 's Ansúd Sa Mhumhain.*

Cork may not have had Carnaby Street, the centre of the swinging sixties in London, but we did have celebrities visiting and performing. I enjoyed an interview with Millie, the Jamaican-born singer who had a hit in 1964 with *My Boy Lollipop*. I had an encounter with a young gentleman singer from the UK, Mick Jagger, who fronted an up-and-upcoming rock ensemble going under the name of "The Rolling Stones." The group were playing in The Savoy in Cork and creating a stir in the city centre. I was the intrepid reporter charged with interviewing this young singer. The proceedings deserve reproduction in their entirety.

Mick Jagger - Rolling Stones Concert, Slane Castle, 1982.

DOD: 'Mr Jagger what brings you to Cork?'

MJ: 'Concerts - Blues, man, blues, we're a rhythm and blues band.'

DOD: 'Something like The Beatles then.'

MJ: 'Naw, nothing like The Beatles, right?'

DOD: 'Have you ever made records?'

MJ: 'Yeah, yeah man, a few. Do you know *Can't Get No Satisfaction*?'

DOD: 'Well no, actually, I used to collect Mario Lanza and Ronnie Ronalde discs.'

MJ: 'You don't seem to know very much about us, do you?'

DOD: 'Well, no actually, should I ... by the way, where do you come from?'

MJ: 'From London – ever heard of it?'

DOD: 'Vaguely, I must thank you and your friends for a most informative and delightful chat here in Cork. I hope we meet again sometime.'

The interview faded into peals of laughter from the interviewer, interviewee and those around us. I do hope that this nice young man went on to carve out a career for himself in music and that a broadcast from Cork may have helped him achieve his ambitions.

I had been a year in broadcasting when I had the opportunity to meet the then president of the country, Mr Éamon de Valera. He was visiting Bruree, his home village, and the home of a good friend of mine, Mainchín Seoighe. Mainchín had taught me Irish in our classes in Charleville. His mother, Nora, had been in the same class as the president in his national school days. We met the 'Long Fella', as he was affectionately nicknamed, in Nora's home. The meeting was private and affable but it was the seed for what was to be my first major breakthrough, a radio series on the president's childhood which was broadcast under the title, *A Boy from Bruree*. I'll return to this later as it was a formative event for me and had some value in developing an understanding of the great man and what was to drive him in later life.

These programmes gave me a new and different insight into what was happening in Munster then. I travelled all over the province and got to meet people who weren't normally heard on radio. Teachers in village schools, priests working in the parishes, the local post mistress, leaders and members of the GAA and the Irish Country Women's Association. I had learnt that the best way to interview someone was for me, the interviewer, to stay as quiet as possible and let them fill the silence with their stories. I followed the same formula in programmes such as *Mid-Morning* and *A Woman's Voice*. It was finding the hidden Munster that drew me to these people and, indeed, it is what drives me still and always will.

Things moved quickly from those days under Síle Ní Bhriain's strict but benign tutelage. I prepared and broadcast a tribute to Daniel Corkery, entitled, *Dónal Ó Corcora Remembered,* at her prompting. Corkery had a major influence on other writers including Frank O'Connor, Seán Ó Faoláin and Séamus Murphy. *Teach In* was another programme that was well received and the late Professor Gus Martin was generous in his praise of it in his review published in the now extinct *Irish Press*:

"The most exciting piece of radio I have heard for many a day was in Donncha Ó Dúlaing's finely edited report from the Cork, 'Teach In'... If you want to get the state of urgency, excitement and intensity of the occasion, tune in..."

One of the people I'm proudest of bringing onto the airways was Edna O'Brien, the brilliant, controversial novelist. Her first novels, *The Country Girls* and *Girl with the Green Eyes* had just been published, banned and in some cases burnt, echoing the treatment meted out to Eric Cross's book, *The Tailor and Ansty* some years previously. *The Tailor* described the life and times of a couple from Gougane Barra in rural west county Cork. It retold their fireside stories and attitudes to life. The Censorship Board banned the book and the local worthies organised a boycott of the couple which lasted until their deaths. Noble senators in Seanad Éireann castigated the book and the couple, accusing them of filth, corrupting youth and moral degeneracy. Censorship, I believe, tells us more about the minds of people who

With Gay Byrne and Ciarán
MacMathúna, celebrating
40 years of broadcasting at
the launch of a new set of
commemorative postage
stamps at the GPO in 2001.

decide what is corrupt than it does about those at whom it casts stones. For me, the book captures a part of Irish life that I cherish and have celebrated in my life. Don't take my word for it, you can borrow a copy from your local library and I don't think that you need worry about being struck by lightning as you exit its portals!

Broadcasting in Ireland changed rapidly through the sixties, driven in the main by television. In a strange way, television, and particularly Telefís Éireann, had a liberating impact on radio, too. Some presenters moved between the two media and there was a synergy between them. One of the most significant events of that era was the establishing of a Friday night chat show called *The Late Late Show,* which came to our screens in 1962, and featured an up-and-coming broadcaster named Gay Byrne. Another ground-breaking series, *7 Days,* took to the air in late 1966. These programmes were expanding the boundaries of broadcasting and allowing us to explore different and, in my opinion, more relevant topics. The advent of *The Riordans,* television soap about farming folk, helped to break down the prejudice against more rural accents.

On the mail boat to England - a fate for many Irish men and women over the years.

I was a magpie in terms of from whom and from where I learnt. Ireland had experienced massive emigration in the fifties and sixties with most going to work in labouring jobs in Britain. In December 1965 I visited the Irish community in England, particularly London, which I knew and understood well. While there, I was keen to make contact with people in the BBC in Broadcasting House and gain some insights into how they achieved broadcasting excellence. Teresa McGonigle from Cobh edited the still-running and even then well-established daily programme, *Woman's Hour*. Teresa introduced me to some of the major programme producers in that corporation.

I was struck how open and eager people there were to help a relative novice like me and I drew on the

Broadcasting outside The Crown Moran Hotel in Cricklewood, the meeting place of many Irish immigrants, during the '40s, '50s and '60s.

guidance I received then for many years to come. I spent some time there and met the famous presenter, Marjorie Anderson. I also got the opportunity to go to a recording of *Friday Night is Music Night,* a firm favourite of the BBC Light Service. This took place in the Camden Theatre, a large former cinema that had an excellent natural acoustic. Its large stage meant that there was room for an orchestra, brass band, soloists and backing singers to perform in the same show. Jimmy Kingsbury presented. It planted the seed that would eventually grow into my own series, *On Stage in Cork.*

There was one famous person I met but sadly never managed to coax to give me an interview. This was the well-known Nobel Laureate, John Steinbeck. I got a telephone call from one of my former workmates in the hotel in Waterville telling me that the novelist was staying with them. It was a cold, frosty night in January 1966 – regardless I didn't hesitate. I left the office, bought ten copies of his books and loaded them into my car. I naturally brought my tape recorder and hit the road for Waterville, roughly a hundred miles on dark, windy roads. It was approaching midnight when I arrived and begged the night porter to call Mr Steinbeck, who at that stage, naturally enough, had gone to bed. After some entreaties, the porter called his room. A while later I saw John Steinbeck descending the stairs with his wife. He was tall, tousled, bearded and wearing his dark red dressing gown. I had barely begun talking when his wife, Elaine, interjected to say that there would be no interview. I could feel that the atmosphere was souring quickly and I pointed out that I had travelled a long way. I proffered my books for signing and suddenly he changed. He took the books and promised to meet me and return them to me autographed the next week when he visited Cork.

He was true to his word and we had lunch in the Metropole Hotel in the city. Again, I had my tape recorder with me but his wife insisted that he was too unwell to give an interview. Nevertheless, we chatted about his writing, his travels and his Irish roots. His father's family were from Germany but his mother's was from Derry. I never got my interview but I still have the autographed books as a memento from those meetings. They took on a special poignancy a couple of short years afterwards when I heard that he had died at the age of 66 – the result of a lifetime's heavy smoking.

My broadcasting career took another turn when Norris Davidson, the head of scriptwriters, asked me to join his team in Radio Éireann's Henry Street Offices above the GPO in O'Connell Street - the centre of Dublin. This was hallowed ground for me. My office looked out towards Cole Lane where The O'Rahilly had given up his last breath in the fight for Irish freedom. I was at the centre of historical commemoration, too, as the GPO was the centre of the commemoration of the fiftieth anniversary of the Easter Rising in 1966, as it had been the focal point of that uprising. It was hard to avoid the sense of ghosts, real or imaginary, looking over your shoulder and questioning what you had done with the freedom for which they had so fiercely fought and died.

The scriptwriting department was the broadcasting home to such radio luminaries as Seán MacRéamóinn, Ciarán MacMathúna and P.P. Maguire. I was flattered and, in a certain sense, intimidated by their reputations. One of the reasons for my selection was that Francis McManus, Head of Features, had found my documentary on Daniel Corkery to be workmanlike and enjoyable. Norris Davidson asked me to prepare a short series to be entitled *A Corkman's Dublin*. He suggested that I dip into Joyce and skim Seán O'Casey's autobiographies for inspiration.

I did as I was asked but walked the streets as well to breathe in the atmosphere that imbued every lane and backstreet of what was then a shambolic city. This was the Dublin of Kavanagh and Clarke, Brendan Behan and Ulick O'Connor, Bang Bang and Johnny Forty Coats, MacLíammóir and Edwards, the Dubliners and Dickie Rock. I revelled in the opportunity and wandered the streets from morn to nightfall until I eventually fell under the spell of that city. My series was accepted and broadcast. Other programmes followed and I began to feel that I had added another notch to my radio belt.

Following my stint in scriptwriting, I decided to return to Cork. While I've described the positive changes that came about with the launch of television, there was continued animosity between the two services as many of radio's best people migrated or were press-ganged into the new service. The Cork studios lost a number of the more senior key people. This delivered personal benefit as it created programme opportunities that probably wouldn't have come my way.

Síle, who had guided and advised me through my nursery days in broadcasting, was becoming increasingly unwell and absent through illness. Her programme output declined and in a short time was transferred to St Vincent's Hospital in Dublin. She wasted quickly and I hardly recognised her on what was to prove my final visit to see her. She didn't lose her interest in the studios and enquired about administrative work that needed taking care of. She discussed plans for the coming year and while doing so, that spirit I'd known, and firstly feared but later came to admire and love, came back despite her deteriorating health. We parted and sometime later, as Alfred Lord Tennyson put it, she crossed the bar.

I was appointed Regional Officer on Síle's passing. I began to pursue new opportunities to reach out to our present listenership and entice new listeners to join us. I engaged directly with communities and groups throughout Munster giving talks on broadcasting. I followed these presentations with a recording for *Mid-Morning,* a radio slot I shared with my colleagues in scriptwriting in Henry Street. It led Jean Sheridan who attended one of these talks to describe me as the voice of genuine Munster. I also met Maeve Curtis, a journalist with *The Cork Examiner* and she inveigled me to attend the ICA summer college in Termonfeckin, Co. Louth. In a short few years, I was delivering a course there on my own. I found the ICA a great well to draw from

On Stage in Cork.

for programme material. The women from that body gave a direct line into the homes, farms and small businesses of Ireland and a voice to a large segment of the population that were under-represented on the airwaves.

I drew on my BBC visit to put together a Saturday night show modelled very roughly one their *Friday Night is Music Night.* Our programme, *On Stage in Cork*, played before full houses in the Cork School of Music Concert Hall. I presented the programme and had guests from all over the province and further afield. It was a great experience and one that I enjoyed thoroughly. I didn't know then, but it was part of my final lap of honour in Union Quay.

6 HIGHS AND LOWS

...Another programme that had its genesis in those meetings was *Sunday Miscellany* one of RTÉ's best known and best-loved programmes. Now running for close to fifty years, it blends music, poetry and storytelling to create a temporal paradise on Sunday mornings. ...

At the microphone in the studio in July 1976 preparing for the next edition of *Highway and Byways*.

TOM HARDIMAN IS A dapper man always well presented in an elegant suit. He is quiet, courteous and a careful listener. He is an engineer and, when engineered himself, he was given a backbone of steel, though carefully concealed. His face can be inscrutable, a classic poker face, but his eyes twinkle mischievously which even he finds hard to disguise. Tom took over as Director General (DG) in RTÉ in 1968. One of his aims was to modernise the radio service and give it the flexibility it needed to provide a service in a fast-moving and changing world. Pirate radio had just sailed onto the horizon in Ireland and pop music was becoming all pervasive. Mr Hardiman had a strong commitment to radio and particularly to its use of the Irish language and retaining the uniquely Irish aspects of the daily output. Tom believed that the use of Irish should come from the heart.

The Radio Steering Committee was formed to translate these aspirations into action. I was appointed to it along with Kevin Roche, P.P. Maguire and Oliver Maloney, who chaired the proceedings. We reviewed our activities totally and after argument, soul--searching and debate, we were able to propose a new direction for the radio service. We introduced a range of new programmes, including *Music for Middlebrows,* presented by Des Keogh which was intended to run for thirteen weeks. It ran for thirty-two years and developed a huge following in its time. Another programme that had its genesis in those meetings was *Sunday Miscellany* one of RTÉ's best known and best-loved programmes. Now running for close to fifty years, it blends music, poetry and storytelling to create a temporal paradise on Sunday mornings.

While I may have helped create some oases of calm for the

listening public, it was far from calm in RTÉ. I was appointed Head of Features and Current Affairs while still Regional Officer for Cork. The senior staff showed little sign of welcoming me to their ranks. I was perceived as being an outsider, a whippersnapper and unfit to fill the shoes of Francis MacManus, the previous incumbent. There was also a misguided belief that I was politically "well got" which arose from the interviews that I had done with Éamon de Valera. This was untrue as these had resulted from personal rather than political contacts and the President eschewed any politicisation of his role. To a certain extent, my lack of political connection contributed to the President's agreeing to be interviewed at all. His speaking only about his childhood in the programmes underlined this.

For my part, I didn't care about the negative views held and occasionally expressed; I was determined to keep alive the magic of radio in RTÉ in whatever way I could. Newspaper columnists repeated the criticism heard from my colleagues within the walls and these fed a negative attitude. One of my intentions was to find new blood to present new programme ideas. Freda McGough was one such person. With an excellent broadcasting voice, she was a talented reporter who served RTÉ well for many years after. Others included Annette Andrews, who moved from continuity, and Terry Prone and Christina Murphy, who brought life to our programmes for younger listeners. One of the people I'm proudest of bringing to RTÉ was Liam Nolan, a fellow Corkman from Cobh. Liam was presenting, among other things, the flagship *Today* programme on the BBC. He also had a great interest and broadcasting track record in sports journalism. I had met Liam a year before in London and he expressed the desire to return to Ireland. He was married and had a young family and, like so many emigrants, wanted to raise his family in his native land. He returned to present the *Liam Nolan Hour* which later became *Here and Now*. Our cup overflowed with excellence at this stage as I was privileged to work with Andy O'Mahony, John Bowman and Brendan Balfe, three consummate broadcasters who have given much of quality to Irish radio over the years.

I have always admired Liam's broadcasting prowess and his ability to describe the minutiae of a game such that you could see it clearly in your mind's eye. These meetings drove the service and managed all of the output. The DG frequently attended to keep his finger on the pulse.

Language was always an issue in RTÉ. Tom Hardiman was supportive of moves aimed at encouraging its greater use of Irish in our day-to-day working. I tried to make our management meetings bilingual and proposed this; it shouldn't have caused any problem as all employees were required to speak Irish on recruitment. Anyhow, for some reason or other, we never managed to bring this idea to fruition and meetings carried on in English.

I made one important contribution towards the advancement of the language during my time as a senior manager in RTÉ and that was helping to establish Raidió na Gaeltachta in 1971. Once again, it was Tom Hardiman who guided and supported this major development and every time I listen to that station I take a certain pride in my role in its establishment.

My domestic arrangements continued to undergo great and joyful change. The Ó Dúlaing clan expanded and we were delivered of five wonderful and healthy children in the sixties. All of them, I'm proud to state, born in Cork although the last, Donncha, only just made it. Our first son, Feargal, arrived into this world on the 4th of July 1963. While it may have been Independence Day in the USA, it was a major change in Vera's and my life. Ours had been a relatively carefree, somewhat bohemian life by the then Cork standards and so the responsibilities of parenthood came as something of a joyous shock to the system. Our youth, love and enthusiasm carried us through.

Baby Sinéad.

Parenting obviously suited us for Feargal was quickly followed by Rúairí on the 8th of September 1964; our daughter, Sinéad, was also a September baby, arriving on the 26th of that month in 1966; third son, Dónal, was born on the 8th of January in 1968 and our family was complete with the birth of Donncha on the 25th of April 1969. Donncha junior had little opportunity to put down Corkonian roots as we quit our family home "Waikiki" in Rostellan, East Cork, when he was just four months old. I named the house after one of Elizabeth Bowen's homes that had caught my imagination when I was completing my thesis. My work meant that I had to relocate to the metropolis that was Dublin.

Our first staging post was in Kilmacud, a south county suburb. We moved soon after this to Nutley Lane in Donnybrook before we finally found the house that has been home for Vera and me and, until they were fully fledged, our children, close to RTÉ's headquarters in Donnybrook. We made summer trips back to "Waikiki" for some time giving the children the opportunity to connect with their family and keep in touch with their paternal roots.

I was working in RTÉ's Henry Street studios at the time. There was a Primary Gaelscoil, Scoil Cholmcille (boys) and Scoil Mhuire (girls), now amalgamated as Scoil Chaoimhín, in the grounds of the Department of Education in Marlborough Street, just a few hundred yards from the studios, and I was fortunate to be able to bring our boys with me on the bus while they attended that school. It was a great school for them, learning through Irish, close to my workplace and within a short walk of the hallowed ground that is Croke Park. Indeed, the Principal there at the time, Aodh Ó Ruairc, used to make the announcements and was the very voice of Croke Park. Growing children keep you grounded and it was a breath of fresh air to chat and play with them, away from the childishness I experienced from some of the adults I encountered doing the day job.

Telegram to Sinéad from Éamon de Valera wishing her a happy first birthday.

While RTÉ was changing in 1969, so was the world, and doing so most dramatically. The Vietnam War dominated international news virtually daily and in that year, millions of Americans marched against the war – thought to have been the largest protest ever to have taken place. Aldrin and Armstrong bounced across the surface of the moon and spoke of giant steps for mankind while we looked skywards at the disk of light tamed forever. Woodstock brought over half a million disaffected youth together for a concert in a small town in New York State.

There was change afoot closer to home too. British troops patrolled streets in Northern Ireland while civil rights' protests spread across the six counties. The trouble in the North built steadily during the year as we watched with disbelief as old certainties crumbled into sectarian and security-force violence. In early August 1969, I was as far from Derry as the man in the moon. Like many "Southerners", I admired the Northern Civil Rights movement from a careful distance. It was, quite simply, none of my business. Career, progress, affluence sometime, these were the immediate priorities,

However, as things escalated, I, along with my colleagues in the Features and Current Affairs department, decided that we should allow the listeners in the Republic the chance to hear in depth what was happening on their own island. We planned two one-hour long programmes: one focusing on Derry and the other on Belfast. We would transmit these on Sunday morning.

I decided to lead from the front – unusual then – and go north with one of the two teams, one to each city. We planned to research each programme and then head home to edit and produce the shows for the following Sunday. I had selected the teams carefully and I joined the Derry team which included, Nollaig McCarthy, Howard

Kinlay, Michael Littleton and Seán MacRéammoin. This was new for all of us. We started in Derry where the people of the Bogside and Creggan, both nationalist areas, were besieged in their own city. I had never been to the "six counties" before.

It was a Friday night when we travelled and we stopped in Monaghan where we decided to spend the night. Three of us visited the local Garda station and asked if it was safe to cross the border at

night. The Garda orderly looked us up and down somewhat critically and even when we repeated that we were an RTÉ team, he gave me a strong impression that offences against some State might, or could, be perpetrated by us. He advised us to wait until morning and as we left, suggested that me, with my Cork accent, better keep my mouth shut when we crossed into the six counties. Shortly after dawn, we crossed the border at Aughnacloy and we were greeted by a large billboard warning us that we were "Welcome to Northern Ireland."

That was scarcely how it seemed some twenty yards later when we were stopped by the B -Specials. This was my first time seeing a "Special" in the flesh and it was scarcely designed to make me anxious to further our relationship. The young man, he seemed all Adam's apple, poked his machine gun in the car window and in a brusque and nervous voice, asked: 'D' ye know where yer goin?' which was the worst possible question for us. We didn't. His two friends, one of whom eyed us over his rifle and the other who sat and trained his machine gun on us, never spoke. One of my companions asked him if his gun was really loaded and dangerous. Happily, he withdrew it from the window. We were allowed to go, although I found the back of my neck prickling as, out of the corner of my eye, I saw our friend swivel his machine gun towards the rear of our car. I did not wish to be "shot in the back while trying to escape!"

Derry was shocking. It felt as if we had driven into a war film. In reality it was a war zone. We could see a pall of smoke from tear gas and burning tyres, as we approached. We could feel the air as the gas stung our eyes and caught the back of our throats. The streets were strewn with rubble; walls painted with slogans and murals; businesses with boarded up windows. The residents had spent their nights and days repelling wave after wave of attack from the Royal Ulster Constabulary (RUC) and the B-Specials, a paramilitary reserve force dominated by Loyalists. Fear ruled the streets and imbued a sense of foreboding.

Young British soldiers had arrived on the scene and they were bemused, unsure why they were there and who was the enemy. The local people welcomed them with some misgivings as possibly being the ones who would save them from the unremitting violence of the hated B-Specials and the repression from the RUC. It was a case of the devil you don't know.

The 12th of August marked a further deterioration of the situation, the day of the annual Apprentice Boys' parade in Derry, when aged apprentices march to commemorate the relief of the siege of the city in 1688. On the 10th the Derry Citizens' Defence Association approached the Apprentice Boys and asked them to change the route

The women presenters and producers of the RTÉ Radio Features and Current Affairs Department with Department Head, Donncha Ó Dúlaing, in February 1969. Sitting on the floor, from left to right, Annette Cusack (presenter of *Woman's Page*) Clare Boylan (interviewer with *Weekend Roundabout*) and Nodlaig McCarthy (interviewer with *The World this Week*). Standing in the back row, left to right, Máire Ní Mhurchú (presenter of *Children Talking*) Christina Murphy (presenter of *Ár bPobal Féin*), Deirdre Ní Laoire, Pamela Perry (interviewer), Terry Prone (presenter of *The Young Idea*), Katherine Rose and producer Áine McEvoy (*Woman's Page* and *The Church in Action*).

to avoid flashpoints in what was already a tinderbox. They refused. There was mass meeting of residents in Celtic Park that evening and all women and children considered vulnerable were evacuated. Most of them joined the streams of refugees who fled south to the Republic. The Bogsiders then began the erection of barricades.

We spoke to the community leaders and community members. Eddie McAteer led the Nationalist Party and had represented Derry in the British Parliament. He was seen as part of the old guard nationalists who were being replaced by the Social Democratic and Labour Party (SDLP) from which John Hume was emerging as a powerful new leader, and also by the rise of the Provisional IRA who were re-arming and moving from purely defensive to offensive attacks. Mr McAteer identified the root of the troubles trenchantly as being the colonization of the city in 1613 and the subsequent repression of the nationalist population through gerrymandering, which allowed one third of the population to control the local administration.

We heard an alternative view from Eamonn McCann who was an activist in the Derry Housing Action Committee and had been prominent in the civil rights' marches in the city in 1968. He saw the problem in terms of class war and the enemy being the system that the RUC and the B-Specials represented. He saw the traditional leaders such as the Churches and the established political parties as being out of touch with the community and the realities on the ground. He surprised me and rattled my traditional view of Irish nationalism by dismissing a role for the South in the changing of the North – instead stressing the need for the South to change and destroy Toryism there, too.

Perhaps though it was the voices of the ordinary residents that resonated most with me and have stayed with me. I met exhausted parents whose eyes were smarting from gas as they talked of the fear that they had for themselves and their children as the RUC baton-charged at random, fired gas into their houses and broke down doors to drag people out to beat them or take them into detention.

The riots of the 12th of August are remembered still as the Battle of the Bogside. Buildings, armoured cars and barriers burnt as Police fired gas and rubber bullets and the citizens replied with stones and petrol bombs. Rumours swirled through the streets faster than the sting of gas and these inflamed both sides to escalate the situation. A few tried vainly to restore order. The following morning, the burnt-out cars and shops told the story of the night before.

Sometimes, the most important thing in the life of a reporter is to be in the right place as the right time. And we were on the 13th of August. It was on the evening of that day that the then Taoiseach, Jack

Lynch, made the most famous speech of his career. Often now dubbed the "We will not stand idly by" speech, the Taoiseach didn't use those precise words. But his comments were significant nonetheless.

> *"It is clear now that the present situation cannot be allowed to continue. It is evident also that the Stormont government is no longer in control of the situation. Indeed, the present situation is the inevitable outcome of the policies pursued for decades by successive Stormont governments. It is clear also that the Irish Government can no longer stand by and see innocent people injured and perhaps worse. It is obvious that the RUC is no longer accepted as an impartial police force. Neither would the employment of British troops be acceptable nor would they be likely to restore peaceful conditions, certainly not in the long term."*

The Taoiseach wanted to involve the United Nations and also stated the intention of establishing field hospitals on the Republic's side of the border. It was interpreted by some, especially those in besieged Derry, that the Irish army would soon pour over the border to save them. The speech "electrified the place" according to Father Ed Daly. Father Daly, who was later to become famous as the "Bloody Sunday" priest talked to me, 'Yes, things looked better now... Of course, the people were moved by An Taoiseach's stirring speech... Certainly they could not endure much more... the British Army... Well, that was a different matter... an uneasy peace... a matter of time... things would never be the same again... were the soldiers really welcome... well , of course, the devil himself would be welcome at this time.' His handshake was warm and his smile, even from tired eyes, was a Northerner's thanks and for more help to come.

The people of the Bogside had felt isolated but now believed that Dublin was listening to them and taking their side. We were fortunate to be on hand to record the reactions and the emotions of those around us and we headed back to Dublin in a cloud of euphoria.

We interviewed priests, bishops, and others whose names were little known then but who became household names in the following years.

When we returned across the border to the peace and normality of the South, it hardly seemed real as we edited it until all hours on the Sunday morning of its transmission. We broadcast our two programmes, *Derry '69* and *Belfast '69*, and I'm proud that we did. They were a great success.

I regard them now among the most important programmes I have

made. I have a few awards from my broadcasting days. I also have some souvenirs one of which is a rubber bullet fired in my direction during the making of these programmes.

Attitudes in RTÉ changed rapidly as the Troubles intensified in the North. A form of self-censorship emerged and affected even the smallest of matters. Songs once accepted as standards in our musical programme repertoire were now re-examined in the light of a new orthodoxy that suspected anything nationalistic as supporting the armed struggle. As someone who loved songs and music from the late nineteenth and early twentieth centuries and who loved broadcasting in the first language, I felt an extra level of pressure as I watched what I believed was the bending of the news and current affairs to match a particular political perspective, and tarring those who opposed it as terrorists. I belonged to a different camp who believed that we should tell it as we found it.

The self-censorship in RTÉ gained official sanction when the Fianna Fáil Minister for Post and Telegraphs, Mr Gerry Collins, instructed RTÉ not to broadcast:

> *"Any matter that could be calculated to promote the aims or activities of any organisation which engages in, promotes, encourages or advocates the attaining of any particular objectives by violent means."*

The station interpreted this as meaning that it was banned from transmitting the voices of anyone from the Provisional or Official IRA or any other 'extreme' group. This ran counter to all that I believed radio broadcasting should be or do. The diktat smacked of repression and for me was tinged with the iron fist of our former occupiers. I was greatly upset by this and found it difficult to work as part of a management team enforcing this repressive direction.

The next time I was in Derry was for the "Bloody Sunday" funerals. I was part of the broadcasting team. It was late at night when we arrived and I joined the media of the world in a city centre hotel and prepared to settle down for the night. Whiskey, brandy and vodka were plentiful and the "craic" was good. I couldn't help but think of the Bogside and the Creggan and wonder how the "craic" was there. I decided, there and then that journalistic mateyness was more than I needed, so two of us set out for the Creggan. The Bogside was quiet. There were no troops about. We stopped a woman on a steep hill. 'Of course, I know the Creggan. I live there myself... I'm out for a wee loaf. You're welcome to come home and share it!' So, a new friend was made.

Her husband and children did not seem surprised: 'Nothin' surprises us in the Creggan. Not even the British Army,' her husband told us. I could well believe it. Later, when we were fed, we went to the church where the victims of the Bloody Sunday massacre lay. The scene will always be part of me. Thirteen coffins exuding the smell of fresh wood and varnish. Hundreds filed by. Others sat or knelt. No one spoke. After all the noise, the speeches, the warnings, the screams, the shouts, the shots, here was the silence of death.

The names of the dead meant little: James Wray, Bernard McGuigan, Patrick Doherty or the others were no more than links in an unbroken chain of fifty years of oppression and destruction.

A young girl near me began to weep. Over and over again she repeated her useless bitter little question, 'Why did they have to do it?' What was it Father Daly had said back in '69? 'The devil himself would be welcome at this time.' Well, the British paratroopers, if not the devil, had outstayed their welcome and Father Daly was there to see his prophecy of a few years earlier realised in the most bloodthirsty and wanton killings ever seen in this country.

The funerals, attended by thousands, were, as I had expected, sombre, pitiful and bitter expressions of the people's sorrow. The only light relief was provided by several members of the Southern Parliament who seemed to spend the greater part of the morning darting around like demented mayflies in their effort to ensure people knew they were present. I remember saying in my commentary that Derry, if it had been alone in its sorrow the previous Sunday, would never be alone again. A somewhat hasty assessment, I fear, one made in the wake of a burning British Embassy in Dublin and the feverish expressions of sympathy and support heard on all sides in the twenty-six counties. Three or four days was quite sufficient to reduce these expression to what they really were, transient responses to Derry's awful predicament.

The next time I visited Derry was several months after Internment and this time I went in the company of Edna O'Brien. Edna, who was then reading her *Country Girls* on *Three-O-One,* had shown a warm and real interest in the people of the North and had asked me to bring her to Derry to meet some of those most actively engaged in the Northern minority's struggle for survival. What I am really trying to say she wanted to meet some of the national majority in the Derry area!

This was pre-Motorman and so "Free Derry" greeted us. First of all, there were the British soldiers. We stopped. I was ordered out, spread-eagled and searched. The soldier seemed to pay special attention to my chest and armpits. I wondered idly how he might react if I whispered "B.O." I'll never know!

Then we drove through the Diamond and I asked for Sean Keenan's house. Sean, a great and loyal Derry Republican, was at that time in Long Kesh, but I had been told that we would receive a warm welcome from his daughter, Róisín. When we reached the little house in the

Edna O'Brien and Bernadette McAliskey at the Forum for Peace and Reconciliation in Dublin Castle January 1995.

Creggan estate it was quite late in the evening and long shadows were stretching across the little streets. It was still, apart from the nattering motor of a helicopter that circled over and over us as we climbed the steep hill to our destination. I almost forgot to say that we had to negotiate an "official" road-block and then a "Provo" questioning before we arrived at the Keenan home.

The greeting was warm without being effusive. A friendly voice whispering in the background was not conducive to relaxing. 'Oh, Róisín, it's the wee fellow from the Free State Radio again.' It was the stress on the word "again" that worried me. Edna was that evening's attraction. Lean young men kept coming in for cups of tea, kept looking in her direction. She was gloriously and magnificently herself. Róisín talked of her father, her brothers, Seán and Séamus, and the difficulties and happiness of living in Free Derry. She wondered how long it would last.

There was another young girl in the room. Her name was Nora. She was Róisín's younger sister. She sat immobile before the fireless hearth on this dusky spring evening. She shivered, did not speak. She had about her an air of insuperable sadness. The TV set , which mouthed voiceless in the corner, threw its grey-black reflections across her bowed head. She raised her eyes and, without moving, began to talk: 'Me Daddy's in Long Kesh, not his first nor his second time inside, nor his last either, I suppose. Me mammy's dead,' she added, almost as a guilty afterthought. 'And me husband, he was lifted last week and the brother, poor wee Colm, he was shot dead by the soldiers and he not even armed.' A pause. 'And me baby, me wee wain, died too, a wee while back.' There was a longer pause. She said, quite naturally, 'Oh, them soldiers, they're bad lads.'

Róisín was talking. 'Would you like a wee present?' she asked. 'Oh, now I know you would and I know my Daddy'd like you to have it, too. She handed me a little tray cloth embroidered in Long Kesh. The inscription under the green, white and gold tricolour, and the volunteer holding a rifle aloft, (for some reason it reminded me of Cúchulainn in the General Post Office in Dublin) was the tattered legend, 'Ireland unfree shall never be at peace.' I took it from her, without speaking. There seemed nothing to say. 'Thanks' is an inadequate word for Creggan hospitality and generosity. I never believed before that there was literally a place in Ireland where they give you their last bit. Such a place and such people are those who live on the hills above the Foyle.

"Long Kesh", "Bloody Sunday", the early mornings, the knock-on-the-door dawns, all seemed far away that warm spring dusk in Derry. Yet, here it was, tangible, brutal, real, every day of the week. 'That's the helicopter,' a young boy in the corner said. We listened. It passed over. Seamus said, 'It's like that here always. You never know what'll happen next.' Two silent young men sipping tea nodded. I thought of a poem written by my good friend Patrick Galvin, a few lines of which run:

> *"Soldier*
> *We are tired of the peace you bring*
> *To Irish bones*
> *We dream*
> *We dream that this land*

Is our land
That one day
Catholic and Protestant
Believer and Non- Believer
Will stand here
And dream
As Irishmen."

It was dark now and I had another visit to make before I could leave for Dublin and *Three-O-One* in the early morning. Edna's encouragement and kindness would soon be well known in the Creggan. We also had to call into the Bogside to meet a friend. Leaving the car outside, I was told it was safe and, looking apprehensively at the armed figures of British soldiers in the city walls and at the masked and armed young men who mounted a barricade nearby, we hurried in.

The atmosphere was smokey, beer-smelling, Derry-accented until the silence fell and it fell like a ten- ton truck when we entered! There were men everywhere. Some had been playing darts. Others drinking, others talking, now they were all watching, watching us. 'What will you have?' I asked. Edna, somewhat nervously, said, 'I'll have a Bushmills.' 'Haven't got it,' the barman grunted. I tried again. Nor had they wine! No coffee! No salads! Hamburger? Yes. By now, it seems we appeared to be more or less human and my Cork accent, dangerous in other areas, was acceptable. The noise as we munched our hamburgers was deafening. I hoped that I might choke, but couldn't. Edna, without looking at me or at anyone else, and certainly without speaking, gave the impression that she coped with this sort of situation every day.

She enquired after our contact. 'Never heard of him,' the barman said. I tried another tack, mentioning the name of the man who sent us. 'Oh,' the barman said, 'you mean...' after saying the very name I had used thirty seconds before. 'You mean... why didn't you say so the first time?!' Our man joined us.

It was time for me to go back to the Creggan. The barman saw me to the door. He called one of the masked young men from the barricade who proceeded to give me a quick lecture on British army philosophy. 'Now,' he said, 'that's Bligh's Lane up that way. When you are going by, don't go wild like. You see,' and he paused, 'if you're going too slow, they'd think you're comin' bombin'. And if you go too fast they think you're comin' bombin'. So, now, you know what to do.' I didn't.

Later I met Eileen, whose husband, Paddy, had been shot by the paratroopers on Bloody Sunday. She brought me home to see the "wains" as they lay peacefully sleeping their fatherless dreams in this sad place. She didn't talk much. A friend of hers who was older and had lost a son, had most to say, 'It's terrible to rear them to that age and then to lose them... God's holy will, I suppose... But, he was so strong, so strong and so happy... Always playing with the wains... Used even lift myself in the air when he'd come in in the early mornings. He was on the run you see and used be coming home early. It's then I miss him most.' A slow tear was following a well-worn furrow as she continued. 'And then in one minute, all gone. All nineteen years of lovin' and carin' and nursin' and grievin', all gone. D'you know why he died?' she asked me. Answering herself with a lift of the head, she declared, 'He died for Ireland, for a united Ireland. That's all we know up here. That's all we ever heard from youse down there. For that, God help us, for that my wee boy died. And now...' she spread her hands, whispered," We're all alone!"

> *"Lord, thou art hard on mothers,*
> *we suffer in their coming and their going*
> *and though I grudge them not, I weary, weary*
> *of the long sorrow. And yet I have my joy*
> *My sons were faithful and they fought."*

from Padraig H. Pearse's, *The Mother*

So the night passed. It was 2.30 a.m. when I drank my final cup of tea. Darkness, now murky, now moon-splashed, hatted over the little houses about Derry. Too soon it was time to go. They came to the gate. Séamus, young Seán, Róisín, one or two others. I know that at home someone would say emotive, emotional, sentimental... I knew, too, that these words have no meaning in an already emotional climate, a war situation. Emotions are... stripped back to essentials. Words, anyway, are meaningless. I turned the car and drove down by St. Mary's Church where I, and thousands of others, had sat all night a few months earlier, and passed by the cemetery, where now, at least, they were at rest. Down the Brandywell and "Free Derry Corner", it was as silent as the grave. Even ferrets and the pigs, not to mention the interrogating pimping helicopters seem to be sleeping.

The filmy greyness of a spring dawn was filtering the darkness and paling the moon as I crossed the bridge. The Foyle, caught between night and day, reflected only its own dark stillness. Across the river, up on the heights, dawn was breaking. Lights were going out in the Creggan. Vigilantes, unshaven and bleary-eyed were going home.

It was another day. The end of another night. Most memorable. Sadder than I had ever experienced. The soldier behind the sandbags beckoned me on. A lone man in a car is always safe except under certain

RADIO TELEFÍS ÉIREANN

Sráid Anraí, Baile Átha Cliath 1, Teléfón 42981

11th January, 1972.

Mr. D. Crawford,
Springfield Service Station,
Springfield Rd.,
BELFAST.

Dear Sir,

Thank you for your letter concerning my programme, "Christmas in Belfast".

The material, gathered mostly from wives of internees and mothers of small and now fatherless children was indeed, as you say, a sad but true reflection of the times we live in. The two male contributors, one of whom is a reputable and highly-respected social worker in the city and the other a journalist who spent six Christmases in internment, gave us their views and opinions of the loneliness and isolation afflicting all segments of the Northern Ireland community.

There was not any intention on my part to use the programme for what you described as, "to recruit ignorant and dangerous fanatics for a cause that is undemocratic and irresponsible". The programme was concerned with the utter and complete break-down of the North's fabric of existence. My own abiding impression of the programme was one of sadness and disillusion with the present structures in these unhappy counties.

I regret that it seemed otherwise to you.

Yours sincerely,

Donncha O Dulaing,
HEAD OF FEATURES & CURRENT AFFAIRS.

circumstances. I turned right and had a last look across the river. It was 3.45. And if I hurried, I'd manage breakfast before my programme deadline. The tapes began to roll and I mentally edited my friends. Their story, perhaps it was too real. I wondered would it be acceptable. Material like that often wasn't. Perhaps it was unacceptable, as unacceptable as it was to the people left behind in the Creggan.

The re-introduction of Internment in August 1971 in Northern Ireland became a breaking point for me. The fact that only people from the nationalist community were taken by the British Army and subjected to degrading and inhuman treatment, compounded my disillusionment. My concern was not only for the men who were interned but for their families – particularly those with children whom I felt would suffer the most. Christmas was approaching and I decided to do something to brighten up the lives of these children and show them and their families that they were not forgotten. I launched a campaign to collect toys for them and make sure that their Christmas had some hope in it. I used the radio and newspapers and my contacts spread around Ireland to gather toys. I made contact with the Central Citizens' Defence Committee through their chairman, Tom Conaty. They were more than happy to help with the distribution of the toys.

The top brass in RTÉ were less than happy with my campaign. They certainly weren't willing to accept the volume of toys now being collected in all parts of the country. While the senior echelons of the organisation frowned on what I was doing, colleagues such as Mick McKeever and Tommy Ryan were more than happy to help. Joe Jennings from CIE helped us to resolve the logistical problem by providing a large storage area for the toys near the Five Lamps, close to Connolly (Amiens Street) Station in the city centre. The newspapers carried stories of children giving toys to the campaign that they themselves were to get for Christmas. And the week before Christmas, a large, happy crowd assembled in Connolly Station to see the toys off.

I didn't travel with them because I was told not to by RTÉ Radio management, who opposed the collection. Vera, Feargal and Ruairí travelled to Belfast though, bringing the toys with them. A week later, on Christmas Eve, I did visit Belfast and met the children who received the presents and could see the joy that we had brought. I was gratified to see that an idea of mine had had such a positive influence. I saw this as an extension of one of the Seven Christian Corporal Works of Mercy to visit those in prison. In this case I wasn't visiting the prisoners, but relieving some of the burden that they had to carry while they were held without recourse to justice.

Needless to state, the executives of RTÉ didn't seem to be all that interested in Corporal Works of Mercy on that Christmas Eve. I was surprised to find a telegraph waiting for me on my return from Belfast. I was summoned to meet the Controller of Programmes telling me to visit a senior executive in his own home. While cordial, the executive made RTÉ's displeasure clear concerning what was described the "Santa Claus Train". He believed that my contacts in Belfast were fronts for the Provisional IRA. It wasn't advisable for someone in my position to engage with such people even though he never doubted my good intentions. Following this, I was offered a glass of whiskey and we toasted Christmas.

This time was a great sorrow in my life. I felt alone and bereft. I was working in a job I loved, in an organisation whose ambitions I supported fully and I found that they had put these values to one side. Here was my place of disaffection – to paraphrase TS Eliot. Indeed, he had already captured much of how I felt at the time when he wrote:

> *"Because these wings are no longer wings to fly*
> *But merely vans to beat the air*
> *The air which is now thoroughly small and dry*
> *Smaller and dryer than the will*
> *Teach us to care and not to care*
> *Teach us to sit still."*

The confluence of working under the constraints of Section 31 and the suspicion of anything that appeared nationalist or republican, even when that amounted to nothing more than making a number of children happy at Christmas, weighed me down terribly. I decided that I should resign from my position as the Head of Features and Current Affairs and return to what I had joined the station to do, and that is broadcasting. I discussed this decision with Oliver Maloney and he advised me to be cautious and consider it carefully. I wrote the letter and cast the die.

I found myself alone and without friends. People who before had wanted to discuss ideas with me, now scurried in the other direction with their eyes averted. I now had the reputation, apparently, as it was told to me much later, of being a heavy drinker and an IRA man and, because of this, difficult to work with. Elements in Raidió na Gaeltachta campaigned against me – something which hurt deeply given that I had done so much to champion them when they had few enough friends in the mother ship. Again, I turn to Eliot who perhaps had people such as this in mind when he wrote:

Difficult times: Donncha and sons at home with Rua, 1982.

"We are the hollow men
We are the stuffed men
Leaning together
Headpiece filled with straw. Alas!"

There were those who offered encouragement and support and to these I'll be forever grateful. Edna O'Brien wrote a kind letter expressing her own upset. I recall, too, Pádraic O'Rathallaigh and Peig Monahan, his wife, stopping their car in Donnybrook to give me a few words of encouragement. These small kindnesses kept me going.

This was a terrible time for me and I hurt deeply. But I gradually realised that I had been freed of a burden, a yoke that would have warped and damaged me forever. I may have been worse off financially and in terms of organisational power, but at least I was free of those burdens also – free to be what I had set out to be: a broadcaster.

7 EXTRAORDINARY PEOPLE

... His father was probably of Spanish origin but may have arrived in New York through Cuba or New Mexico. There were several forms of his name used including Valero, de Valero and de Valera. His father was a sculptor and musician and apparently suffered from ill health. He died in 1885 leaving young Éamon's mother without the means to support her son. There is no confusion about his mother's origin; she was Catherine Coll, an immigrant from Bruree in County Limerick. ...

The Ó Dúlaings at Áras an Uachtaráin with President de Valera and his private secretary, Máire Ní Cheallaigh.

A PRIVILEGE OF BEING a radio presenter is that you have the opportunity to interview the luminaries of the day and learn something more about them, their public persona and also occasionally their private self. Interviews are always a snapshot of someone at that particular time. They are affected by their health, their current successes or difficulties, their age and popularity. Empathy from the interviewer for the subject helps them divulge something of their inner self. I don't see my role to judge or criticise, I'll leave that for others; instead, I saw my purpose as being to pose the questions that I imagined the listener would ask if they were present.

I also felt it was important to let the interviewee express what they understood as the truth, not try to catch them out in untruths or errors but to find out what they believed to be true, and why it was true for them. There is little truth that is agreed by everyone and much of what is interesting in life happens in the grey areas. Memory is selective – just as this book is. Memory is also defective and what was told to me was not necessarily how the story began, but the version polished in regular retelling. There were stories, too, that were simple fabrication and it is well worth exploring where these came from and what motivated their telling. There are other stories that have since been overtaken by further information and clarification.

I've chosen to re-examine here just some of the interviews that stand out in my mind. They have a special significance for different reasons: Mícheál Mac Líammóir, an actor who reminds me still of my early desire to run off with the fit-ups; Éamon de Valera, a revolutionary, politician, father of the State and family man; Gene Kelly, legendary Hollywood actor and dancer; women of 1916 who retold the story of the most important days of this country's history – a recounting that had been almost ignored up until that time; Christy Ring, Cork hurling legend and neighbour of my mother's people. There were many more interviewees who deserve a place on this list but I've forced myself to choose the few who have impressed me most, and who have changed me or my broadcasting career since carrying them out.

The Actor and Dreamer

One interview that stands out because it wove truth with fable to yield a colourful, wonderful tale was with Micheál MacLíammóir. The great actor was born Alfred Wilmore in London, the son of English Protestant parents who encouraged him to take to the stage, for money apparently, and he became a renowned child actor with, among others, Noel Coward. He trained in art in London and travelled to Europe where he developed a great love of Ireland and the Irish language. He studied the language and became fluent in writing and speaking.

Micheál MacLíammóir.

He came to Ireland and worked in the fit-ups where he met his lifelong partner, the opera singer and actor, Hilton Edwards. MacLíammóir was an active and enthusiastic promoter of the national language, writing and performing through that medium throughout his life. Together with Hilton, he founded The Taibhdhearch Theatre in Galway and shortly afterwards The Gate Theatre in Dublin in 1928. Micheál was one of Ireland's greatest actors and had an enormous impact for the good on Irish theatre.

"The Boys", as they were commonly known, set up home at No. 4, Harcourt Terrace and it was there that I went to interview the great actor in the autumn of his life. I still believed then that he was a native of Cork and of Irish Catholic parentage. It was, therefore, as a fellow Corkman that I went to meet him. He was tired and in poor health but still wove a spell with words that entranced me. His voice was sonorous and his accent tinged with Cork when he spoke of his childhood in that city. My friend, Jimmy Keenan recorded the occasion.

Our conversation traced his life and the people he had known and worked with. He spoke of WB Yeats and his prickly relationship with that great bard. He found Yeats humourless but then added the aside that nobody who fell in love with Maude Gonne could have much of a sense of humour. He described Countess Markievicz as being charismatic but devoid of humour. The conversation moved to Pádraig Pearse whom MacLíammóir had never known personally. He was, nevertheless, willing to expound on the hero as a man. He commented, somewhat cryptically, that Pearse had two guilt complexes, one being that he was half-English (ironically given that Micheál was fully English) and the other he refused to elaborate on other than to suggest that he had something weighing his conscience.

He spoke of his lifelong friendship with Noel Coward and how they had first acted together as children in a play entitled *The Goldfish* and how the young Noel was sure, even then, that he was bound to be an actor, and how even on his deathbed he pointed out to Mac Líammóir that while they were born in the same year, he, Coward, was the younger and that could never be changed.

Mac Líammóir offered an interesting perspective on our political leaders. He had been pro-Treaty and though he had never met Michael Collins, he professed a fondness for him and such a belief in his leadership that he accepted the pro-Treaty argument. Yet he disliked Collins's militaristic persona. Micheál seemed to have always been interested in the person behind the political mask. Perhaps as an actor he could see through the public face into the politician-player underneath, and it was the less obvious character that he warmed to. He distinguished, too, between de Valera's political face and his human side. He disliked his politics but found the person charming and someone he came to like immensely.

He was similarly interesting when addressing Ireland's current troubles. He used George Bernard Shaw's metaphor to explain it. A healthy man is unaware of his backbone and a healthy nation is not conscious of its nationhood. Once a man's backbone is warped or injured, then he thinks of nothing else. It is the same with nationhood, once injured it becomes an obsession and all efforts are directed towards putting it right. That is what he saw as Ireland's problem: she could think of nothing else but ridding herself of the stranger.

Throughout the interview, Micheál spoke of the great loves of his life: art, music and the theatre. He quoted poetry, reminisced about the works of Michelangelo, pointing out that all the women he painted resembled men and how his "David" was one of the most ravishing things he had seen. He expressed a love for Chopin's music and commented on Oscar Wilde's, another of his Muses, referencing a Chopin nocturne in *Dorian Grey*.

As we moved to the final stages of our talk, we turned to discussing God and the afterlife. Mac Líammóir was religious but perhaps not in the conventional sense. He expressed a strong belief in reincarnation but not necessarily in this world, rather that the spirit is born into another body and using its past life experiences it tries to learn what it failed to do before. Not surprisingly, he compared this to rehearsing a play where you keep working at it until you get it right, the perfect production would lead to Heaven.

We finished the interview by my asking him what made him happy now. He was silent, thoughtful before stating simply, 'Hilton being well and happy.' Hilton was not well then. And so it ended with a declaration of true love. Micheál was a true Irishman because he wanted to be such and he loved the country that he had chosen loyally. He expressed this love through giving us all the gift of theatre and his own passionate performances. For the private person, I realised then, he had only one other thing left and that was his love of Hilton. It was a great romance that spanned the years from the time that they first met in The Athenaeum in Enniscorthy, Co. Wexford, in 1927 to his death in March 1978. The words of Eden Ahbez's song *Nature Boy*, famously rendered by Nat King Cole, came into my mind as I walked back down Harcourt Terrace moved by those last words. Nat King Cole sang:

> *"And then one day, a magic day*
> *He passed my way, and while we spoke*
> *Of many things, fools and kings*
> *This he said to me,*
> *   'The greatest thing you'll ever learn*
> *Is just to love and be loved in return'."*

A Boy from Bruree

My interviews with Éamon de Valera explored the difference between the man and the legend, the child and the man. At that stage, he was President of Ireland and a figurehead representing our struggle for independence and the shaping of the State. He was depicted as cold and austere, with a fanciful commitment to a mythical Ireland with the words "comely maidens dancing at the crossroads" used as a lazy shorthand to summarise his national view. These dismissals were as disingenuous as they were lazy. After all, he had served as leader of those opposing the treaty with Britain. He led Sinn Féin into democratic politics and was one of the founders of Fianna Fáil which was to become the main party in government for most of the life of the State to date.

His political life was well documented but his personal and his early life remained something of a mystery. I had been fascinated by him from my early school days in the Christian Brothers. His picture, along with those of his peers, adorned the school wall and I recall the frequent references to him and the reverence in which these were made. I knew his home place, too, as I had frequently cycled from Charleville to Bruree and passed his homestead in Knockmore, close to the village. I had, you recall, shaken his hand when he visited Charleville and this personal connection made him all the more intriguing.

Áras an Uactaráin,
PRESIDENT'S HOUSE

Baile Áta Cliat.
DUBLIN

27th August, 1970

Dear Donncha,

I received your letter, and appreciate how you would like to get a personal interview with the President in connection with the biography to be published on November 2nd next. He has had similar requests from quite a number already, but to all he is quite adamant - "he will not be giving any interviews on the biography to be published on November 2nd....this book is that of the authors and, therefore, their responsibility should interviews or comments be necessary". The President has made this clear to Telefís Éireann also. and to the B.B.C.

However, I would be grateful if you would give me a ring when you return to Dublin so that we can arrange for you to drop up. I would like to fill you in on the background etc., to this biography as I feel sure you would find such information both necessary and useful to anything you may be doing on it. He was very glad to see An tAthair Ó Fiannachta's name mentioned by you as one suitable for inclusion in a panel to be interviews. Fr. O'Fiannachta has put his heart and soul into the Irish book - the first part published over a year or more ago, and the second part due to be published almost immediately. The President was most anxious all the time that the Irish should come out first. Although it is not a translation of the English, needless to remark were the English to precede the Irish the language would likely suffer. Although the President has no financial interest whatever in either book, at least he was able to lay down the fact that the Irish come first on account of making both the documents and himself available to the authors. He also insisted that the book be printed in Ireland - "and by Ireland I mean the 32 counties" as the President said. You can see from these few remarks that there are some useful facts that I can give you. At this point I think you should know that the President was very upset to receive a proof copy of the book when he had not even seen the typescript of whole chapters and portions of the book; and to learn that the proof copy had been sent to newspaper offices etc., I'll tell you more about this when I see you.

We are delighted you are enjoying yourselves down in your native south and that the weather has been so good for the past week.

Give me affectionate regards to all.

Marie O'Kelly

A Munster Journal was one of my first programmes as a rookie reporter in Union Quay in Cork. I was keen to interview Mainchín Seoighe, the writer and Irish scholar, who lived in Tankardstown close to Bruree. In due course I did. While visiting him, I spoke to his mother, Mrs Nora Joyce, who had been at school with de Valera in Bruree and referred to him as "Eddie", as she had done as a child. She mentioned that the President often called to visit her when he found himself in the area and she suggested that I might like to meet him the next time that he did.

So it came to pass that I was invited to come to the Joyce household when the President would be making an unofficial visit. I recall the morning vividly. It was grey, misty. The house had been cleaned and tidied as if for a station Mass or the visit of royalty. Everyone maintained a nervous silence, broken only by occasional whispered comments.

The great man arrived, accompanied by Máire Ní Cheallaigh, his private secretary. I told her of my desire to interview the great man about growing up in Bruree and she, in turn, put this to the President. He wasn't willing to do it there and then, and frustrated me further by chatting about his childhood, with vivid details, for the next hour or so. The contact was made though, and sometime after, I received a summons to meet the President in the Áras. His secretary gave me names of people in Bruree to speak to in advance so that I could build up a picture of childhood at that time.

The details of Éamon de Valera's early childhood are confused and sometimes there are contradictory claims about his father's country of origin. Dev was born in New York on the 18th of September 1881. His father was probably of Spanish origin but may have arrived in New York through Cuba or New Mexico. There were several forms of his name used including Valero, de Valero and de Valera. His father was a sculptor and musician and apparently suffered from ill health. He died in 1885 leaving young Éamon's mother without the means to support her son. There is no confusion about his mother's origin; she was Catherine Coll, an immigrant from Bruree in County Limerick. She sent her son home with his uncle Pat to be reared by his grandparents in Knockmore, north of Bruree on the road to Drumacomer. Dev was approaching three years of age.

The absence of a father and almost no relationship with his mother may have made de Valera even more attached to the place that he called home and those who cared for him there. I wondered how the President, then in his eighties, would respond to my probing his early life. It had been something less examined until then and I was afraid that his memories would have faded or been sanitised over the decades. I need not have worried. He wanted to tell the story of his early life and the importance of a rural upbringing in shaping his worldview.

The series of interviews began with him telephoning me and inviting me to the Áras the following Tuesday. Our first meeting there was a lunch with the President, his wife, Sinéad, and a professor of history whose name escapes me now. His wife was particularly warm and welcoming and she agreed to my recording her reciting poetry, that was her passion. The President was very amenable and agreed to my recording thirteen hours of interview over the coming months. We sat across a big table in the Áras with a mobile unit outside the windows recording everything. Paddy O'Donovan was in charge of the recording and made sure that the technology didn't damage the rapport between the President and me.

The RTÉ authorities were in two minds about these interviews. There was some resentment on the part of senior broadcasters in Dublin that a young Cork upstart had got such a scoop without their knowing. The other view recognised that this was an opportunity to gain an insight into a founder of the State who had remained enigmatic despite his prominence. There was nothing that they could do about it, though, as the President had expressed his desire to record this material and made it clear that I was the person he wanted to do it.

The interviews went very well as I found the President to be warm, engaging and with a strong wish to share his past with a wider public. In interviewing him, therefore, I found that I was pushing an open door. His love of the Irish language was clear and he moved between the two tongues with fluency and clarity. He had learnt much of his Irish from Sinéad who was a teacher and it was an obvious, strong bond between them both. Family was important to him and his love of his wife and children came through clearly to me.

The President's love for his absent mother was still evident, even after all of these years. This love wasn't quite unrequited as he recalled a woman in black who visited during his childhood but only later did he work out that this was his mother. One of his most treasured childhood possessions had been his first book, an alphabet book which was sent to him by his mother from the States. Even after more than eighty years, the President could still recite the short paragraphs for each letter:

> *"A is for ape who has four clever hands, he lives in the woods*
> *in the tropical lands. B is for boar, a savage wild pig...."*

all the way to "L" when he stopped. I found it hard to know whether he finished then because he could no longer remember or whether the memory was too vivid and loaded with emotion.

The President recalled his first night in Ireland when he was still under three years of age. What marked this memory was that it was the only night he spent in what he described as, "the old house." His grandparents moved into their new house the day after he arrived. The President remembered later helping to knock down the old house and remarked how thick and solid the mud walls were. I can only imagine that this must have raised conflicting emotions for the young boy as he was demolishing what had been his mother's home.

De Valera was a normal, if somewhat mischievous, young boy. His schooling was basic. He attended the local school and there, the half of the class who were writing got to sit in the desks, while the other half stood. He had distinct memories of being in a group of children who challenged each other to point out exotic, far off places such as Christmas Island or Kamchatka on the map of the world. There were arranged fights in the school yard and one of his schoolmates put the broken tip of a shoe through the palm of his hand and marked him for life.

His childhood world was a tranquil and slow-moving one. His teacher, Paddy Kelly, cycled to school on a penny-farthing and de Valera remembered watching a penny-farthing race in the village. He talked of smoking turf and rattan stems with fellow youngsters although he omitted to recount the outcome of this activity. Like all boys, he played wherever there was an opportunity. The village railway station was a favourite haunt of his and he described how he used to slide empty coal wagons down from Sutton's store back to the bumpers. His companions and himself clung to the side of the carriage and controlled the wagons with the footbrake.

De Valera had a fondness for horses and horse riding which I think may have surprised many.

It's not surprising considering where he grew up and the great horse tradition there. What came as a surprise to me, and what would surprise many still, is that he had ridden race horses on a few occasions. The fact that the owners allowed him to suggests that he was skilled around horses and able to handle them properly. He told me of coming across a local man one day by the name of Willie Daly riding home on his horse. The man was obviously the worse for drink and he and the horse were weaving from side to side.

The horse, "March Boy", was well known and had won the Charleville Plate. Young Éamon was afraid that the man would fall and injure or kill himself and was worrying what to do when the man's steward and another came along in a horse and trap. They put the drunken rider into the sidecar but it needed the two of them to control him. Dev was asked to ride the horse to the man's home and he was delighted to do so. He exercised a horse for a Mr Barron which also raced at Charleville. In that case the rather heavy owner was looking for someone lighter to give the horse a gallop – something Dev enjoyed thoroughly.

Much of Dev's time, outside school hours, was taken up with farm work. He worked closely with his uncle and many of his memories involved both of them together attending fairs where a freezing Dev recalls one time having a pint of mulled stout – a drink he found wonderful. Perhaps an early political act was when the young Éamon acted as lookout while his uncle grazed the cattle on the 'long farm', the grass margins by the road side. Dev could identify the policemen's gait from a half-mile away and they were able to move their few head of cattle to another road.

With President Éamon de Valera in Áras an Uachtaráin in 1966 are Vera, Feargal,
Ruairí and Donncha.

With Uachtarán na hÉireann, Michael D. Higgins at Áras an Uachtarain, in August 2014 were
Feargal, Ruairí, Donncha, Vera, and Donncha Óg. President Higgins presented a specially
commissioned sculpture to Donncha in recognition of his contribution to Irish culture.

Dev milked the cows and mashed the turnips for their feed. His uncle only owned a half acre and hired out land to graze the young steers he bought in the market for fattening. Dev gained a detailed knowledge of the tightrope existence that farmers and rural people lived at that time. It affected him profoundly and had, I'm sure, a deep influence on his future policies of self-sufficiency and independence.

Dev's earliest exposure to politics came at home. He listened to his uncle reading the newspaper to his grandmother. He heard of William O'Brien's agitation and his escape from prison. Although very young, he remembered the Mitchelstown massacre when the police shot three rioters following a rent strike against the Dowager Kingston. His early political memories include the decline and fall of Parnell and the difficulty that a staunchly Catholic rural community had dealing with this. Dev's first political activism that he could remember was attending a boycotting meeting led by Father Sheehy, the Land League priest.

Fr Sheehy was appointed to Bruree parish after his release from prison for his part in Land League agitation. Dev recalled the Fedamore Band attending and he being fascinated by the band's large drum. His uncle's election to the Kilmallock District Council must also have helped politicise the young boy. Here was someone with a strong commitment to the land and labour organisation and also someone that Dev looked up to. Dev perceived the local community as being strongly nationalistic and, doubtless, he absorbed this sense in his daily life.

Dev had a strong sense of place and community. It was obvious from talking with him that the village society was important to him and something that shaped the views that he would espouse later. He admired Fr Sheehy's sermons and his eloquent portrayal of the historical importance of Bruree stretching back to mythical times. It is evident that the young Dev had a great love for village life and those who lived there. His recollections of his childhood friends, playing and working there, his professed enjoyment of the social aspect of village life, the dances, missions and fairs, all point to the foundation of his later political motivation.

I interviewed the President over several months and I like to believe that I got an opportunity to see something of the real man. He was sharp and insightful even though he was then in his eighties, and distinctly unimpressed by plámás or flattery. An example of this came towards the end of the series of interviews when some senior officials at RTÉ felt that they too should be present at the final interview. I explained this to the President and he didn't seem best pleased. I gather that word went back from the Áras to RTÉ and nothing further was mentioned of others being in attendance.

The President was warm and friendly. He was very much a family man and expressed a great interest in my own family and how the children were faring. He was very keen that I bring the children to the Áras to visit and have their photos taken with him. I was struck by how great he was with them, despite being practically blind at the time. He let them play around the Áras and let them play with a ceremonial sword that President John F. Kennedy had presented to him during his visit. For my part, I was petrified that one of my young fellas would inadvertently run the Head of State through with this weapon. Thankfully, nothing untoward happened.

The interviews with the President opened up the opportunity to meet his wife, Sinéad. She was more reserved than her more outgoing husband but still warm and friendly in conversation. I had the pleasure of sitting with them both as they sipped from glasses of port and reminisced. She had written and published books and plays for children and she had an excellent memory for poetry and was fond of reciting – almost always in Irish. She was an extremely well-spoken woman with a fund of tales about her family and friends that reached back to 1798, the year of the Wexford uprising and also the year that her father was born.

She retold stories that she had heard as a child about her father's surviving the Famine. She recalled meetings with Douglas Hyde, Dr Hyde as she called him, and the great Fenian, John O'Leary. Pádraig Pearse had impressed her and she admired him greatly but she did not warm to him personally. It was a joy and privilege to hear at first hand of the lives of the people who had shaped this nation of ours from one of those who had played an important part in it.

There are many who have asked me since what Dev was really like. The passage of time and his portrayal in films and television programmes has turned his memory into something of a caricature.

Dev replaced his parents' absence with the community of people who took him into their hearts in Bruree. He summarised this beautifully when he said:

'Oh, I think that loving one's immediate surroundings is very natural and we naturally widen it as our horizon gets wider. If you love your parish and your own little community, you'll widen it so as to embrace the nation as a whole. I like to think that my love of Ireland originated in Bruree.'

The Man Beside the Fire

In the early 1970s I wrote an entertainment show with the warm encouragement of Senator Labhrás Ó Murchú, his wife, Úna, and my many Comhaltas friends.

The show I called *Where now, Caitlín?* and it was a reflection of my thoughts and actions when the Lord answered every call for national freedom.

Anyway, I was invited to present a reflection of my thinking in the lovely village of Puckane, County Tipperary, on many a warm summer weekend. I did and a wonderful and talented local joined me in the entertainment.

The other day, when thinking of this chapter, I was talking to my Céilí house friend, Kieran Hanrahan, and my long-time mentor

Gene Kelly.

and head of Comhaltas, Senator Labhrás Ó Murchú. Could I forget Puckane and that wonderful summer in the early '70s and those we entertained and the audiences who entertained us? No, I could not.

I know I was taught in college that "tempus fugit" which, of course it does but happy memories and thoughts remain.

I remember Paddy O'Brien now, alas, gone from us and his wonderful accordion playing, and his daughter, Eileen, whose fiddle playing enhanced those long-ago summer weekends in Puckane. I used go to Eileen O'Brien's salon in Nenagh; she always cut my hair when I'd be passing through. Recently when I talked with her, she reminded me of happy fruitful days.

Indeed, those Puckane evenings reflected much of the welcoming Comhaltas world and of the yet-to-come *Fáilte Isteach* nights.

I remember Eamon de Stafort and his heart-warming singing and a young Roy Galvin playing the tin whistle. There were others, too - an island storyteller, a fine dancer and lady recitationist.

Our audiences loved us and none more than a quiet man who sipped tea as he listened by the open fire. On his second visit, he caught my eye and smiled. There was something about him that drew me to his side. The question was as inevitable as it was stupid, 'Have we met before?' 'We could have,' he answered with a gentle smile. Reflections and memories were singing in my mind. 'Do I know you?' His quiet American accent said, 'I doubt it!' He told me that his name was Kelly. I was transfixed when he said, 'My Christian name is Gene.' I gulped. 'Did you sing and dance in the rain?' 'That's me,' he said. I was astounded, delighted and humiliated. Here was one of the greatest Hollywood stars visiting our show in Puckane.

We shared a few beers later during which he asked, 'Were you ever in Hollywood?' 'Not in America,' I replied. 'You'd enjoy it and might do well there,' he said and invited me out. Who knows what might have been? My only real Fáilte was in RTÉ's Radio Centre, but Gene Kelly and my Puckane friends are ever dear to me.

Women of the Revolution

The Easter Rising has always been close to my heart and an inspirational presence in my life. The men of the Rising, their bravery, their belief in their cause, their faultless, unselfish fight and death for the freedom of our country inspired and fostered my love for Ireland. Their almost inevitable defeat spread and opened the grey wing of revolution in my heart.

Women? What women? There were never any featured in my schooldays' history of 1916 or in the stories or tales that I read or heard. It wasn't until the 'Northern Troubles' that the beliefs and ambitions

Rosie Hackett at the Fiftieth Anniversary Commemorations of the 1916 Rising in 1966.

of these women resurfaced. A chance meeting with Síghle Bean Uí Dhonnchadha, one of the most extraordinary women I have ever met, changed my heart and my broadcasting life forever. Síghle, a veteran of the War of Independence and a lifelong republican, was to be my guide and mentor in my various attempts to meet the cheerful and lively survivors of Cumann na mBan and the Citizens' Army who sometimes met at her house in Donnybrook close to Montrose, RTÉ's home, in Dublin.

On one particular night she invited me to meet "a few friends" and not to forget "my little tape machine" which I never did anyway. It was a night that changed my life and opened a door on the very heart of the republicanism that led to the foundation of the State. Through this initial contact, I was to meet Julia Grenan, one of the last women to leave the GPO in Easter Week; Phyllis Bean Uí Cheallaigh who acted as a messenger during the rising and subsequently married the then widowed Seán T. Ó Ceallaigh, future President of Ireland; Margaret Skinnider who fought alongside Countess Markievicz in St. Stephen's Green; Eily O'Hanrahan-O'Reilly whose brother, Mícheál Ó hAnnracháin, was executed for his role in the Rising, and Nora Connolly-O'Brien, the daughter of James Connolly.

These women were to point me to others also, and make the introductions I wanted in order to gain a broad appreciation of the role these women played in the birth of the nation. I later interviewed Leslie Bean de Barra, who gave me a vivid account of what it was like to be in the GPO during the few short, glorious days of Easter week and I talked with Rosie Hackett, whose hand I shook knowing it had been anointed by the still-wet ink of the Proclamation.

These women were primarily involved in communications and maintaining a supply of weapons and explosives. This description understates their real contribution. Cumann na mBan was an auxiliary force and excluded from involvement in direct action. Women in the Citizens' Army did become involved in direct action and played an important role in engagements throughout the Rising. The attitude towards women fighting was highlighted very recently with the release of the records of the Military Pensions Archive in 2014.

I had spoken to Margaret Skinnider about her active involvement. She had led five men in an attack on houses in Harcourt Street with the aim of cutting off the advance of British reinforcements. She suffered two gunshot wounds to the shoulder and another within a quarter of an inch of her spine during this fire fight. Some years later and after the founding of the State, she applied for a military pension as a wounded soldier. She was refused initially as it was believed that the term 'soldier' was inherently male and a woman could not therefore qualify. She was eventually granted a pension but only after more than a decade of paperwork and bureaucracy. Leslie Bean de Barra too told me of how she was left in no doubt about her role when in the GPO with Tom Clarke and Seán MacDiarmada.

Talking to these gentle, elderly ladies gave me some insight into the fear and excitement that they had experienced in those tumultuous years. Julia Grenan's story stood out for me as she typified the tremendous service that these women gave in the background and were subsequently largely ignored. Julia, '"nurse" Elizabeth O'Farrell and Winifred Carney were the last women to leave the GPO. On Easter Monday, Julia carried dispatches to Dundalk and Carrickmacross with orders for the uprising. She returned and reported to the GPO. She made various forays carrying messages and gathering intelligence during the week. She put herself in great personal danger, going out searching for food for the Volunteers. Later Pádraig Pearse entrusted her with a letter to the British Commander telling them that they had razed a Red Cross Unit and threatening hostages that they held in the GPO should there be a recurrence. She spent the whole week hungry and didn't remember having anything at all to eat.

What was most striking about Julia's tale was the wave of emotion that came over her as she recounted her story – particularly when she addressed those final hours as they retreated from the GPO to Moore Street. She had tears in her eyes as she described the inevitable surrender from those houses. She recalled her friend asking Connolly, then on a stretcher, how he was. He replied, 'Bad, the soldier who shot me did a good day's work for the British Parliament!'

A very poignant moment was speaking to Nora Connolly O'Brien about the last hours of her father before his execution. She told of British Army soldiers bringing her mother and herself to visit Connolly in Dublin Castle. It was an emotional scene, one which moves me still whenever I reread her words. Her recounting of Connolly's own word to his wife, 'Haven't I had a great life, Lilian? Isn't this a good end?' captures the courage and commitment of these people. For Nora this must have been the most traumatic ending of what had been an exhausting and draining two weeks. She had begun by travelling north to Belfast on Easter Monday in an effort to persuade Volunteers there to join the Rising. This didn't prove successful and, with her sister, she had to walk back south as the trains had been commandeered by the British military. The sisters slept out in the fields. In Swords they met a contingent of British soldiers and for one brief, ecstatic moment they believed that the British were retreating and the uprising had been a success. She heard then of the surrender and the wounding and serious condition of her father

THE PROCLAMATION OF

POBLACHT NA H EIREANN.

THE PROVISIONAL GOVERNMENT
OF THE

IRISH REPUBLIC
TO THE PEOPLE OF IRELAND.

IRISHMEN AND IRISHWOMEN: In the name of God and of the dead generations from which she receives her old tradition of nationhood, Ireland, through us, summons her children to her flag and strikes for her freedom.

Having organised and trained her manhood through her secret revolutionary organisation, the Irish Republican Brotherhood, and through her open military organisations, the Irish Volunteers and the Irish Citizen Army, having patiently perfected her discipline, having resolutely waited for the right moment to reveal itself, she now seizes that moment, and, supported by her exiled children in America and by gallant allies in Europe, but relying in the first on her own strength, she strikes in full confidence of victory.

We declare the right of the people of Ireland to the ownership of Ireland, and to the unfettered control of Irish destinies, to be sovereign and indefeasible. The long usurpation of that right by a foreign people and government has not extinguished the right, nor can it ever be extinguished except by the destruction of the Irish people. In every generation the Irish people have asserted their right to national freedom and sovereignty; six times during the past three hundred years they have asserted it in arms. Standing on that fundamental right and again asserting it in arms in the face of the world, we hereby proclaim the Irish Republic as a Sovereign Independent State, and we pledge our lives and the lives of our comrades-in-arms to the cause of its freedom, of its welfare, and of its exaltation among the nations.

The Irish Republic is entitled to, and hereby claims, the allegiance of every Irishman and Irishwoman. The Republic guarantees religious and civil liberty, equal rights and equal opportunities to all its citizens, and declares its resolve to pursue the happiness and prosperity of the whole nation and of all its parts, cherishing all the children of the nation equally, and oblivious of the differences carefully fostered by an alien government, which have divided a minority from the majority in the past.

Until our arms have brought the opportune moment for the establishment of a permanent National Government, representative of the whole people of Ireland and elected by the suffrages of all her men and women, the Provisional Government, hereby constituted, will administer the civil and military affairs of the Republic in trust for the people.

We place the cause of the Irish Republic under the protection of the Most High God, Whose blessing we invoke upon our arms, and we pray that no one who serves that cause will dishonour it by cowardice, inhumanity, or rapine. In this supreme hour the Irish nation must, by its valour and discipline and by the readiness of its children to sacrifice themselves for the common good, prove itself worthy of the august destiny to which it is called.

Signed on Behalf of the Provisional Government,

THOMAS J. CLARKE,
SEAN Mac DIARMADA,   THOMAS MacDONAGH,
P. H. PEARSE,   EAMONN CEANNT,
JAMES CONNOLLY,   JOSEPH PLUNKETT.

when she arrived at friends in Drumcondra. I can hardly imagine how devastating this must have been for these two young women.

Nora continued the struggle after her father's execution. Using false papers, she travelled to the United States to spread word of the Rising to appreciative audiences there. Banned by the British from returning to Ireland, nevertheless she snuck across the Irish Sea from Liverpool disguised as a young man. She spent time on the run and worked with the ITGWU during the 1918 election campaign. On the anti-treaty side, both she and her husband, Seamus, were imprisoned for a short period. She remained politically involved throughout her life. She corresponded with Leon Trotsky on her belief in the possibility of creating a workers' republic and the development of socialism internationally. Hers was a lifelong commitment to a struggle for true independence from oppression, whether from a conqueror or capital.

I couldn't mention the women of 1916 without mentioning the indomitable spirit of Rosie Hackett who fought for the rights of her sisters in Jacob's and the freedom of the country in 1916. She is now rightly remembered in Dublin City where a new bridge has been named in her honour. She told me how that great document, *The Proclamation of the Republic,* was put together in Liberty Hall, the night before the Rising. The printing machine was faulty and she helped to patch up the missing type on the plate before the print run. She appeared to take special delight in the fact that her fellow male workers were put out that a woman was playing such a role in the production of such an historic document. Rosie was active in the revolution itself. She was part of the group, along with Michael Mallon and Countess Markievicz, who occupied St Stephen's Green and then moved to the Royal College of Surgeons. She was imprisoned briefly for this before being freed on a general release.

Rosie gave out an infectious sense of enjoyment of life. She was a true activist and believed in direct action over rhetoric. On the first anniversary of James Connolly's execution, the ITGWU decided that they would mark the day by hanging a sign from Liberty Hall saying, "James Connolly murdered 12th of May 1916." The police arrived quickly and removed it. Rosie, along with three other women, would not accept this and printed another poster and took it to the top of the building and hung it there. The police mobilised quickly but this time the women were ready and had nailed shut the door and barricaded it with bags of coal. They kept the banner on display until six o'clock in the evening when the police finally broke through. Rosie boasted that it had taken four hundred police to overpower four women.

I interviewed other women of the Rising and was struck by their dignity and quiet courage. They were just as much a part of the Rising and its success as any man. It was a great shame that as a nation we lacked the courage to recognise this contribution. The new State adopted the same discriminatory policies towards women as our oppressor applied in Ireland and other parts of the empire. It has taken a long time and much further agitation to right these wrongs where they have been righted. I wonder how different this country would have been if we had stayed true to the original beliefs set out in the Proclamation which was addressed to "Irishmen and Irishwomen." It was clear when it said:

> *"The Republic guarantees religious and civil liberty, equal rights and equal opportunities to all its citizens, and declares its resolve to pursue the happiness and prosperity of the whole nation and all of its parts, cherishing all of the children of the nation equally and oblivious of the differences carefully fostered by an alien government, which have divided a minority from the majority in the past."*

Perhaps as we approach the centenary commemorations of the Easter Rising we'll examine these words again and honour fully the promise that they hold. It's an outrageous dream, perhaps, but then so was the Rising itself.

Hurling Legend

Christy Ring is a legend in Cork. Ask anyone to name the best hurlers ever and his name will be the first, or one of the first, mentioned. A legend in his own lifetime, and since his passing, he featured on the hurling team of the millennium and if our species survives to live for another millennium, I doubt there will be many who will surpass him in terms of skill and determination. I have a special fondness for Christy Ring because of an early connection – tenuous enough in the scheme of things, but there nonetheless.

Christy came from Kilboy, a townland close to Cloyne. I suppose his home was about six miles from my grandparents, my mother's people, in Ballyshane near Cloyne, where I spent so many happy summer holidays. I remember well seeing him walking around in

Interviewing hurling legend Christy Ring, in his home in Cloyne village, County Cork, in January 1979 during Donncha's Travelling Roadshow.

Cloyne during those years just as he reached his peak in terms of fame. He was a quiet and kindly man who carried his fame lightly. Everyone wanted to know how he was and what he thought as key matches approached. The county hung on his word and prayed for his good health.

His sister was married to the postman who delivered to my grandparents' house and I remember he'd bring the letters into the fields where we were having our tea during a break from haymaking or whatever we were doing, and he'd be asked, 'How's himself? How's he for Sunday for the Munster final?' and so on. Every word and phrase of his answer were weighed and parsed as if it were a direct quote from the Prophecies of St Malachy.

Christy's origins were humble. He was born on the 12th of October in 1920, the year of "Bloody Sunday" in Croke Park. He was Nicholas and Mary Ring's fourth child and was christened Christopher Michael but was forever known as "Christy." His father had a great passion for hurling and he passed this on to Christy. He'd cycle eighteen miles each way to games in Cork with the young Christy on the crossbar. Christy went to national school in Cloyne. He was a good student and could apply himself when there was a purpose to it. His teacher, Maurice Spillane, once offered a prize of a hurley and sliotar to whoever was the best in the school. Christy put the head down and won the prize. On leaving national school, he became an apprentice mechanic and later went on to become a lorry driver for CIE and then a delivery man for Shell Oil. His rise in hurling deserves the appellation "meteoric." Even as a youngster he had winning ways with Cloyne, St Enda's in Midleton and then with the mighty Glen Rovers.

Christy carried his hurley everywhere and he practised shooting against the walls of the local coal store. He positioned himself thirty yards away and hit the ball, aiming at a particular shutter which was less than a foot wide. He'd prove his accuracy to anyone doubting his prowess by dipping the ball in water before hitting it so that it left a damp imprint on the shutter. Christy went on to win eight All-Ireland medals, three national league medals and nine Munster ones. He played for Cork for twenty-four years and won eighteen Railway Cup medals – a record in itself. Christy was a prolific scorer, breaking records throughout his career.

I had met him at the end of matches; the first one I remember was between Cork and Tipperary in 1949. He was would always talk to you and listen politely to spectators' comments, and seemed genuinely surprised by their praise. I got his autograph on that occasion and it is one of my great annoyances that I have lost it now. I don't know what happened to it. Another day that stands out was when Christy visited Charleville on his way to the United States. He stopped the car and walked through the town shaking hands and talking with everyone along the way. This was the mark of the man – giving generously of himself and his time with a smile.

Robert Kennedy and Peter O'Farrell (centre) meet Christy Ring.

I recall, too, welcoming Christy to my home on the eve of an All-Ireland final. He was accompanied by two of the then stars of the Cork team, Tom Cashman and Dermot McCurtain. Christy watched over them as intently as any Irish mother would and made sure that they ate correctly, taking the fresh ham and avoiding the cakes and rolls the rest of us were having. At his insistence, they headed back for a pre-match early night. As Christy left, he shook hands with my son, Dónal, and, referring to the two others, he told him to, 'Always remember tonight, a great night, and who you met in your home.' Of course, we all remembered that night having spent an evening with the great man on the eve of a final.

I interviewed Christy on a number of occasions and was struck by his quietly-spoken modesty. The interview which remains with me still is one he gave me just two weeks before his untimely death. It was luck that I was able to interview Christy at all that day. I was doing a television programme on a parish priest in Ballycotton who was an excellent artist, when I got a call from Canon Bertie Troy, the Cork coach, telling me that Christy was back home in Cloyne and to get myself and the crew over there for an interview. I asked him about the priest that I was already filming and was told that he'd be happy painting away on his own. I don't think the priest ever forgave me as we skedaddled for Cloyne. Christy had promised to give an interview to me many times when we had met in Páirc Uí Chaoimh and he had said it would be just the two of us. 'Alone' in television terms meant the two of us and a watching camera crew and sound engineers.

What interested me in that interview was what motivated Christy and what was it that had driven him to become such a great sporting hero. I asked him if he had any special training techniques. His answer gives a real insight into his thinking, 'I always tried to do the impossible. It's hard to explain. I thought that there was always more to be done, that you never got to the top in hurling really. You could do anything with the stick; there was no end to one's skill.' Christy practised incessantly. He didn't set out to be better than his opponent, rather he worked to better himself. He brought a hurley with him everywhere when out on his delivery round and if there was a break in his schedule, he was happy to introduce himself to anyone and knock around the sliotar with them. This small insight is revealing in two ways: firstly, the obvious fact that he devoted as much time as possible to honing his already near perfect skills; secondly, he felt the need to introduce himself when he was known the length and breadth of the country.

His self-belief marked him out, too. It was a quiet confidence but as strong and as deep as the man himself. It was this characteristic that made me compare him to Cúchulainn and label him the 'Cúchulainn of Cloyne.' In interview, he commented that he had never come across anyone else stronger than him on the field. 'It was a decided asset,' he continued, 'although I never used it. I knew that if I had to, I could go through.' It was that strength, both inner and outer, that confronted opposition players and few felt strong enough to challenge.

Christy Ring had a deep love and affection for Cloyne. He returned to the village every Saturday and met with family and his pals from his school days. He described having great friends in Cloyne who had helped and supported him and that he had always been very happy in that village. Indeed, friendship was core to the man and something that he valued highly. He said, 'You can't play the game too seriously and when the game is over, there's no point in having post mortems or bad feelings because that's what the game is all about – friends.' In a sense, it's hard to believe Christy when he said you can't take the game too seriously for there was no one who took it more seriously than Christy in terms of preparation and commitment. Once the game was over, though, it was finished and it was the people he played with and against who were important to him.

Humour helps if you're at the top. Christy had a wry, self-deprecating approach to life. He told how, after the 1946 All-Ireland Final against Kilkenny, when he had played one of the best games of his life, but had missed two scoreable frees early in the match, he was coming out of the gate when he heard a voice shout, 'By God, you played a great game but, how did you miss the first two frees?'

In our interview, he emphasised that hurling had meant a lot to him but, as he said, 'There's always a time comes when your family or your home has to be reckoned with as well..." Christy didn't regard any game as having been his last game. He stepped quietly from the limelight and left the pitch clear for other, younger men.

The game of life was harsher on the great man though. Christy was clear, adamant even, that this was the last interview that he would give. He asked that his wife, Rita, and his children be included in the interview as he said, 'This is their day, too.' We shook hands after that interview and there was talk of a book at some time in the future. A little over two weeks later, Christy Ring suffered a massive heart attack while walking past the College of Commerce on Morrison's Island in Cork city. He was 58 years of age. He was such an enduring presence in life that his absence seemed unthinkable.

His passing was mourned throughout the county, the country and those places in the world where hurling is enjoyed. I had been fortunate to grow up with Christy's career and privileged to have witnessed some of his greatest triumphs. Those memories are as strong today as they were so many decades ago and they still warm my heart when they come to mind.

Christy is remembered and honoured throughout the county of Cork. There is a cup named after him and a stadium, too. There is a bridge in the city in his name while visitors arriving into Cork airport are greeted by a statue of him with his hurley in mid-strike, forever hitting the sliotar into the sky. Another life-size statue of Christy stands at the entrance to the playing pitches in Cloyne – and perhaps this is the memorial that would have made him most proud.

8 HIGHWAYS AND BYWAYS

… There were strange adventures along the way. I was at the Bogside Festival in Derry recording set dancing while all around us rubber bullets flew up the street and stones back down. The programme wasn't judged suitable and was never broadcast. John was uncomfortable about it but had to do his job. The attitude in RTÉ seemed to frown on anything that questioned the status quo in the North or indeed the South. It was unhealthy for a State broadcaster to pay such attention to a political agenda …

With American country music singer Glen Campbell in Bunratty, County Clare, in July 1983. Campbell was headlining the Siamsa Cois Laoi festival in Cork.

THE CENSORSHIP OF PUBLICATIONS Board banned Edna O'Brien's *The Country Girls* when it was first published in 1960. The book tells of the lives of two young girls, childhood friends, and how they learn to make their way in the world. It is not pornographic or obscene but a lyrical account of growing up in rural Ireland – an experience I knew well. I had been in contact with the good lady author in the past and indeed she and I had met in Derry on one of my trips to that city. It isn't too surprising therefore that she features again in my broadcasting life.

On my resignation as Head of Features and Current Affairs, I was assigned a programme imaginatively called *Three-O-One,* after its afternoon starting time. I expected to produce this and was surprised then that I was assigned a producer, as if my previous years of radio experience had been expunged from memory. John Skehan was appointed as my editor. He felt uneasy with this arrangement but he had to live with it, as did I. He asked Brendan Balfe to choose the signature tune and he proposed *Flower Among Them All* by Horslips. Perhaps he was delivering a hidden message with his choice but it suited what we were trying to achieve with the new programme. John and I slowly built up a relationship that proved to be creative and friendly as we wrestled with the problem of just what the programme should cover. We positioned the programme as an Arts programme in the broadest sense, with an eclectic mix that dipped into folklore, music, literature and aspects of contemporary Irish life.

Returning to Edna, I decided that it would be a great coup if we were to get her to read *The Country Girls* in serial form on the programme. We debated this extensively as it was banned but I argued that it was only banned in book form. No one had considered or mentioned the oral version and I believed therefore that it was not covered by the original ban. I visited Edna in London and she agreed to the serialisation. It went ahead and was well received by a grateful audience; there were no repercussions afterwards. I'm still not sure if it broke the law but I'm still at liberty so I figure it mustn't have, or else the censors mustn't have listened to afternoon radio.

Off the Beat, 1980 - Frank Hall, Brendan Balfe and Hugh Leonard.

It's hard to describe just how eclectic the programme content was. We kept the mix broad and were always willing to try something different. It is often easy to stick with safe programming, returning to the same issues that interest people. Our intention was to broadcast items that were different but we felt, with the right airing, would catch the listeners' attention. Live broadcasts were an important part of what we did. There are some broadcasters who avoid going live, fearing that the spontaneity will run riot and anarchy will prevail. I've always been a bit of an anarchist and know that the spontaneous can spark great creativity and interest. Going live on air is like attending a concert, there is an added frisson for the audience in knowing that something could potentially go wrong.

One unforgettable programme was the one held to celebrate the ninetieth birthday of Kathleen Behan, mother of famous writer, Brendan. This was in 1979 and the celebration was held in The Embankment, Tallaght, and I was there with my microphone to capture the moment. It was all very Behanesque. I began announcing the programme when the guest of honour launched into *The Tri-Coloured Ribbon,* a song written by her brother, Peadar Kearney, also author of our national anthem, and no one paid any attention to

Personal

64 ST. PATRICK'S STREET.
CORK.

14. 2. 1977

Donncha A Cara,

Thanks very much for your very generous reference to me in yesterday's "Sunday Independent". I can return the compliment as you were the most understanding and fairest of the many who interviewed me. And thank you too, for your fine programmes which I hardly ever miss. I like particularly the selection of poetry with which you intersperse the programmes; today's reading of the mother talking to her baby as she moved towards the river which is to be their grave was though sad, very fine indeed.

I smiled at the hidden meanings in parts of your interview.

Give me a ring when you are next in Cork.

Good wishes to you Donncha and your wife and family for a good life.

Your friend
Tom Barry

anything else. Ulick O'Connor spoke with great affection that night also.

I look back over that time and marvel at the variety and scope of what we covered. I recall Andy Allen, the memory man from Aughrim in Co. Wicklow contrasting with Kingsley Amis, the novelist, and how these contributors blended together. Arthur Askey, one of my heroes from the BBC *Light Programme,* delighted me with his stories and reminiscences. General Tom Barry and his wife, Leslie, then in the Red Cross, told us the details of their first meeting and this was an unplanned precursor to *The Boys of Kilmichael*, a radio documentary broadcast in 1970, fifty years after the event. I enjoyed meeting with Elmer Bernstein, the American composer renowned for his film music, who led me through the composition of scores such as *The Magnificent Seven, The Ten Commandments,* and *The Great Escape* – all films that I had admired and enjoyed.

There were strange adventures along the way. I was at the Bogside Festival in Derry recording set dancing while all around us rubber bullets flew up the street and stones back down. The programme wasn't judged suitable and was never broadcast. John was uncomfortable about it but had to do his job.

The attitude in RTÉ seemed to frown on anything that questioned the status quo in the North or indeed the South. It was unhealthy for a State broadcaster to pay such attention to a political agenda. The invidious impact of Section 31 was that its spirit was applied well beyond the strict application of its regulation. Mine was a minority view, apparently, as Liam Cassidy was to point out in a letter in the Irish Independent in 2007:

"...For 20 years from 1975 to 1995, I was a permanent fixture on the IT&GWU (now Siptu) *branch committee in RTÉ, on which I served as chairman for many years. Accordingly, I*

am well placed to correct the false notion that RTÉ workers did not support Section 31. In fact, most workers in RTÉ, just like the majority of TDs in the Dáil, and the majority of the public, either supported Section 31 or at least had no objection to its operation. I know this because not once in all my years on the branch committee, was a motion proposed, at any level, in any section or branch of the IT&GWU in RTÉ, to remove Section 31. It was neither raised nor discussed.

As my union represented the vast majority of the RTÉ workforce, I can conclude from this that most employees in RTÉ either actively or passively supported Section 31 because they saw the necessity for it.

The demand for the removal of Section 31 in RTÉ was confined to a small number of journalists. They didn't understand then, and some in RTÉ still do not understand now, that a democracy has no obligation to allow freedom of speech to terrorists. This applies as much to the IRA as it does to Islamic terrorists."

I belonged to the small number of journalists I mentioned there who demanded its removal. Frankly, most staff did not have to make these decisions directly. If one worked in administration, catering or marketing then you didn't have to worry about Section 31. It was the journalists who had to deal with it. Looking back at Mr Cassidy's letter now and his comments about Islamic terrorists, I can't help but smile wryly as, while I write this, RTÉ's website has a short film of Abubakar Shekau, the leader of Boko Haram, a Nigerian Islamic fundamentalist group, kidnappers of two-hundred and eighteen unfortunate young school girls, in which he calls for the killing of all Christians and the stopping of young girls attending school. I don't think that people in RTÉ, or in Ireland generally, will be tempted to support this gentleman but may, instead, be jolted to push for action to prevent this type of terrorism now and in the future.

There was a great freedom with *Three-O-One*. Since it was a tabula rasa, we could move and change with our listenership. I heard one day that *Fáilte Isteach* was planning an interview with Canon Sydney MacEwan, the famous tenor. I managed to winkle the Canon's telephone number from one of those working on *Fáilte Isteach* and got in touch with the great priest directly. I arranged to meet him in Glasgow and interviewed him about his life and times.

I flew to Glasgow early one morning and met the Canon for lunch. He had inherited a great interest in Ireland from his mother who came from Portadown. As a child, his family had been chronically short of money but somehow his mother had scraped together enough to give him a musical education. Caught between his love of music and the Lord, he entered the Jesuit novitiate in London but left after a year to study in Glasgow University. John Count McCormack and Sir Compton Mackenzie encouraged him to pursue his musical dreams. He recorded for Allophone in 1934 and toured nationally and internationally.

His religious vocation drew him back to the Church and he trained and was ordained in 1944. He now combined his twin loves, music and Church, and continued to tour and play music – now using the profits to renovate his church and for other good causes. We had a wonderful lunch together. I told him of Irish people's fondness for his recording of *Flowers of the Fairest* and how it was played faithfully every first of May on RTÉ. Once we'd finished lunch, I dashed back to the airport and was back in RTÉ that evening. I met some of the *Fáilte* lads in the corridor and with, I admit, no little glee, told them that I had the Canon's programme recorded for *Three-O-One* and so there was no need for them to concern themselves with it further.

There was some chance to travel with *Three-O-One*; travel to the Nordic region stands out for different reasons. Denmark was our first port of call and due to the extreme parsimonious approach of our travel section in RTÉ, we were booked into a cheap but clean hotel where the cubicle-like rooms had paper-thin walls. I never slept a wink, nor were the guests in the other rooms sleeping either. It was a busy place with people constantly arriving and leaving. Next day at a lunch at the Irish embassy, we mentioned where we were staying; the embassy staff effected a rapid change of accommodation for us as they didn't like the idea of Irish broadcasters being put up in a brothel.

Our travels took us to Finland and this was more exciting for all of the right reasons. We started our visit in Helsinki, a wonderful city, steeped in history, that is spread over several bays and inlets. It has been under Swedish and Russian control over its five-hundred-or-so-year history. We were fortunate to attend a great concert in the then Sibelius Hall and later travelled to Rovaniemi, in the Arctic Circle. Someone had told John Skehan that Finns always carried an extra pair of shoes when visiting someone's home. This seems to have been a misinterpretation of the tradition in some Finnish homes to leave your shoes at the door and walk around in your socks or slippers. We duly arrived at people's houses with extra shoes in plastic bags to be greeted with blank looks from our hosts who had never heard of this idea.

I met a veteran of the early WWII "Hundred Days' War," when the Finnish army held out against a Soviet one that was ten times larger and much better equipped for one hundred and three days. The Finnish troops made use of their knowledge of the forested terrain and the freezing conditions. They wore skis when attacking and white camouflage that allowed them blend in with the snow-covered terrain. The Finns lost 25,000 in the struggle but inflicted losses amounting to 127,000 on the Soviets. It was an heroic struggle that had echoes for me of one of Barry's Flying Columns during our own War of Independence.

I revisited London during my time in *Three-O-One*. There I met Patrick Galvin, the Cork poet, and his reading of his stories and verses remains sharply etched on my mind. He regaled me with tales and songs in a strange Cork-London accent. He had grown up in the harsh environment of Cork city in the 1930s. His experience in Daingean industrial school, where he was exposed to the cruel abuse that characterised these institutions, shaped his early writing. He abhorred Ireland's neutrality in the Second World War. He joined the Royal Air Force when he was only 16 and had served in bomber command and had seen the bombing of cities in the Middle East, and later, Europe. He lived between Ireland and Britain for many years before he finally settled in Cork where he died in 2011. I can still hear him half-read, half-declaim his poem *The Mad Woman of Cork*. The last verse is of immense power and suggestion:

> "*I am the madwoman of Cork*
> *Go away from me.*
> *And if I die now*
> *Don't touch me.*
> *I want to sail in a long boat*
> *From here to Roche's Point*
> *And there I will anoint the sea*
> *With oil and alabaster*
> *I am the madwoman of Cork*
> *And today is the feast day of Saint Anne*
> *Feed me.*"

Patrick was to feature in many of my programmes from then on. His voice and style of recitation were ideal for radio and something that listeners treasured.

Another broadcasting treasure was the inimitable John B. Keane from Listowel. There are few people who are recognised nationally by their first name and an initial, as John B. was. His voice was instantly recognisable and his ability as a storyteller was unsurpassed. He regaled listeners with tales of Jones, the chemist in Doneraile. He told me how Jones had made his name with a singular medication known simply as "Jones, Scour Specific." John B. told how he spent much of his time when working there blending the ingredients that made up this unique cure and thus brought health and comfort to many calves thereafter. Another guest who graced our afternoons and beyond was Leo Maguire, whose voice evoked memories of the sponsored programmes in the earlier days of broadcasting when he was the voice of *The Walton's* programme, and his exaltation at the end of every show that "if you do like singing, do sing an Irish song", is lodged in the memory of many older people.

Seamus Murphy was another inspirational raconteur. A sculptor from Cork, he brought his talent living and vivid into the studio with mystical elements of his own philosophy and art. Once, outside the radio studio and in his own studio in Cork, we looked at his work. He touched his bust of General Tom Barry and smiled, 'He was very patient... a most interesting man. I don't have to tell you that.' He didn't! He looked around him at all of his creations, De Valera, The Tailor, Seán Ó Riada, John Montague and the Countess. I wondered what would happen if all these sculptures could talk. Seamus passed away in 1975. There is a co-incidence in that Seamus sculpted a well-known bust of Michael Collins, while one of Patrick Galvin's best

John B. Keane (centre), on the set of his play *Many Young Men of Twenty*, with members of the Mountjoy Drama Project 1988.

remembered poems was *The White Monument,* also about the great leader.

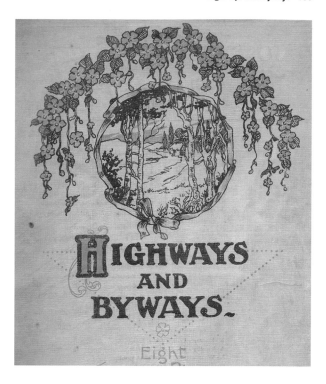

There is a profound difficulty with naming a programme after the time at which it is broadcast; any change in the scheduling nullifies the name. So, the RTÉ planners, in their great wisdom, changed the *Three-O-One* programme time on the schedule by fourteen minutes to a quarter past three. John Skehan gave up as producer and I thanked him for the fun, creativity, the blending of outside broadcast with studio work and above all else, his honesty. I remember him still fondly. May he rest in peace, and if voices are heard in heaven, his is the best.

I got the opportunity to choose the name for the replacement programme and I settled on *Highways and Byways.* Little did I realise that this name would grow into a broadcasting legend. There was hardly a town, village or townland that we didn't touch in some way or other. Our aim was to capture the lives and knowledge of real people throughout the country. My choice of name was to reflect this and we aimed to reach out to all parts of the country and bring their communities to a national audience. My aim was to celebrate the ordinary heroes who contributed to the richness of our communities and made them special. Daniel Corkery's, *The Hidden Ireland,* which studied Irish poetry and culture in eighteenth-century Munster, inspired me and his philosophy formed a cornerstone to the programme.

I have so many wonderful memories from my time exploring our highways and byways and today I still meet or receive correspondence from people I've met in the programme's production or, indeed, they may have been contributors themselves. The programme became a national fixture and I was swept along with it. I was invited hither and thither and it is hard now to pick any particular one – in fact, sometimes I find that the recollections of one event mingles with another and it is hard to separate them out.

I do recall a visit to Tullyvin to record the happenings in Nobby Clarke's Pub. Tullyvin is in drumlin country between Cavan and Cootehill; it is archetypal rural Ireland with a great sense of love and passion for the place. The visit was extraordinary. Peter Smith and Mickey Brady made sure that I arrived safely into this Cavan heartland. As with a great many other events that the programme recorded, it took place late at night. Bill O'Donovan, head of 2FM, a man immersed in the national lore, and brother of the late Fred, a great radio and theatrical impresario, was there, as was Lucia Proctor - also from 2FM – so that the station was well represented.

Nobby and his wife were very busy that evening. They had to minister to a full house as the midnight hour approached and also look after the fish supper. They still found time to invite me in and introduce me to the local Garda sergeant and Cavan legend, the late Mick Higgins. Mick was one of the greats of Cavan and, indeed, Irish football, and had been a member of the Cavan team that won the All-Ireland Senior Football Championship which was played in the Polo Grounds in New York in 1947 – the only time the All-Ireland was played outside Ireland. Mick told of that great occasion. Tony Tighe, who played right half forward in the great New York game and scored a vital point in the defeat of Kerry, was also with us. Obviously, this was a one-sided reminiscence as there wasn't a Kerryman in sight. The big Dungannon country singer, Gene Stuart, formerly a frontman for the Avons, was there too and pressed into service to sing *Lovely Leitrim*, something that he did with aplomb.

"Trup, trup a capaillín ar an mbóthar": out on the highways and byways.

Late night was slipping into early morn. Nobby spoke with emotion: 'You saw that monument to the boys who died for freedom as you came in.' There was a respectful silence along with murmured, 'Lord, have mercy on the dead,' as he recounted his tale. This concerned a Volunteer in the Troubles who, 'died in my arms,' said Nobby, 'and as he went to meet his maker he turned and said, "Fight on Nobby, I'm f***ed."'

A man in the corner sang *The Hackler from Grouse Hall*. Hackling was the final stage in the preparation of flax before it was spun into linen. The song told of one such elderly hackler with a fondness for poitín who was pursued by a zealous RIC officer. Peter Smith, a local man, penned the song in 1880 when the protagonists were still alive. Some of the words stick in my mind:

> *"When I was young I danced and sang and drank strong whiskey, too,*
> *In a shebeen shop that sold a drop of real oul' mountain dew*

With poteen still on every hill the peelers had no call
Round sweet Stradone I am well-known, round Lavey and
Grouse Hall

I used to go from town to town, for hacklin' was me trade
Nor can deny I thought that I an honest living made
Where ever I'd strayed by night or day the youth would
always call
To have the craic with Paddy Jack the Hackler from Grouse
Hall."

This was sung with a beautiful Cavan lilt befitting the tale. As it drew to an end, a huntsman arrived with three beagles and sounded his hunting horn. It was the signal to leave and I felt like the fiddler who had been taken into the fairy rath and was now emerging from their gentle place. I dared not look back for fear of finding that it had all disappeared. Instead, I struck south for RTÉ and that day's edition of *Highways and Byways*.

Another occasion was a visit to Granard. This was again made in the company of Bill O'Donovan and we were welcomed and serenaded by the late Larry Cunningham. Larry was so well-known nationally that you needed only to mention his first name for everyone to understand who you meant. I made my recordings there and was amazed when a man brought in a uniform that General Seán McKeon, the renowned blacksmith of Ballinalee, had worn. We visited the hotel where Michael Collins's fiancée, Kitty Kiernan, once lived. Eddie Macken, the great show jumper was there with his father, James. Songs were sung and tales told and the tape ran, filling the archives for the programme.

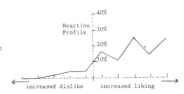

Audience Research Service
Radio Telefís Eireann

confidential

Radio programme report R/598/73 Wk. 36

THREE-O-ONE

Friday, 7th September 1973: 1501 – 1600 hours

This report is based on evidence from 51 completed questionnaires which were received from those members of the Radio Panel (10% of the total membership currently estimated at 500) who had heard more than half the programme as part of their normal listening.

Reaction Profile and Index

Their use of the ten-point Indicator Scale to sum up their reaction to the programme is indicated on this Reaction Profile (the height of the curve above the horizontal line showing the proportion of respondents choosing each position).

This gave a Reaction Index of 76; in Weeks 25 and 34 the programme had respective R.I.s of 73 and 76.

Interest

Most respondents expressed some interest in this edition of 'Three-O-One', over half enjoyed it 'very much'. John D. Steward's talk of Belfast affairs was by far the most popular item.

'He has a genius for injecting humour into everything he says' (housewife).

Fergal Molloy on forest walks sparked off much interest, while Des Moore on Dublin hotels, Hilary Boyle on the canal trip, and the 'War and Peace' item were appreciated by smaller groups. Also well liked was the feature on traditional music. Most of these items came in for sporadic criticism, but the only item to receive censure from more than a few was 'Sebastian - the Teddy Bear' which several considered 'stupid'.

Donncha Ó Dulaing

'Very good' according to six in ten and not less than 'satisfactory' for the rest, Donncha Ó Dulaing was shown to be still a highly regarded presenter. Comment endorsed his consistently high standard of presenting, pinpointing such aspects as his skilled interviewing technique, his 'relaxed' manner and 'pleasing' personality.

p.t.o.

The third Sunday in September, 1973, marked new and distinctive departures for *Highways and Byways*. That day, I returned to my roots in a way that would soon colour much of my broadcasting. Up until then, my career had been bound up with the world of the arts, folklore and local history. Now, I added the wide-ranging world of the GAA. This was a homecoming of sorts to my boyhood dreams and emotions.

I was sitting at home watching Cork footballers win the All-

Top: Interviewing An Taoiseach Jack Lynch at Croke Park.

Above: President Patrick Hillery with, on left, Michael McGrath and Donncha during the Brian Boru Clare-to-Dublin March.

Ireland title in Croke Park, thinking vaguely of the last time that they had done this, in 1945. I had listened to Michael O'Hehir on the wireless then. Names flooded back over the years: Tadhg Crowley, the captain, Derry Beckett, Jack Lynch, Eamon Young, Mick Tubridy, Caleb Crone and very many others from the past. They had been joined that day by Jimmy Barry Murphy, Ray Cummins, and captain, Billy Morgan. It was, in fact, Billy's speech in Croke Park that made me load my tape machine, and with my very young children on board, drive to the team hotel to meet them and the County Secretary, Frank Murphy.

I'm reminded of a lovely day in Thurles when Taoiseach Jack Lynch discussed with me in his analytical way a hurling match between Cork and Clare and then passed me on to President Paddy Hillery for a slightly sadder analysis. Cork always beat Clare back then! I met Dermot Halpin from Newmarket-on-Fergus on my return to the side-line. He was gazing in his mind's eye at that mystic and romantic hurling stronghold of East Clare. 'Listen boy,' he said. 'You know that Clare were never beaten. The shadows of Tul Considine, "Goggles" Doyle and Jimmy Smith, all of whom you know, will lead us yet! We'll leave behind us the world of Biddy Early and some fine day in September, the heroes from Clare will bring McCarthy back to the banner.'

He was now in full flight and turned impassioned to Denis Conroy, the great Cork County Board man from Carrigtwohill, and said, 'Oh God, wouldn't you die happy to see Clare winning an All-Ireland.' Conroy looked at Halpin, then at the *Highways* microphone and said, 'Christ, Dermot! If that's the case, you'll live forever!'

I was now recording material in Croke Park on big match days. I vividly recollect the All-Ireland final between the hurlers of Cork and Wexford in 1977. This was pure joy. My two favourite hurling counties, in full flow. I roamed the side-lines, talking here, recording there and reflecting as best I could the great atmosphere that pervaded that arena.

The year 1978 was surely a Banner year on *Highways and Byways*; some might say "Banner" with a distinctly Western bias, because most of my attention was centred on West Clare.

A note from Mary O'Gorman, of the West Clare Tourist Association, began it all.

> *"Please meet members of the West Clare Tourist Association at the Aylevarroo Caravan Park, not far from Kilrush at 2.30 p.m."*

This is precisely what I did, and what followed was in the nature of a broadcaster's idea of Tír na nÓg.

The month was June and the Clare countryside, varied and multi-coloured, blazed with the sun swept and cloudless glory of mid-summer. Roads, narrow and winding, gave tantalising glimpses, through honey-suckled hedgerows, of hayfields, yellow and fecund, with the promise of long days when the hay would soon be saved and..... and, being an honest Corkman, I never completed that famous, or infamous, sentence. It all depends on your point of view!

Kilrush, which is the second largest town in Clare, was the launching pad for "Operation Banner Highway", and soon, I was driving past Cappagh pier and along the tortuous coast road that winds itself round the waters' edge. The estuary was blue, a blue, however, flecked with leaping bars of white spray. A boat lay uneasily at anchor and, in the distance, St Senan's Scattery thrust its round tower into the afternoon sky·. It looked like the place from which the Banners have lift-off for Heaven.

'That salmon,' said Fr Pat Culligan, 'was caught last night out there in the bay.' As with the O'Gormans, Michael Kelly and Michael Fennell, he urged me on to hearty feats of eating with the odd good drop (the legal variety!) thrown in for good and flaithiúl measure.

"Now,' they all said, "we'll show you the glory of the Banner.'

A convoy of cars soon sets off and we began, where one should, at the beginning, where Kerry and Clare meet on the throbbing back of the Killimer Tarbert Ferry. Here, cars, trucks, travellers, tourists, children eating icecreams, edge nearer and nearer to their twenty-minute ride over two-and-a-quarter miles of water.

A lorry-load of seaweed nudged in between an elegant French Peugeot and a somewhat beaten-up Ford, the driver of which asked me, 'Are you here for the fun of it?' I said, 'Yes and No!' He squinted in the sunlight. 'Oh! You're a Corkman, alright. Still, whether you're here for the craic or business, you're saving eighty-five miles of road.'

We turned our back on the tourists and faced up the hill in the path of the fast-receding figure of Fr. Culligan. He was now on home ground, and didn't we all know it! 'A wonderful place, this,' he said, as I puffed alongside him. And, surely, on that lovely day in June, it was hard to imagine any other vista, even a heavenly reflex, surpassing this wind-rippled and heavenly day of summer.

We were in a cemetery, nothing unusual for me, but this was different, for here lay the mortal remains of Eileen Hanley, the "Colleen Bán", Eileen, whose body was taken from the estuary and lies in a hospitable, if unmarked, grave in this ancient cemetery on the hill overlooking Killimer. It was strange and quiet standing there, reflecting that this quiet fire had been the inspiration for Gerald Griffin's *The Collegians;* Dion Boucicault's *The Colleen Bawn* and, later still, Benedict's *The Lily of Killarney*.

Not too far, from here, too, is the birth place of Eugene O'Curry, the famous Irish scholar, and if you go further West, as I did, you will cross the remarkable bridges of Ross and on to Moneen, where "The Little Ark", that great symbol of Clare endurance and faith, is preserved.

Towards dusk on that June day, we found ourselves in "The Wood", which was formerly the Vandaleur Estate and where a fine car-park marks the site of the landlord's Big House. The Wood, now picturesquely developed as a picnic and forest walk area is owned by the Department of Fisheries.

I was deriving a typical Ó Dúlaing satisfaction from the fact, that, while the landlords had departed, the West Clare people and myself now stood on the sod, when Michael Fennell, in an excess of zeal, suggested that we turn up in the morning for the dawn chorus. We didn't.

Carrigaholt and its Teach an Cheoil provides another memorable occasion for my broadcasting scrapbook of 1978. Old and young gathered in for a great evening of Irish music and song and, of course, that great Clare gift: eloquent and entertaining conversation.

The logs crackled and hissed on the open fire as the children of West Clare jigged, reeled, hornpiped and sang their way through a broad and varied · "repertoire". An American lady sitting near the fire sat profiled against the dark warmth. What memories of West

Clare would she carry home? Her answer to my question was simple, 'The people. The people, their hospitality and their kindness, their generosity and, above all, their welcome. You know, I felt like one of them.'

What better can be said! My few days in the Banner were full. My waking hours were filled with new experiences and old folk memories.

In West Clare, they are proud of themselves, and their Dalcassian traditions. They are so proud, in fact, that their best tribute to their visitors is to make them part of themselves. Surely, the finest experience of all. And, then late in the night, when the body and spirit have shed the stress of day, they will invite you back for, as an old man said to me, 'There is only one thing better than a visit to Clare, and that's two visits.' That is another story, for another time, le cunamh Dé!

Dungiven, Co. Derry, became another home for *Highways and Byways*. Anne Brolly, later to become a Sinn Féin councillor, invited me to record in her home. Her husband, Francie, who went on to become a member of the Legislative Assembly of Northern Ireland, was a traditional musician. Their children were very small at the time but I well remember Joe Brolly who was to become the most famous Derry footballer of his generation and now a well-known commentator on the game.

Some years later, I was walking down the sideline in Croke Park on All-Ireland day when I was hailed by a child's voice, full of certainty and confidence. I stopped and looked up into the Hogan Stand. 'I'd like to come down,' said this chirpy little fellow. 'Who are you anyway?' I asked. 'I'm Brolly from Dungiven, I'm Joe!' Before anything further could be said, helping hands were passing him across the wire to me. He was still talking, 'You know, Anne and Francie Brolly. You stayed in our house.' Say no more. We walked around by the canal end. He was taking in everything. 'Will you be passing the Kerry dugout?' he asked. I would, and why did he want to know. 'I'd like to watch the match from there,' he said. A friendly Kerry mentor gave the nod and as I left, I heard him introducing himself to the men of the Kingdom. A few years later he needed no introduction.

And that was Joe Brolly's first appearance in Croke Park and I am very proud to have been part of it. I often marvelled at his lethal skills and speed, taken, perhaps, by osmosis, from Pat Spillane!

By the early 1980s, I had a small chair on which I sat in between action in Croke Park, taking care never to obscure the advertising hoardings as I had been instructed. I recall sitting in front of the canal end on the first Sunday in September in 1981, reflecting on the tricolour of Offaly hurlers and the more conservative maroon of Galway. It was approaching half-time and it looked as if the men from the West were on their way to victory and the throng from the faithful county would return home empty-handed. A bag-carrying Ossie Bennett, the physio, told me, 'We'll have them in the second-half.' He was "rubbing" for Offaly.

During half-time, I pressed on with the recording of the game. A small boy in an Offaly cap asked, 'May I talk to your programme?' No doubt. Everyone talks on *Highways*! A rhetorical question, 'Who will win?' The reply was distinct even in a babble of sound, 'Offaly, of course.' I could not resist, 'I'll be in Lourdes tomorrow, there will be a miracle there, too.' Great applause from those all around.

Offaly won. A mixture of Johnny Flaherty magic; Damien Martin courage; flair and skill from the late Pat Carroll; calmness under pressure from Pat Fleury; never mind the raking pucks of Pat Delaney who a few years later sang *The Offaly Rover* for me in his home; or the flashing black helmet of Joachim Kelly. All the great Connollys and their lionhearted friends crossed the Shannon back to Galway empty-handed.

There is a postscript. Later that Sunday night, I arrived uninvited, but heartily welcome, to Offaly celebrations in the Gresham Hotel. Liam Fleury introduced me to Brother Denis, a north Cork man now naturalised in Offaly, who has wrought wonders in school and adult hurling in Birr. He invited me down to Tullamore to meet the hurlers the following evening. The *Highway's* tape machine worked overtime and to my great delight I was introduced with the team to a great hurling throng and as I took my bow, I heard a voice distinctly say: "Aha, you Cork man, we won and you don't have to go to Lourdes!" Indeed, yes, everyone listened to *Highways and Byways*!

The GAA training pitch in Belfield in the university grounds in Dublin was where I relaxed and played all-star hurling with my young lads, Feargal, Rúairí, Dónal and Donncha and Sinéad. On a certain evening, however, we stopped to watch the energetic training of members of the great Kerry team. Here it was that Jack O'Shea and teammates answered every call of their Dublin trainer, Micheál Ó Muircheartaigh. In the gathering dusk of an evening, we continued to puck around. A flying sliotar clipped my glasses and off flew the lens. Soon a bunch of burly Kerry men were on their knees before a Corkman. As Micheál said, 'An unlikely happening Donncha, especially on Munster Final Day!' They found the lens.

Ger Power was one of the great and friendliest Kerry men of his generation. I travelled down to Tralee to record a programme with him. Like the Rings in Cloyne, his room was a shrine to our native games. Mrs Power made the tea and Ger casually introduced me to his father whom I had never noticed until then. The penny dropped. This was the great Jackie Power of Ahane and Limerick fame. I checked my tape. There was a little left for Ger when I finished with Jackie!

There aren't that many people who can claim to have shaken hands with and spoken to a saint, but that is now one of my claims to fame. Few of us will forget the Papal visit in 1979 when Pope John Paul II, now canonised, visited our country. I travelled to Rome before the visit in a state of great excitement to a Papal audience in St Peter's Square where I stood near a great crowd from Limerick who sang *There is an Isle*. I held my microphone near the Pope as he looked at their banner which read: "Limerick." The blood was up and Conor O'Clery of *The Irish Times* said, 'You have a scoop.' The late Larry Lyons, an old friend from *The Cork Examiner* had a "contact" or so he thought, and felt that we could get a tour of the Papal apartments. We never did but it was a good try!

We did, however, visit San Clemente, the Roman home of the Irish Dominicans where the hospitability flowed as sweetly as in their Irish House in St. Mary's in Tallaght. There was an old priest sitting on my right and we talked. 'What is your name?' I asked. 'Heuston,' he said. 'As in the station?' I asked jokingly, referring to the railway station in Dublin named after one of the 1916 heroes. He looked at me quietly. 'Yes,' he replied, 'his brother.' I topped up with multitudinous cups of black coffee and before the night was over, one of the great occasions on *Highways and Byways* had taken place.

The papal flight to Dublin was unique. Tape machine in hand, I braved the international pack of paparazzi and legitimate Irish journalists and photographers who surged towards the Pope. I taped a few unmemorable words and was then photographed by Pat Langan of *The Irish Times*, with the Pope. I thank Hubert Gordon of the Gardaí who brilliantly secured everyone! Flying in over the Phoenix Park over a Dublin still and empty apart from the huge crowds in the park, was a moving experience.

Liam Nolan and I were soon to describe another huge event as North came South to greet the Pope in Drogheda. By now I was not just hung-over but exhausted and finding it hard to force out descriptive words. Liam, who was armed with a missal and a lot of research material, was in full flow. I was not at the races! Until, suddenly, it struck me: I had shared something with the Holy Father that morning that few others had. I turned to Liam and said, 'Do you know, Liam, I shared black puddings for breakfast with the Pope this morning?' I was up and running and the rest of my commentary went smoothly.

On the Papal plane with John Williams, producer, PA Margaret Costello and fellow media members.

Cathal Ó Gríofa, who was editing *Highways and Byways* set off with me across "the quiet land of Éireann" through the long night to our sacred destination, the holy place at Clonmacnoise, the ancient home of St Ciarán. The Pope was about to pay a private visit here and I would be the only commentator privileged to broadcast from this place.

The dawn was grey and cold which made the tea all the more welcome as was the splendid poitín shared with me by a kindly, uniformed pilgrim. The quiet of the early morning was gently disturbed by thousands of feet walking the tiny roads of Clonmacnoise. Among them my own family, whom I met later in the field. The walking, driving, cycling throng loomed up out of the grey mist of dawn, surprising the quiet and sleepy Offaly cows that woke ruminating to a morning of history, and a morning repeating itself because many generations had trodden these roads in times past.

William Bulfin in his *Rambles in Éireann* re-draws the scene in words as only he can:

Interviewing Pope John Paul II on the Aer Lingus flight from Rome to Dublin, September 1979.

> *"On all the roads between Banagher and Athlone there are troops of people facing westward. There are vehicles of every kind, from the dashing excursion break to the humble donkey cart, and every kind of bicycle procurable is also in evidence. Hundreds of people are tramping the roads in the dust; hundreds are footing it over the fields and the hills; and there are many boats on the Shannon all laden to the very gunwales with people from Connacht."*

So William Bulfin described a "Pattern" in his own time, when torrents of people descended on Clonmacnoise for the annual blessing of the graves. It was great to be part of that great throng of history and now writing our own chapters in the ongoing story of Clonmacnoise. It was a morning in my broadcasting career when, with the help of John Joyce on Outside Broadcasts and with the tacit encouragement of my editor, who snored quietly in the little shed behind me, I felt proud to be Irish and a broadcaster with RTÉ.

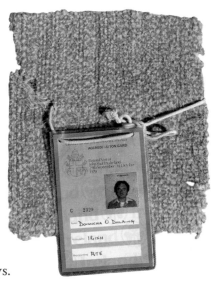

Donncha's Official Idenity card for Pope, now Saint, John Paul II's, visit to Ireland in September 1979. The card is attached to a piece of carpet that was harvested from the altar at Clonmacnoise after the Pope had left.

The Papal visit of 1979 was a high point for the Church in Ireland. It enthused communities across the country and brought light and celebration to many homes and villages. There were tales told of how people had trekked great distances to be in the Phoenix Park, where they had slept along the way and how they had experienced the Pope in their own individual ways. Things changed after that as news of scandals and abuse crashed like waves over the bow of Peter's ship and the darker side of the pomp and splendour was exposed. I was shocked too and greatly unsettled by the revelations that have since emerged. But good may yet come from it, not for the victims sadly, but for the organisation itself. I have had very many friends, priests and higher, who impressed me with their warmth, generosity and kindness, but I have known others too who were self-absorbed, worldly and mean-spirited. The latter were the minority but they stultified the Church for the others. Perhaps now, the more caring and spiritual may come to the fore and follow metaphorically in the footsteps of the man who started it all, as I would literally at a later stage.

It is extraordinary to find oneself watching on television the canonisation of a man who you have met and been physically close to. Saints used to be distant characters from a bygone age but now,

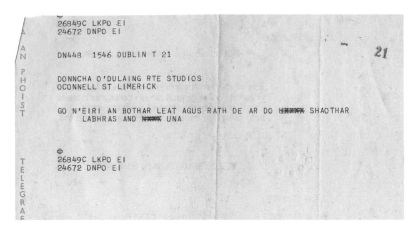

With news broadcaster
Michael Murphy and Father
Maguire.

perhaps it's a sign of age, the saints are getting younger and closer.

Comhaltas Ceoltóirí Éireann is a marvellous organisation dedicated to promoting and preserving traditional Irish music. I first came to appreciate that organisation's work through the friendship and hospitality of Labhrás Ó Murchú and his wife, Úna. I attended and recorded part of their summer entertainment seisiún for *Highways and Byways* and then, out of the blue, Labhrás asked me if I would like to write and present one of their North American Tour Shows. I didn't hesitate and accepted – thus beginning one of my worst contretemps with RTÉ, one which left me, and certainly middle management of that illustrious body, with wounds that have never healed.

The fact that I left without informing anyone speaks volumes in itself and may well have merited the words "gross dereliction of duty through ultra vires behaviour," but certainly didn't deserve that "you usurped the function of the editor of *Three-O-One."* There was no such programme any more anyway nor could one exceed my authority as I, generally, during my *Highways and Byways* time, recorded alone, early and late and without either assistance or direction.

In fact, material to cover the period of my proposed absence had been recorded by me on the weekend prior to my departure. It was transferred to Dublin for the attention of the editor of *Highways and Byways*, all properly linked and arranged. It was then found to be unsuitable, perhaps, because I'd made the recordings on portable equipment without regard for RTÉ's "standards." When the dust and the modicum of bad-humoured codology had settled, all of the material recorded by me during my "ultra vires" days was broadcast unchanged, to my editor's and my great satisfaction.

I went on Comhaltas tours on the following two years and on each occasion, I informed the powers that be in RTÉ of my intentions and suffered no further anxiety. From the distance of so many years now, I regret what happened and for that I feel sorry still.

The tour party was made up of some of the great traditional music performers in the country at the time. These included a young Paddy Glackin, Séamus MacMathúna, Ann Mulqueen, Celine Hession, who recently celebrated the fiftieth anniversary of the founding of her dance school, and the Siamsa Céilí Band – all of them great artists and wonderful company.

Anyone who knows Ireland and Irish culture recognises the important role that the Fleadhanna Cheoil play in keeping our music alive and vibrant. These were the gatherings that breathed life into a music that had been hampered by an elitist approach by some academics. Young musicians came on the streets of towns and villages and played with enthusiasm unhindered by the preconceived notions of what traditional music should be. The Fleadhanna movement has grown beyond all recognition and the recent Fleadh Cheoil na hÉireann in Derry attracted close to a half a million people. This was the first time that the Fleadh moved North of the border and the people there responded with enthusiasm and joy.

Together with sessions in the Piper's club in Thomas Street, these were my first recordings of traditional Irish music and I'll never forget it. The Club was not only a venue for good music but also for great and friendly company. It had a curiously tatty atmosphere in those days, but this was counteracted by the enthusiasm and warmth of the fear a' tí, Jim Nolan. Jim was well known for his somewhat eccentric introductions of guests. Allegedly, he introduced Seán Connery as "Mr O'Connor, I think." Ulick O'Connor was a regular guest but, despite this, a confused Jim often referred to him as "eunuch". I got the same treatment as Jim introduced me in the following way, 'Ladies and gentlemen, we have a very famous man from the radio here this evening'… pausing he leaned towards me and asked, 'What is your name, please?' Then he raised his voice again and declaimed, 'Mr Donaki O'Donaki.'

The programme was now demanding all of my waking, and was eating into my sleeping hours. I travelled the length and breadth of the country many times over, chasing the unusual or as yet uncaptured

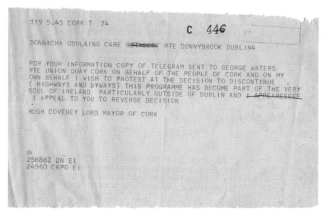

Telegram from Hugh Coveney Mayor of Cork, protesting against the discontinuation of *Highways and Byways* on Radio One.

nuggets of our history, folklore or culture. There were also sessions in parish halls, schools, club houses, public buildings, hotels or pubs. I often operated by sitting my participants in a circle and working my way around the group. There were plenty of times where my questions were answered with a nod or a single syllable response – not the best for a radio broadcast. On other occasions, the event overtook individuals and they became loquacious beyond the listeners' capacity to comprehend and I had to act swiftly to prevent the programme being taken over or led astray. I liked to keep the programmes fluid and open to a change of direction, if a new direction presented itself that seemed better than the one we had planned. These were the lucky breaks that we were able to pursue but I found that the more homework I did, the more lucky breaks we had.

There was one trip that stands out in my mind during my time with *Highways and Byways*. It took place in 1980 and was a visit to Argentina during the turbulent times of the generals' rule in that country. There was disturbance, conflict and outright revolution in various measures and this made it difficult to visit without a very good reason. I was presented with a very good excuse in the form of an invitation from the Aer Lingus staff hurling club who were travelling there as part of their regular overseas' programme. The club organised an annual trip to places where there was an Irish community, both expatriate and the descendants of immigrants. Their boast is that they've travelled to countries from Argentina to Zambia. I was recruited as an honorary member of the club with the help of the airline's public relations' department. Thankfully, for myself and everyone on the team, I didn't actually play during this trip, thus relieving potential pressure on the Accident and Emergency departments in the Buenos Aires hospitals.

I got great help and encouragement from Mary B. Murphy of the Irish Argentine Society who made contacts, suggested places to visit and advised on the practicalities of visiting that country.

The club brought sufficient players to field two teams – thirty in all, with a full complement of hurleys and other gear. The players used their travel concession to get to their destination. This meant that they travelled on stand-by. Obviously, they couldn't all go on the same plane so they had to spread themselves across a range of flights. Some went through New York, others through Madrid; I travelled with the club's public relations' officer, Rory Gallagher, with Paris our intermediary stop. It presented me with the opportunity to pay a brief visit to that beautiful city and rekindle my acquaintance with its magnificent beauty.

The Irish Argentinian Society helped organise the trip and were on hand to welcome us at the airport. These were, in the main, the

Hurling in the Pampas, Buenos Aires, while on tour with the Aer Lingus hurling team in 1980.

descendants of people who had left Ireland because of the Famine, together with those who had migrated at the turn of the twentieth century. A Dominican priest, Fr Fahy, inspired and facilitated the first migration. Most of those he helped came from the Midlands. The men travelled first, with women following to marry, settle down and farm in the Pampas. It must have been an extraordinary change for those early settlers, leaving the central plain in Ireland for the vast plains of the Pampas in Argentina.

I had planned to record interviews with these Argentinian-Irish. I was taken by their accents. Here were Argentinian-born people who were second, third and sometimes fourth generation whose first language was Spanish, yet when they spoke English, it was with an Irish accent. How important this must have been to their forefathers that they strove to keep this small relic of their origins, and they passed on this yearning to the present day. I was surprised but not too much for I was familiar with the plight of émigrés through Bulfin's *Rambles in Éireann,* which was to become a bible for many who had left Ireland for new lands and found solace in that volume's pages.

Bulfin emigrated to Argentina from Birr in 1884 and, with his brother, Peter, they quit the city of Buenos Aires to work on a ranch owned by Juan Dowling – a distant relation of my own perhaps. He was involved in the establishment of a newspaper for the Irish emigrants called *The Southern Cross.* This is still being published. Indeed, I had been receiving copies of it prior to my visit. Bulfin described the lives of the gauchos and the Irish who were working and making a living on these tough, unforgiving plains. He eventually became the editor of this journal and is fondly remembered there.

Brother John Burke, a North Corkman, whose late mother I got to know well subsequent to the visit, was then the Principal in Newman College. Brother Burke had gone to the Christian Brothers School in Doneraile so there was a great personal connection between the two of us.

The Aer Lingus hurlers held one of their games in a ground called Hurling in the Hurlingham district of Hurlingham Partido in greater Buenos Aires. This club derives its name from the Buenos Aires Hurling Club formed by some of the early emigrants. Today the club has a strong hockey team but its origins live on in the club and area names. The teams were made up of ten Aer Lingus lads on each side supplemented by five locals who wanted to try their skills. I posed for a photograph pucking a sliotar around on my own. It was my only sporting involvement. The Aer Lingus lads also played an exhibition match where they provided the full complement of players for both teams. They demonstrated their skills in the first half and in the second they got down to a truly competitive game.

I had to be circumspect about how I behaved and conducted my business while in Argentina. I interviewed some Irish nuns on one occasion and they would only speak to tape in the garden, out of earshot of the building. There was a fear of being bugged or being informed on by someone who overheard them. These fears were well-grounded. Some Passionist Fathers brought me to the scene of a vile murder where some young Passionists had been killed while they watched television. The room remains untouched and is a cold disturbing place.

We had arrived in Argentina just a year after another incident which acted as a warning to me and the Aer Lingus hurlers. Willie Anderson, an Irish rugby player from Sixmilecross in County Tyrone, was arrested and imprisoned for three months for allegedly demeaning a patriotic symbol. It seemed that the patriotic symbol was a flag that he had allegedly taken from a public building. He was completely cleared of these charges but only after he had suffered three months' incarceration. The players were very careful and only went out in small groups and were very careful not to do anything to cause offence in any way. For me, given my own trenchant opposition to Section 31 at home, this was evidence of how censorship can become invidious and suppress openness and freedom of speech.

There were a number of official functions during that visit but I still had time to do my own thing and follow my nose in checking up on stories. One that interested me deeply was the story of the great German battleship, the KMS Admiral Graf Spee. This ship took part in the great battle of the River Plate. We had the opportunity to visit the river itself. This is a fantastic estuary between Uruguay and Argentina. The Graf Spee had been attacking Allied convoys in the Atlantic in the winter of 1939. Finally, it was trapped in the Plate estuary by three British warships. It was outnumbered but attacked nonetheless, inflicting severe damage on HMS Exeter. The German vessel was badly damaged in the exchange and partially disabled. Its fuel and water systems were damaged and it had only sufficient fuel on board for twelve hours' sailing. In addition, the British had created a web of signals that suggested there was a larger fleet on the way.

The ship's captain, Captain Hans Langsdorff, decided to scuttle the ship. He did so on the 18th December, 1939. He transferred the surviving crew to shore but chose to remain on board himself rather than face the ignominy of surrender or capture. The remaining munitions were detonated and he went down with his ship. By chance, I was introduced to some of the surviving German sailors who had settled in Argentina after the war. I interviewed a number of them and learnt at first-hand what it had been like to take part in that battle and watch from the shore as your ship sank at sea.

There was raw and real emotion there as they described the events of that fateful December day. It was as if it were only yesterday. Passions were high towards the end of the evening and my companions launched into a rousing chorus of *Deutschland! Deutschland! Über alles*. I didn't know how to react and so did the only thing I could, I responded with *Amhrán na bhFiann*.

Evita Peron's grave and the wonderful River Plate football stadium were inevitable ports of call. Diego Maradona was playing that night and I can remember the whispers growing to roars that greeted his every move: "Maradona, Maradona, Maradona" echoed around the stadium. John Joseph Scanlan, a Limerick man and founder of St Brendan's school in Buenos Aires, helped with many of the arrangements for our trip but excelled himself by getting me into the commentary boxes and I met their famous broadcaster who burst forth with an elongated GOOOOOOOALLLLL! whenever his team scored.

There was a televised press conference afterwards and I was invited to ask a question to their Bogartesque manager who sat elegantly smoking with his coat draped over his shoulders. I proffered the question, "Do you think that Liam Brady is as good a player as Diego Maradona?"

He looked quizzically at me through a haze of his smoke, and smiling replied, "Ah, Irelandese, you are welcome, sometimes I like to make a joke, too!" His smile hardly reached his eyes. I asked no more questions.

We spent a Sunday on the Great Pampas where we were served magnificent barbecued Argentinian beef. Father Fidelis Rush said Mass and later spoke to me of Tang with great affection. He quoted from John Kearns Casey's (known as "Leo") poem, *Among the Flowers:*

> *"In leafy Tang the wild birds sang-*
> *The brown light lay on Derry's heather*
> *But years have passed since we the last*
> *Sat courting in the summer weather.*
> *The tender light of stars at night*
> *That soothes the wanderer so weary,*
> *Could only show the silvery glow*
> *That lit your glance, my Darling Mary."*

Another recalled the words of Leo's immortal *Rising of the Moon*:

"Oh, thank God, there are still beating
Hearts in manhood's' burning noon,
Who would follow in their footsteps
At the rising of the moon."

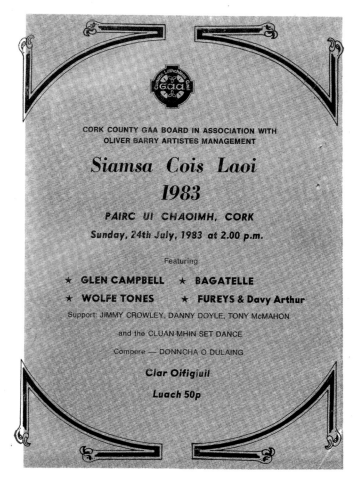

We were entertained royally during our visit. The embassy and the broader Irish community couldn't have been more welcoming and helpful. We had a final farewell in the library of Newman College. It was a magnificent room and packed with lay and clergy, Irish and Argentinian, hurlers and soccer players. Songs were sung; steaks eaten; drinks taken; gifts offered and received; memories laid down forever.

I still hark back to those few wonderful days in Argentina. There was something very special about that visit – perhaps it was the marriage of two cultures, the Spanish and the Irish, on South American soil. Or it may have been the attitude to life and adversity that won me over. It later years I've read the writings of Jorge Luis Borges and one poem, *Instants*, resonates with me:

"If I could live again my life,
In the next - I'll try,
- to make more mistakes,
I won't try to be so perfect,
I'll be more relaxed,
I'll be more full - than I am now,
In fact, I'll take fewer things seriously,
I'll be less hygienic,
I'll take more risks,
I'll take more trips,
I'll watch more sunsets,
I'll climb more mountains,

I'll swim more rivers,
I'll go to more places – I've never been,
I'll eat more ice creams and less (lime) beans,
I'll have more real problems – and less imaginary
ones..."

With former Taoiseach
Charles J. Haughey TD
near Newcastle West.

I echo those sentiments entirely.

Time flies by and now I find myself marking fifty years of broadcasting. Is it an award for endurance or familiarity? The time has passed almost unnoticed and, being honest, I still see myself as a man in my prime, even if my body is raising questions about this.

It would be wrong to leave this part of my life without mentioning the Siamsa Cois Laoi festivals staged in Páirc Uí Chaoimh in Cork in the eighties. These were the main musical events of their time with major international acts joining local heroes. They were televised, too, and I became involved in interviewing the stars, introducing the acts and interpreting the proceedings for the viewers and listeners in their homes. I have vivid memories of interviewing the great Don McLean in a field of recently cut hay on a sunny day in Cork. Glen Campbell showed up, too, as did Joan Baez, Paul Brady, Bono and U2, the Wolfe Tones and many

The concerts were an eclectic mix and attracted a disparate audience. One such was the then Taoiseach, Charles J. Haughey, or "Charlie" as he preferred to be known when mixing with the masses. He turned up to Siamsa in 1980 and was there during The Dubliners' set. Charlie inveigled his way on stage and insisted on singing with them. He was not a renowned singer and his version of *Take Her Up to Monto* failed to impress the audience. If the late Ronnie Drew's reaction was anything to go by, it definitely failed to impress The Dubliners.

9 RAMBLES IN ÉIREANN

... The trip opened up Ireland to me and the joy of travelling, accompanied by the sound of horses' hooves. There was a welcome in every town and village, with crowds turning out to cheer on our progress. We made a detour to visit my home place, Doneraile and I had the honour of turning on the Christmas lights there outside the Court. ...

Law-abiding, safety-conscious citizen, doing his utmost to keep within the speed limit.

Pages 184-5: '... And the world lay spread before me' - Donncha 1960.

Interviewing British Air Service Group air hostess at Cardiff airport.

Discussing the merits of a pint of Murphys with Donal Crosby, then MD of the *Cork Examiner* and Wilf Regan of Murphy's Brewery, at the Press reception for Charleville Cheese Festival, in the late 1970s.

Advising President Patrick Hillery planting a tree during the Brian Boru Clare to Dublin March 1988.

On stage in Cork with tenor and RTÉ broadcaster, Liam Devally.

With Rita Coolidge at Siamsa '82.

Watching poitín being made in a still in a cottage in Ballycastle, County Mayo, September 1979.

During the recording of RTÉ Television's *Donncha at Adare* in March 1980. With Donncha are, l-r: conductor Colman Pearce, Lady Dunraven, Lord Dunraven, singer/harpist Mary O'Hara, and American tenor, Robert White.

In discussion with Fr Dermod McCarthy, Director of Religious Affairs at RTE.

With Matt McNulty Director General of Bórd Fáilte at the Ambassador for Ireland awards in 1989.

Children entertaining Donncha at 'This is your Life' in Charleville.

Opposite: With Producer Dick Warner, at the back of the Bank of Ireland, College Green, with Tom O'Neill's vintage car heading off for the "Tipp Remembers Kickham Weekend".

JOHN STEINBECK'S BOOK *Travels With Charley* tells of the author's trip to discover the real America. Charley was the author's faithful poodle (actually his wife's) and both travelled in a camper van from New York to Salinas Valley in California. He made the trip in 1960, a year of major change in America when John F. Kennedy was campaigning to become the US president and to lead an administration that would usher in an era of major social and technological change. The book fed my ideas of travel and exploration and these dreams were always close to the surface as my broadcasting career advanced. I travelled regularly in Ireland and abroad to the UK and further afield. Yet, I didn't feel that this was true travel. My trips were short and confined. I enjoyed the contact with people that these trips allowed but the pressures of the radio schedule didn't allow me to truly explore the people and places I visited.

I also had a desire to give something back to the communities that had been generous to me in the past. I received many a helping hand along my career and I felt I had a duty to repay this generosity, using the popularity I had achieved. I didn't come to this realisation overnight; it was a slow, gradual awareness. The toys' train for the children of the interned in the North started the ball rolling, when I realised the power of radio to unleash the extraordinary generosity of ordinary people. The memory of that campaign lingered and I kept reflecting on it with a certain pleasure of a job well done. Another event stuck in my mind and that was a visit to a wheelchair holiday resort in County Monaghan and here I came into close contact for the first time with people with physical disabilities. Peter Stokes from the Irish Wheelchair Association had extended the invitation to me. Around this time I received several Rehab Entertainment Awards and this put me in touch with Frank Flannery and Stephen Farrelly.

These benign feelings might have remained such, if it hadn't been for a meeting with Nicholas O'Hare, the chronicler of all things equine and a man with a passion for ponies and horses. Nick introduced me to two Connemara ponies: "Hullaballoo" and "Let's Go". The latter was a television personality in his own right having featured in a programme called *Let's Go* which had traced his training and development. Nick was an enthusiast, and proposed a jaunt with him in his gig. From that proposal came the grain of an idea for a trip from Dublin to Cork as a pre–Christmas fund-raiser for charity. Without hesitation, I telephoned Peter Stokes and despite surprise at this sudden turn of events, he was delighted to have his charity associated with the trip.

Such events as this need planning and a team to handle the details. Here I was blessed in that Dick Warner was producing *Highways and Byways* at the time. Dick had an innate understanding of the project as his later work on voyaging through Irish waterways shows. Ted Berry, my good friend, and outside broadcaster par excellence, was to travel with us and look after the crucial technical side of this adventure. For it was an adventure. It was winter and that imposed additional constraints caused by the cold and dark. It was a real challenge: would we make it all the way? Would we raise any funds?

Having a chat with Mrs Hussey and her friend, just outside Roscommon.

I needn't have worried. It was a success from the very outset. We were seen off in Tallaght by Bishop Joseph Carroll from the Dublin archdiocese, Síle de Valera, the Fianna Fáil politician, and Jim Ryan from Dunnes Stores – all supported by hundreds of well-wishers.

Our convoy travelled along the main N7. It was bitterly cold and snowed much of the time. One of the ponies pulled our trap while the other went a few hundred yards ahead in a truck. This allowed the ponies to stay in contact with each other – something that they found reassuring. We had a van from the Wheelchair Association leading, with collectors carrying buckets. There was plenty of enjoyment and entertainment along the way. The nights were spent in long sessions with stories, poetry and music while we defrosted with warming glasses. I recall that we received a particularly warm welcome and a celebratory party when we reached the Curragh Camp.

On another occasion, a man cycled beside the trap and passed us in a glass of whiskey to warm us on the road. On another occasion the same medicine was given to the pony. We were met by a band as we entered Cashel, something that upset our four-legged companions. I don't know whether this was because they didn't like the music or the way it was played, but Nick managed to soothe their nerves. Another upset was caused by the motorists flashing their lights in support as they drove past us – this seemed to unnerve the horses a lot.

The trip opened up Ireland to me and the joy of travelling, accompanied by the sound of horses' hooves. There was a welcome in every town and village, with crowds turning out to cheer on our progress. We made a detour to visit my home place, Doneraile and I had the honour of turning on the Christmas lights there outside the Court. It was strange to enter that town by pony and trap, a form of transport that was common when I was a young boy there. There was refreshment aplenty before we hit the road for our final destination, Cork.

That first journey for charity reawakened my love of travel. I wanted to get to know more of our country and to do it on my own two feet, walking rather than riding the route. There was a degree of apprehension in RTÉ about taking this literal as well as metaphorical direction – charities that weren't supported on our trip from Dublin to Cork had raised their concerns with senior people in the station, but I marched on regardless. Walking the country offered a unique chance to experience the countryside in a way that had become almost extinct with the arrival of the motor car. I wanted to re-find that spirit within me. As the poet Walt Whitman had commented in his *Song of the Wanderer*:

> "*Afoot and light-hearted I take to the open road,*
> *Healthy, free, the world before me,*
> *The long brown path before me leading wherever I choose.*
> "*Henceforth I ask not good-fortune, I myself am good-fortune,*
> *Henceforth I whimper no more,*
> *postpone no more, need nothing,*
> *Done with indoor complaints,*
> *libraries, querulous criticisms,*
> *Strong and content I travel the*
> *open road.*"

Fundraising.

Indeed, done with indoor complaints and querulous criticisms, I was taking to the road and with a light heart.

We were broadcasting live every day. This is always a great challenge as it means that you have to get to wherever it is that you've chosen, by whatever the means of transport involved, to be miked-up in time to go live on air. Things could easily go wrong – weather was always a potential hazard, recalcitrant interviewees another. There is nothing worse on radio than an interviewee who nods quietly in response to a question. This was more likely to happen when on the road and with less, or no, time to prepare the interview or the interviewee. Many of you will have heard my plaintiff comment, 'You're nodding there...', only to receive a silent nod in affirmation! Silence is doubtless golden but my listeners and the authorities in RTÉ didn't necessarily welcome it too frequently during broadcasting hours.

Enjoying a well-earned cup of tea in Athlone.

I do recall an instance of enforced silence. I was engaged in a lively and entertaining interview with a parish priest in North Cork when all of a sudden, everything went dead as we were on air. 'Oh Mr Dowling,' said one of the local ICA women. 'I'm very sorry; we plugged you out to make some tea.' Ted Berry let out an involuntary curse and plugged the sound system back in. The parish priest was shocked and asked if Ted was always like that, and I assured him that it only occurred in the most extreme circumstances. It's funny but it is these small things that stick in my memory long after the substance of many of the seemingly important interviews have faded into the mists.

Bantry Bay, Co. Cork to Ballycastle, Co. Antrim, was my first long-haul charity walk. This was a true test of endurance. It must be remembered that I was coming to this without any previous experience or interest in walking. I hadn't been training secretly for years prior to this, climbing hills or engaging in endurance trips to the North or South poles. No, I was a walking novice without any of the physical or mental attributes that you might associate with such activities. Perhaps my walking exertions reflected the onset of a mid-life crisis – it's hard to know and I'll never truly understand but I took to it with enthusiasm. One thing I had learnt from my years in broadcasting was that to do anything properly, you needed a good team. And these needed to be the very best that could be found.

I turned to Ossie Bennett for help with my feet and the general maintenance of my body. Ossie had been "rubber" for the Offaly hurlers when they beat Galway in the 1981 All-Ireland final and I had had the chance to chat with him in Croke Park. At half time, Offaly were trailing Galway but he confidently predicted Offaly's final triumph. Ossie was a fellow Corkman from Ballinhassig. Apart from three other All-Irelands for Offaly, he had "rubbed" for Tipperary (6), Galway (1) and Cork footballers. Ossie had no official training but had inherited the art from his father, Bill, and had honed it during his time as an athlete, cyclist and boxer. Commdt. Bernie O'Callaghan, an All-Ireland champion walker, trained and advised me on the art and science of walking properly, and for long distances as opposed to the pleasant ambles to and from the studio that up until then I had given the broad description of "walks."

I won't bore you, dear reader, with the details of each and every walk I have completed. I've taken part in far too many to be able to do so and I have to admit that many of the details of these individual walks have slipped from memory or have merged with others to become one global recollection. I and others have written about these walks and runs and I don't want to regurgitate them here. Instead, what I'll do is take you through some of the walks I've taken part in and how they affected and changed me over the decades.

One of the abiding memories from all of the walks is the kindness, friendship and love shown to us by the people we met on our routes. These selfless acts happened so frequently that I would not be able to mention even a fraction of them. We were housed, fed, watered and had our spirits revived on every walk. Indeed, a greater part of the endurance needed for these walks was surviving the great, often night-long singsongs and parties that punctuated our days on the road. There were times when the prospect of walking twenty or thirty miles came as a blessed relief after a long night of uproarious celebration. There were many times when the lyrics of that great Scottish traditional song *The Parting Glass* came to haunt me on a morning after a night before. The first verse captures much of what went on as we walked the land:

> *"Of all the money that e'er I spent*
> *I've spent it in good company*
> *And all the harm that ever I did*
> *Alas it was to none but me*
> *And all I've done for want of wit*
> *To memory now I can't recall*
> *So fill to me the parting glass*
> *Good night and joy be with you all."*

I argue in my defence that these late night activities were mostly for the purpose of fundraising. REHAB, for example, showed an almost military precision in arranging nightly and some times more, events or collections. These bore all the hallmarks of a Garda raid on some unfortunate country pub. We'd arrive at the pub, loudspeakers blaring and music blasting. I'd come in shortly afterwards and following a quick introduction, would sing, speak, entreat – whatever was needed – for a short while until we unleashed the bucket squad who rattled through the assembled customers until their loose, and not so loose, change had been prised from their grasp.

Walking was one thing, but running? That was a different matter altogether. Running or jogging takes preparation and training. I had never "trained" for my walks with any great intensity, or, indeed, enthusiasm. I relied on muscle memory. Growing up in the Ireland of the 1930s and '40s, I walked a lot – not for fitness but simply to get from A to B. Outside of team sports and school sports days, running was something that you did to catch a bus, or if you were late for

Sheep shearing.

school or college. Thus, my body was historically predisposed towards walking. In 1983, I was inveigled to get involved in marathon running. Training for a marathon is long-term and requires dedication and commitment. This was a novelty for me. Firstly, I had to create space in what was a busy work day, to allow time for training.

A few quotes from my diary of 1983 give an idea of what was involved:

"The whole family left Dublin at 9.15 am en route for Clonea. A typical St. Patrick's Day: cold sunshine and spitting rain. There is much ado about Mike Flannery (hard-line republican fund-raiser) *heading the St. Patrick's Day parade in NY. The drive to Clonea, apart from the usual family skirmishes, was uneventful. Sliabh na mBan was shrouded in womanly mystery. We arrived at 12.30. We are the very first to stay in the hotel. Did a six-mile run to Dungarvan after lunch. Met Bridie, Pete and Fr Brendan later. The family listened in great excitement to the ear-splitting delights of Top of the Pops. Found it hard to sleep. The bed is quite solid!*

...Six miles on the beach. Attended function to celebrate John and Ann McGrath's new hotel. Recorded Austin Deasy, Minister for Agriculture. The evening was pleasant with talk

of Cork, hurling and soccer with Dan Hurley, a Northsider who is county manager in Waterford. The family all dined well in our room...

...Had lunch early (light!) in the Seanachie. Six miles on the beach at Clonea. Exhausting and strength sapping. All to Cork: in at Conroy's, later with friends in Currig. Arrived back at 11.45 pm. The moon in glory over Helvick...
We all returned in the car from Clonea. Seven miles on the circuit. Great welcome from Rua (who was our little dog). We're all tired..."

Another day shows the other side of training, this time in Dublin:

"Rain came. It's now 11.00 am and I'm debating whether or not to go to Belfield. The rain is absolutely spearing down. Even the garden looks waterlogged. 1.00 pm had a bath after three miles of raining cold agony on the track. There was just no way of avoiding rain, wind and tiredness. New shoes behaved well, at least they didn't stop. Two-mile walk to work... Seven-mile run around the block, good form no real problems. "To the Lighthouse" on TV: manic intellectuality and depressing..."

Vera with all the children at home in Donnybrook, Christmas in the 1980s.

I had signed up for the 1984 marathon. My son, Dónal, was running with me. He was a relative veteran at this stage having already run three marathons. Radio Two were sponsors of the event and so there was a strong RTÉ contingent running or waving. I had watched the first Dublin marathon pass close to the gates at Montrose and was somewhere between bemused and amused at the dashers, prancers and stragglers who pounded past. Ruairí Quinn seemed to struggle as did some of my RTÉ workmates who were probably wishing that they had volunteered for an extra day's work inside the gates rather than running past on the outside. I never imagined myself so engaged, or finding such a thing to be of importance.

Dónal and I headed for the St Stephen's Green where most of the runners had gathered. Dónal took care of the car keys and my keys. I tend to lose them and forget where I parked the car. I didn't feel at all confident. It was cold and the weather dubious, with a tendency towards wet. We made our way to Hatch Street and soon the wheelchair contingent was away, along with what the organisers described as "elite ladies." I was unsure what defined an "elite" lady but knew that this was someone that I'd best not try to compete against.

There was a wave from George Waters, the then Director General of RTÉ. I wondered who would occupy that post the following year. At that time, DGs seemed to change with the seasons but they were always there to wave to you and smile, which is a great consolation when you needed support. Bill Wall, Radio Two's controller, was also on the dais.

We run, or half run, at what seems to me to be a brisk pace. The people along South Circular Road cheer and clap. I spot my friend, Helen Cole, wife of Paddy, the jazz man. Helen waves me good luck. We reach our first water station with its ubiquitous paper cups. I avoid it, thinking longingly instead of a little tincture of poitín and how that would have raised my spirits, stimulated the mind and deadened the aches and fears.

We make our way across the Suir Bridge and into Bulfin Road where my mind wanders once more to Bulfin's *Rambles in Éireann*. A few yards later we are in Emmet Road and my thoughts move to the great revolutionary hero and his struggle for freedom.

At the three-mile stage, I feel great and am filled with a type of euphoria. A handshake from the TD, Jim Tunney is surprisingly encouraging. The runners towards the centre of the road are silent with an air of grit and determination. I prefer to run closer to the kerb and feed from the spectators' enthusiasm. On we climb up the Kylemore Road, much longer now by foot than I ever recall it when driving. As you run, you note the lovely, understated architecture of this dear, dirty city. From there, we weave through the city until we cross the flyover and here, Peter Stokes from the Irish Wheelchair Association, approaches, 'You're doing great,' he assures me and gives me a bottle of Lucozade and a Mars bar, which go down well.

Suddenly, my friend Bill O'Donovan of RTÉ 2 grabs me and wheels me into the van to have a quick word with Jimmy Greally, 'Are you bunched?' he asked. 'You look a bit tired.' Refusing tea or coffee, I hasten up the hill like a demented hedgehog – just as the rain began to pelt down. Onwards and onwards past a rock band blaring out from a roadside stand. 'Dance, Donncha! Dance!' some spectators call and I wave my arms and gyrate, a dervish cut loose on the capital's streets.

Dónal and Donncha ready for the off in the Dublin City Marathon 1984.

We pass beneath a bridge that someone says is the twenty-two-mile mark. A young Garda promises that it won't be long now. The firemen in Tara Street clap out a rhythm that barely registers. A kind man in green encourages me with reminiscences of my long walks. We lope into Lincoln Place and around the square and discuss the beauties of Georgian Dublin and decide that life in the eighteenth century was good for some at least. My man in green talked of Bath and I admitted that I had never visited that wonderful city, but I knew that Jane Austen thought well of it, which was good enough for me.

We proceeded through the streets until the finishing line hove into view. Feargal, my son, shouted to me if I would stop for a photograph. That wasn't what was at issue; it was whether or not if I did stop, would I be able to start again. And finally, the crowd takes over, urging, cheering, cajoling, willing, and dragging us by mental force alone along Leeson Street and into St Stephen's Green.

I feel like all of the greats together as I crossed that finish line. I am Ronnie Delany, John Treacy and Roger Bannister, all rolled into one. I feel the exhilaration of completion through my body's exhaustion. RTÉ's DG congratulates me and Noel Carroll of Dublin Corporation, gives me a warm and generous welcome – a proud moment to receive recognition from one who has excelled as a runner. Peter Stokes tells me that he never doubted me. I say a few words to Jimmy Greally again and stand and clap and clap all of those who've run that day. The words of the poet, Brendan Kennelly come into my mind when he wrote of Dublin's eccentrics in his poem *The Fool's Rod*:

> "*Gibbering tattered souls pass by*
> *Raising their strange and distant cry*
> *For something lost in the air or ground*
> *That may be sought but never found*
> *As they, poor souls who crave and moan*
> *Are always seen but never known*
> "*The city, built in mire and mud,*
> *Is refuge for the poor and mad;*
> *The busy man and watchful God*
> *Suffer the lash of the fool's rod.*"

We were neither poor nor lost, but there was a madness about the joy that day in 1984.

There are ideas that seem good at the time. Walking from Croke Park to Thurles for the GAA's centenary celebrations was definitely one of these. I was caught up in the excitement and general bonhomie that surrounded this centenary. Michael Cusack had called a meeting in Hayes's Commercial Hotel, Thurles, on November 1, 1884. This was the first meeting of the 'Gaelic Athletic Association for the Preservation and Cultivation of National Pastimes.' Maurice Davin was elected President, Cusack, Wyse-Power and McKay were elected Secretaries and it was agreed that Archbishop Croke, Charles Stewart Parnell and Michael Davitt would be asked to become Patrons. These humble beginnings gave birth to a great amateur sporting movement that has gone from strength to strength since then.

I had launched my *Donncha's Sunday* on Radio One to capture the spirit of the vibrant celebrations being held all around the country to mark this significant event. I wanted to do something myself to mark the occasion and decided that I'd walk from Croke Park, the headquarters and spiritual heart of the GAA, to where the All-Ireland Hurling Finals were being held in Semple Stadium in Thurles, Co. Tipperary. I chose to do it for Concern, the charity that works with the poorest people to transform their lives.

People had begun to look on me as Ireland's greatest walker and I suppose to an extent I wanted to live up to their belief and expectations of me. I was proud to be Ireland's greatest pedestrian but this challenge was more daunting than anything I had taken on before. I planned to walk continuously, without a break for sleeping, from Croke Park to Thurles. This was more than 160 kilometres or over one-hundred miles in old measurements. The plan was to leave on the Friday at 6.00 a.m. and reach Thurles around midday on the Sunday of the game. Donncha Junior, then only fifteen, volunteered to accompany me and I was delighted to have such close support and the time to spend in his company.

Michael O'Halloran, the Lord Mayor of Dublin saw us off as did Liam Mulvihill, the Director General of the GAA. Dublin was deserted and there was an eerie feeling walking down O'Connell Street, the capital's main thoroughfare, and finding it completely empty of anything living other than scavenging seagulls screeching overhead and diving down to pick up the discarded scraps from the previous night's fast food. The aim of any charity walk is to raise money for the cause and so our route took us through as many towns and villages as we possibly could, while still reaching our destination on time. I would like to say that the Gods looked kindly on our venture but much of the time it was raining and cool, despite the fact that our walk spanned the last day of August and the first two days of September.

Our walk took us through Lucan, Palmerstown and then on to Celbridge. Carbury GAA organised a replay of their 1960 final to mark the walk's passing while a band marched with us into Naas and Superquinn organised a reception with a giant cake that caught

Donncha Junior's eye. We reached the Curragh at about six or seven o'clock in the evening and had an equestrian escort into the army barracks. I recall it was raining heavily there and we paused for about an hour. Then it was on into the gathering gloom of the evening. We passed through Portarlington for a midnight seisiún to raise money for famine relief in Ethiopia. Then breakfast in Montmellick, where the Sisters of Charity recharged the batteries at six o'clock in preparation for the second day of purgatory after twenty-four hours of near continuous walking. It was a battle of endurance and I remember walking that night towards Monasterevin in the blaze of the blinding lights from the oncoming trucks and cars and occasional silent pools of darkness as the night thickened and enveloped us all.

Saturday's dawn was weak and uninspiring and the early morning quickly settled into rain. Father Finucane joined us at various points to encourage and inspire. An accordion band brought us through Portlaoise. Micheál Ó Muircheartaigh and Brother Liam Ó Caithnia, author of *Scéal na hIomána*, a history of hurling from its early beginnings to 1884, stopped on their way to the match to support and greet us.

DONNCHA O DULAING of Radio's
Highways and Byways & Across the Water

Dusk came and with it, rain, in a water-filled County Laois. We had tea in Abbeyleix and the great march paused for more sustenance in Ballycolla. Rathdowney reminded me of the stop we had made there when travelling by pony and trap. It had been our first stop then. I found my mind wondering how the two heroes of that trip, "Hullabaloo" and "Let's Go", were getting on. My thoughts were disjointed and fragmentary and I felt as if I were sleep-walking, zombie-like along the road. We reached Errill at 2.00 a.m. I could see the occasional curtain pulled back, yard light coming on and dogs barking a distant warning. The cold, pre-dawn wind whipped across our sweaty faces; it was like having a hot and cold shower at the same time. We didn't talk now; we just slogged on, putting one foot in front of another and thinking only of one step at a time.

Father Finucane joined us at dawn and we wandered uneasily into silent Templemore, where the Garda training school is based. The young guards there gave us a great welcome. We attended Mass in the training centre and followed this with breakfast and a short rest. We had now been walking for forty-eight hours non-stop. I felt pain, stiffness and exhaustion throughout my body. I found it almost impossible to recall the detail of the previous night's trudge and was vaguely aware of having met Dermot Kelly, the hurler and other sporting personalities. Now though, there was only eight miles to go and I was determined to put my best foot forward. I felt a sudden energy surge engulf my battered body – where it came from I cannot tell – and I reached Thurles at an unlikely speed.

Thurles on that All-Ireland day was unique and special. It was full of excitement and celebrations everywhere. We were led to the Bank of Ireland and I was presented with a cheque in the square outside. The Bank of Ireland itself was open and welcoming and Jim Whitty put a tot of Paddy into my outstretched hand. It surged into the very deepest recesses of my body and spirit – truly uisce beatha, indeed.

I had to test the reviving capacity of whiskey when I had to get back on my feet and walk the final steps to the game itself. The stadium was resplendent in the colours of Cork and Offaly, the two finalists. I was greeted, patted on the back and had my hand pumped until it felt that it would drop off.

Play the Game in 1987 - Donncha, Dermot Morgan and Larry Gogan.

CELEBRITIES Give a Day BY Fasting

MIKE MURPHY
PAT KENNY
MARTIN SHEEN
ANNE DOYLE
DEIRDRE PURCELL
DAVE FANNING
DONNCHA O'DULIANG
RICHARD CROWLEY
JIMMY GREELEY
MAXI
CHRISTY MOORE
OLIVIA O'LEARY
MICHAEL LALLY
MARIAN RICHARDSON
RONNIE DREW
AONGHUS MC ANALLY
FLO MC SWEENEY
BRYAN MURRAY
TWINK
GERRY RYAN

Christmas Fast 1986

CONCERN Christmas Week which takes place nationwide from December 11 to 18th will be launched on Thursday 11th December at 11.30 a.m. in O'Connell Street Dublin.

The Lord Mayor of Dublin Mr. Bertie Aherne, T.D. and a host of celebrities who are fasting this year for CONCERN will launch the CONCERN Christmas Week. The fast will be launched countrywide at the following locations:

FAST
LOCATIONS DECEMBER

Location	Dates
CARLOW	11, 12, 13
CAVAN	22, 23, 24
CLARE	10, 11, 12
CORK CITY	8, 12
CORK COUNTY	
EAST RIDING –	not confirmed:
WEST RIDING	12, 13, 14
DONEGAL	22, 23, 24
DUBLIN	11, 12, 13
GALWAY CITY	11, 12, 13
GALWAY WEST	19, 20, 21
CLIFDEN	12, 13, 14
GALWAY EAST	21, 22, 23, 24
KERRY	19, 20, 21
KILLARNEY	4, 5
KILDARE	11, 12, 13
KILKENNY	12, 13, 14
CASTLECOMER	19, 20, 21
LAOIS	11, 12, 13
LEITRIM	15, 16, 17
LIMERICK	11, 12, 13
LOUTH	5, 6, 14
LONGFORD	9, 10, 11
MAYO	10, 11, 12, 13
CASTLEBAR	10, 11, 12
WESTPORT	10, 11, 12
MEATH	5, 6, 7
NAVAN,	
KELLS, TRIM	22, 23, 24
ATHBOY	13, 14
MONAGHAN	22, 23, 24
OFFALY	11, 12, 13
ROSCOMMON	21, 22, 23, 24
SLIGO	15, 16, 17
SLIGO TOWN	11, 12, 13
BALLYMOTE	11, 12, 13
TIPPERARY	21, 22, 23, 24
WATERFORD	12, 13, 14
W FORD CITY	15, 16
FERRYBANK	15, 16
DUNGARVAN,	
ABBEYSIDE	22, 23, 24
WESTMEATH	9, 10, 11
ATHLONE	12, 13, 14
WEXFORD	12, 13, 14
GOREY	19, 20, 21
WICKLOW	Part of Dublin, Carlow, Wexford.

Special offer in Quinnsworth this Christmas

CONCERN Christmas Box

It's a bargain not to be missed.
Pick up your Christmas box – absolutely free at Quinnsworth Stores in Dublin.
Offer lasts from 3rd to 6th December.
Or you can apply to CONCERN Christmas Box Appeal, 1, Upper Camden Street Phone:(01) 681237.

Finally, I reached the interview point and spoke to Jimmy Magee. I was disorientated and found it hard to answer his questions coherently. My confusion was complete when I finished the interview and I had to ask him for directions to the stand. This was ridiculous – here I was in Thurles, a place I knew so well and I couldn't remember the layout of the stadium. I was exhausted and all but crawled into my seat. I slept off and on through the pre-match celebrations and the game itself. At one point, I fell from my seat. Cork won. All of the excitement had passed me by. 'Wake up, Donncha! You're the only Corkman asleep as ye get the cup,' were the words of the late great Tipp hurler Tommy Doyle, who sat near me during the match, when John Fenton took the MacCarthy Cup. I finally got back to Dublin and bed around midnight. I could neither talk nor rest. My body was still walking when my head hit the pillow for my first sleep in nearly seventy hours. These were certainly my longest days.

I take great pride in that walk for Concern. We walked to help relieve the impact of famine in Ethiopia. This was a tragedy that mirrored our own national experience a little more than one hundred years previously. We were ahead of the posse in this walk as Band-Aid only launched its hit single, *Do they Know it's Christmas?* for the following December. It is good to know that Ireland provided some small leadership in the fight against this terrible tragedy. Of course, it was another Irishman, Bob Geldof, who was the main motivator behind the whole Band-Aid movement.

There is another walk that stands out in my memory. It was a joyful one that now is overlaid with great sadness. I completed "Donncha's Winter March" for the first time in late 1986, early 1987, as we followed in the steps of the great O'Sullivan Beara. My memory of this great adventure is entwined with that of my co-walker and companion, my daughter, Sinéad. It was something that we shared and on which I now look back wistfully. We were following in the footsteps of the thousand people who marched with Dónal Cam Ó Súilleabháin Beara on the most fearsome march, or retreat, in our history. While a thousand set out, only 35 reached the fort of Ó Ruairc of Breifne. They retreated from what should have been the greatest Irish victory of all time and one which would surely have changed the course of our nation's history, when Mountjoy outmanoeuvred the Irish forces under Red Hugh O'Donnell and Hugh O'Neill.

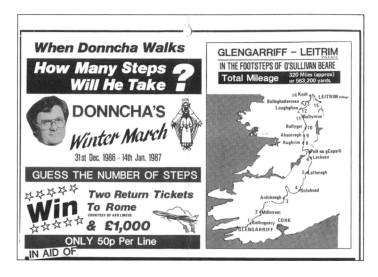

The Ó Suilleabháin Clan at the start of the O'Sullivan Beara walk in 1986.

The march commemorates the O'Sullivans forced march from Glengarriff in West Cork north to Leitrim. They travelled in the depths of winter at a time when the country was gripped by a mini-ice age. It was inhospitable countryside where ambush and treachery dogged each step. We walked for another reason – not retreat from an enemy but to help friends, a charity known then as the Irish National Handicapped Children's Pilgrimage Trust, now The Irish Pilgrimage Trust. The charity organises annual pilgrimages to Lourdes for children with disabilities.

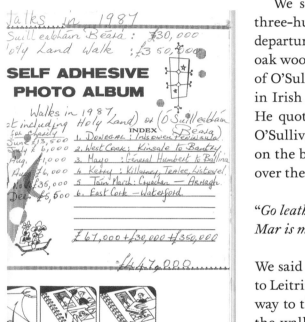

We set out from Glengarriff on the last day of 1986, three-hundred and eighty-four years after Ó Súilleabháin's departure. Our setting off point was Doirín na Fola – the little oak wood of blood - above Glengarriff. We were in the midst of O'Sullivans, and Bernie O'Sullivan wished us a bon voyage in Irish and English on behalf of his fellow clan members. He quoted from Canon Dineen's famous poem imagining O'Sullivan's feelings as he set out on his march home. He calls on the bright sun not to set until he has gazed one last time over the mountain and valleys of his home place:

"Go leathad mo shúil ar na sléibhtibh seo ailne
Mar is mór é mo dhúil iad d'fheiscint uair eile."

We said our farewells and slid down the hillside on our way to Leitrim. Glengarriff still slept as we passed through on our way to the first long climb. Joe Earley was chef d'equipe for the walk and he watched over us carefully. He told us that I looked "sweaty." I had dressed for a cold and snowy start but I had failed to take account of the continental climate that cossets the coastline there. I was soaked in perspiration by the time that we reached Derrycreha National School. I had to struggle out of my thermals there before talking to Gay Byrne for his radio programme.

At Kealkill Post Office, Barry Murphy and his wife indulged us with a feast of Christmas cake and whiskey before we struck out for the dark forbidding Pass of Keimaneigh. Here, we climbed beyond the reach of Glengarriff's benign influence and into torrential rain.

Night fell as we climbed to the sopping windy heights of Gort a' Chladaigh. Dozens joined us and laughter and the fluting of tin whistles drove away the ghosts of the gathering night. Tales, tall, funny and often ghostly, filled the night. There were Christmas candles glowing in the windows across the valley. We dropped down slowly. The backs of our legs ached as the sound of the bagpipes rose eerily up the hillside. Donal Cronin emerged from the gloom in his full piper's regalia and welcomed us to his land as the rain fell once again upon us. The O'Sullivans spent their first night at the Teampaillín at Eachros, an event so eloquently described by Aodh de Blácam, *"It is likely that no camp fires were lit, lest spies from the heights around should detect the lodging place of the fugitive 1,000. Twenty-six miles the column had marched on one terrible day."* As we had done, too!

Oliver O'Brien recorded Dónal as he played O'Sullivan's march. There was a memorable party in Cronins. Mrs Cronin had just had a baby, and I sat by the fire holding the baby, another Dónal, in my arms while all celebrated his arrival. Sinéad, my daughter, sat quietly on the other side of the hearth; the baby snuggled contentedly in the crook of my arm. He would never remember this night but Sinéad and I would and now I hold that peaceful memory alone. It was a strange counterpoint to the death of an O'Sullivan baby on the same march centuries before. The field where the child is reputed to have died in still known as "Páirc a Leinbh."

New Year's Day is a day of rest and relaxation for most but for Sinéad and me the year began with our marching over Maoileann Mountain and recalled that this was where O'Sullivan lost his great mare, "An Chearc", so called because of her liveliness, in a boghole hereabouts. Dónal MacSuibhne brought us to Baile Mhúirne and towards the shrine of St Gobnait. Here lay Seán Ó Riada, his wife, Ruth, and among a great many others, the poet Seán Ó Riordáin.

Seán O' Sé joined us, and given his great regard for Ó Riada, sang *Mo Ghile Mear*, Seán Clárach Mac Domhnaill's poem. The assembled crowd joined us in the chorus. We continued, making a brief stop at the Mills in Ballyvourney for lunch. We then headed for the steep climb up the side of Mullachanish heading north; Helen Ní hAodha from Raidió na Gaeltachta interviewed me there.

We left the crowd behind and trudged past the RTÉ transmitter towards the dark woods now flecked with lightly falling snow. The mast offered little comfort against the cold that now began to bite hard. The mountains were ghostly and shadowy, like some Japanese painting, before us. Hail shafted down. A woman was waiting for us in a clearing; Máire Ní Cheallacháin, who would become President of the Camogie Association the following year and hold that post until 1991.

Fr JJ Ó Riordáin, the Redemptorist, joined us as we walked into Millstreet. We crossed the bridge over the Blackwater, dark and forbidding except for the torches that glowed on every side. It was night by the time we reached the Millstreet Road where a great crowd was waiting. The Millstreet Pipe Band fell into step with us and we

Crossing the Shannon in a handmade replica currach during the O'Sullivan Beara walk.

were joined by several hundred supporters. We reached a place called "the Boeing", a traditional ford across the Blackwater. We heard it before we saw it that evening and I wondered how Ó Súilleabháin had managed to cross the river here.

Our two boatmen were waiting stoically for us in the cold. We were to cross with the aid of a rope thrown to us from the other side. We caught it to the accompaniment of a loud cheer and many willing hands pulled us up and ashore where we were addressed by Dónal Ó Síocháin and Tom Meaney. We were now in the Barony of Duhallow in Cork and dined there with the O'Sullivan family. People from the Irish Chiropody Association tended to our poor feet. Clare Edwards from Killarney, the Kerry team physiotherapist, brought rest and calm to aching limbs. Each evening after the march, we broadcast the daily edition of *Donncha's Winter March* which soon caught the national imagination and helped many share in our mid-winter trek, eavesdropping on our travels and travails, all of this before enjoying a well-earned night's sleep brought on by twenty-four savage miles of hard hiking.

We faced a march of forty tough miles on the third day. We set out at 7.30a.m. in torrential rain. Raymond O'Sullivan reminded us

of another savage encounter where the O'Sullivans put the attacking Barrys to flight, suffering the loss of four of their own party. Don Philip O'Sullivan Beara describes it thus:

> *"The ford was contested with red-hot balls from both sides for about an hour. Four of the Irish fell; the Queen's men lost more and were forced to retreat... There by the ford somewhere beyond Liscarroll, the dead were buried."*

It was evening by the time we actually visited the place. Dan Brennan and his wife, the landowners, accompanied us. Dan cherished this sacred place and its tree grove. We had still twelve miles to go before we got to Ballyhea and we heard that there were hundreds waiting for us there.

And so it was each day; we trudged through the cold and wet fortified by the well-wishes of the many who came to welcome us or walk a little of the way with us. We had been told that the O'Sullivans set upon the O'Dwyer clan on the following day as they searched for food; they then stopped close to the village of Solohead in County Tipperary. On one occasion, we spent the night with the hospitable Collins family. On the first march, we halted in the village in the company of Archbishop of Cashel, Dr. Clifford, who later joined us in Dundrum House where we were guests of Austin Crowe for that evening.

Osmond Bennett arrived and by bed-time Sinéad and I were fit for the rigours of another day. Rigours there truly were, for through the rain, sleet and floods, we set off to the Tipperary uplands, marching as best we could. Hollyford was first and on to Milestone where a car flashed its lights and a cheery voice shouted: "Fáilte." It was Willie Corbett, a well-known historian. He was astounded when I told him that we had started our walk that day at 5.30 a.m. We turned our faces for Upperchurch, which we reached for breakfast after four-and-a half hours' walking. Pearse Duggan and Eamon de Stafort led the greeting party while some of the local ladies provided an ample and welcome breakfast.

Daylight emboldened us and we set out to cross the Sliabh Félim Mountains, running wet with streams of yellow rain water. We took a short break in one of the many Ryan homesteads along the way. My throat muscles flexed and relaxed to a liquid welcome. It was a rough, uncomfortable morning and I had yet to make a live broadcast in Templederry Hall. We planted trees and prepared for the day's last trek into Latteragh in the barony of Ormonde. The O'Sullivan army, now greatly diminished, holed up there and as Don Philip wrote:

"He halted in the village of Latteragh, and threw his men into a rather small church and its enclosure. There was, in this village, a fort from which he was annoyed the whole night with firing and sallies from the garrison."

We stayed nearby, close to where the church had been. I wasn't in bed until 2.30 a.m.

The following morning we had an almost vertical climb up a hill and near the summit we met Nancy Murphy, the historian. It was calm and peaceful. The sun was rising pale pink in the wintry dawn, lighting the Devil's Bit away to our right. Knocksheegowna showed across the great valley of Ormonde.

We reached Cloughjordan around 1.00 p.m. to a welcome from Canon White and there, too, was Sergeant Michael McMahon who would be our guide and advisor across the Shannon. It's amazing how frost and night seem to fall together in the winter and this they certainly did under the romantic hill of Knocksheegowna. As we struggled towards that day's end, I met Mary Cahalane whose kindness in planning and in helping to organise this great march are unforgettable.

Indeed, we dined with herself and her family in her lovely home and broke bread there after another brutal day. The summit of Knocksheegowna had been "lit up" for the occasion and it was not difficult to imagine its importance in folklore as we crunched past on the icy road. Later that night we were guests of the late Michael Joe Egan from Castlebar who was now owner and loving carer of Redwood Castle, on the east bank of the Shannon, the ancestral home of the McEgans, scholars, bards and sometime sheriffs. He had renovated the old castle. The late Canon Martin Ryan from Lorrha joined us as another welcome guest on what seemed an historic night. I couldn't help but muse that this was a far cry from the terrible place when O'Sullivan and what was left of his little force settled down for another night of fear in the boggy lea of this ancient castle. They had reached the Shannon and it had to be crossed.

They spent two days here *"building two ships of osiers and trees covered with the skins of twelve horses which they killed and whose flesh they all ate except for Ó Súilleabháin, Diarmuid of Dursey and Diarmuid Ó hUallacháin."* The field has been known since as "Poll na gCapall" and as I crossed it with Mr and Mrs Comber and a great throng from the Tipperary side, the full horror of what took place then engulfed me.

We paused to attend Canon Martin Ryan's lovely and gentle Mass in Lorrha. Later on, Canon Martin commented that history was greeting us every day and that this was a place in which it was a privilege to live. Indeed, I couldn't disagree with that and it was a great privilege to be there on a Sunday morning and to be greeted so hospitably by the Canon and his housekeeper.

Our crossing of the great river Shannon took place on a misty morning with rime on grass and trees as the last Munster bonfire blazed near the water's edge. The pupils from the Vocational School in Kilcormac, Co. Offaly, made the coracle in which we crossed the great river. This is an almost circular boat, six-feet in length and over four-feet wide. It consisted of hazel twigs bound together and covered with leather and impregnated with linseed oil. It was hard not to recall the fact that there were two coracles used for the Beara march: one made by Diarmuid of Dursey and the other by O'Malley for the Connacht men. The former crossed successfully, the latter sank. I could not help but note that our coracle was the same design as the Connacht one. There was some trepidation in the air as I climbed into our craft – the tension heightened by Eileen O'Brien, playing a slow air on fiddle. Canon Martin's housekeeper sprinkled us with holy water as we cast off and our two oarsmen struck out for the opposite bank.

O'Súilleabháin's crossing captured many writers' imaginations. Thomas Davis described it as "The Great Romantic Achievement of the Age." For me there is no doubt but that this was the highlight of the great march and I'm unlikely to ever cross a great river such as this in a coracle ever again. Bishop Fogarty described the earlier achievement thus, 'O'Sullivan crossed the Shannon with the corpse of Ireland on his back.'

It was ten miles more to the sitting-room in Gortnamona in the home formerly occupied by the Lynam family, one of whom, Ned, was a friend and colleague of Percy French. They say that it was here that Percy French wrote the great lament *Gortnamona* . It was close to dusk when I went to the piano, the same one used by Percy himself. I played the chord of C and Patrick Kenneally sang the song.

Joe Earley told us that it was six miles to Aughrim and Tom O'Sullivan, an old friend who had travelled from Lahinch in Co. Clare, joined us for this part of the march. It was dark and bonfires flared and glowed as we stepped out. There were lots of people around, cheering and encouraging us along the way.

Aughrim represented another cathartic moment for Ó Súilleabháin Beara and his decimated force. Here they faced a renewed onslaught from an Englishman, Henry Malby and Thomas Burke, brother of the Earl of Clanricarde. They had five companies on foot, two troops on horse and a local force. They attacked ferociously and their horsemen, with gleaming armour, their trumpets and drums, brought fear to the

Ó Súilleabháin's advance guard and dispersed them in all directions. Facing annihilation, Ó Súilleabháin urged the remainder by saying:

"Since on this day our desperate fortunes have left us here without means or country, or wives or children to fight for, the struggle with our enemies before us now is for our bare lives; we have nothing left that we can lose.

"In God's eternal name I ask you men, will you not rather fall gloriously in battle, avenging your blood than die like brute cattle in a cowardly flight? Our ancestors surely would never seek by flight to avoid an honourable death.

"Let us then follow in the footsteps of our sires: there is no other salvation. See around you that the country is now bare of woods or bogs; there is no concealment; the people of these parts offer us no aid. Roads and passes are blocked, even if we had strength to fly. Our only hope is in our own courage, and the strength of our own arms.

"Up then and attack the enemy, whom you excel in spirit, in courage, in achievements past, and holy faith! Had I the breath for it, which I hadn't, I'd have cried: 'Up the Rebels!'

"Remember that everywhere hitherto enemies who attacked us were routed by the Divine Mercy. Victory is the gift of God. Let us think then that Christ Our Lord will be with His servants in their most dire need; and that 'tis for His name and holy faith that we are at issue with the heretics and those who cleave to them.

"Fear not this worthless mob; they are not men of such fame as we, nor used to fight as we are. When they see us, heartily defy them, I do hope that they will turn tail, even as I look to it, that you will shew forth your courage and your faith."

Ó Súilleabháin's men rose to the challenge and fearlessly faced the enemy in hand-to-hand combat. Ó Súilleabháin's men were victorious, losing only fourteen men while the opposing army scattered and ran in disarray. Ó Súilleabháin took the colours, his men ate some of their horses before pressing northwards, leaving one-hundred of the enemy's dead behind them.

Our entry into Aughrim was a good deal less violent and greeted with great applause. Sinéad borrowed my scarf and kept it, of course. She had walked without complaint and was to continue to do so – despite the terrible weather conditions. Her care, her courage, her strength, I shall never forget. She is ever deep at the heart of me.

211 Rambles in Éireann

Ahasgragh was home of Bríd and Seán 'ac Donncha. Here Mattie McDonagh, the famous Galway footballer met us and marched on to Mount Mary. We walked on with snow and frost surrounding us. Aodh de Blácam's commentary states: *"Snow was everywhere on O'Sullivan's march."* I looked back at this wintry scene as we swung left for Glinsk. The early morning cold had a mystical intensity and my thoughts were with those who formed the small force's rearguard. These were mercenaries, galloglasses, and brave unyielding fighting men. A.E. Housman summarised this succinctly in one of his last poems:

> *"These in the days when heaven was falling*
> *The hours when earth's foundation fled*
> *Followed their mercenary calling*
> *And took their wages and are dead."*

The poet put it accurately in the next verse, *"What God abandoned, these defended."*

A welcoming party met us approximately six miles from Glinsk. Horses, pipers, cars and children made up this welcome. We received cheers and speeches of welcome at Glinsk Castle – a place that had turned Ó Súilleabháin away. We planted a tree and indulged in a medieval style banquet. Indeed, these memories make Glinsk special. Glinsk was, and ever is, special.

We left a silent, still-sleeping Ballinlough just after 5.30 a.m. We were alone with the bitter cold as we marched alongside Sliabh O'Flynn and then on to Lake O'Flynn. Nearby, a bonfire blazed in a farmyard into which we diverted for a bit of heat with the Carthy family who may be descendants of some of the original Beara marchers.

Our thirteenth day on the road began beside the grave of Ireland's first President, near Frenchpark, Co. Roscommon. We received an early morning welcome from children from the local national school. We began our day's recording here where Paddy Ryan played a slow air on the fiddle while I recited a poem by President Dubhghlas de hÍde, Úlla den Chraobh:

> *"Guth na gaoithe is na taoide*
> *Ag síorthroid le cogadh cumhachtach*
> *Muir, tír, spéir, séideadh na gaoithe*
> *Och! Uile go léir is uaigneach."*

It was easy to feel the loneliness that the past president described on our winter wander through that bleak white countryside. We were on our own for a short while as snowflakes swirled around as we trudged to Ballaghaderreen and the welcome of the school band. We had now entered a land of beauty and myth as we moved towards the grey-faced Bricklieve territory. The texture of the landscape reminded me of south Lebanon during my winter visit in 1978. The morning sun shone brightly but not warm. In the clear distance I could see Maeve's Knocknarea across the skyline from Ben Bulben and the Sligo drumlins. Nearer was the Hill of Kesh with its echoes of Diarmuid and Gráinne. Colmcille and the battle of the books had his own place in this lunar landscape.

Joe Earley told us that the radio said that Ireland had seized up. It seemed that even the birds were freezing on the bare branches. We moved on slowly towards a tangled wood and by later afternoon we were entering our last great climb. Our feet were cold and sore. I looked towards the distant hilltop where Lloyd Praegar discovered the great Bronze Age Cairn of Carrowkeel. We stood not far from this strange and wonderful place some thousand feet above sea level as Fr Pat pointed out to

Observing peace-keeping activities of Irish UN forces in the Lebanon 1978.

me some ravens flying from Kesh; the Ox Mountains, and there in the distance was Croagh Patrick. This was the last conversation we ever had. 'This is a great thing,' he said, 'but you know, I feel for them lost in time and place. Their past gone forever and their future, well, doubtful.' He drove away into the afternoon sun and we carried on our way.

At Mass in Ballinafad later that night we heard inspiring words from Bishop Dominic Conway. It was in this very place that Don Philip tells us, 'a man clad in a linen garment, his feet bare, his temples bound with a white wreath ... an appearance well-calculated to inspire awe.' He led the remaining marchers through the night. They groped their way, feet slipping on loose stones, snow had heaped up in the wind, as, quite exhausted, the unhappy fugitives struggled on their way.

Our final day on the march was cold. We walked an ancient pathway above the beautiful Lough Arrow and often looked through the driving snow up towards yesterday's climb. We were an emotional little party that left McDonagh's Pub to tramp the last seven miles into the vast desolation of Leitrim. The lake was rimmed with snow.

A few swans sailed uncaringly by and a robin twittered on a holly bush. Gerry Enright and the pupils of Carraigín Rua National School enchanted us. There was great temptation to linger. Ted Berry said with truth, 'It's time to go lads; we have a place to go and a programme to make.'

Fr Dermod McCarthy, who first mooted the idea, shook hands silently. We unveiled a plaque to Sinéad and myself at Knockvicar and crossed the Shannon for the second time. It was dark; a great moment before a blazing bonfire. St Patrick had crossed once near here. We were all together on this dark winter's night. There were pipes again to play us and the hundreds who were with us into Leitrim village. Beth Earley handed me an Irish coffee. My hands were too frozen to hold it but my throat responded well and I let the warm liquid slide down slowly. I thought again of the words of the Chronicler:

> *"They reached Leitrim Fort about 11 o'clock, being then reduced to thirty-five, of whom eighteen were armed, sixteen were sutlers (army providers) and one was a woman... I am astonished that Dermot O'Sullivan, my father, an old man near seventy, and the woman of gentle sex were able to go through these toils."*

They were all received *"with most honourable hospitality."* And indeed, we were, too. Sinéad was the first woman since 1603 to complete this journey. I was truly proud of her that day and glad now to have that memory.

I was interested to read recently of a charity cycle through the thirty-two counties in aid of Console, the national suicide awareness charity. It took me back to one of my own around-Ireland adventures, my all-Ireland walk.

I've never been a lie-on-the-beach sort of person; I enjoy activity and meeting different people in their own places. Thus, holidays have always been a challenge for me and I like to find something that allows me be active and have time with my family. I decided to devote my summer holidays for 1985 to fundraising on behalf of REHAB. I aimed to devise a walk that allowed me to walk in every county in Ireland within thirty days. Added to this, I pledged somewhat bizarrely not to shave until I had completed the entire walk. Two of my sons, Dónal and Donncha, agreed to accompany me – splitting the walk between them, with Dónal taking the first week and Donncha the rest.

This was to be a high point of my walks up to that time. We collected over IR£100,000 due, in great part, to the unstinting efforts

Donncha's Winter March 1987
l-r: Fr Dermod McCarthy,
Sinéad, Donncha and
Joe Earley.

of the regional committees, Eileen Kerr and Noel Greene, great and enthusiastic fundraisers and my companions for the entire thousand miles that strayed into every county in the country. I had a great sense of achievement when I finished, even if the walk nearly finished me in the process.

We began on the 1st of August on what was a quiet, dry morning – one of the few that we were to have over the next 30 days. Our starting place was Slane, an historic and beautiful village with a wonderful "Square," which is actually an octagon. We had a pre-walk celebration in Trim Hospital and further ones in Dunleer and Slane Castle where my good friend, Paddy Reilly, performed.

There was a great buzz in Slane for our official start. Trucks, cars, flags, banners and people turned out in abundance. Dónal was at my side, as he had been on many walks and the marathon. I drew upon my two sons' youthful energy and unbounded enthusiasm. It gave me the lift that I needed for a telephone interview with *Morning Ireland*. 'Of course, I'll complete the course,' I'd said and then silently added for my own ears only, 'even without training.' Television news cameras were there, too, and I spoke with a confidence that was somewhat exaggerated, smiled the smile of the overly-optimistic and hoped vainly for good weather every day.

We were waved on by a lone Garda, and so we were off; the first day of my beard growth had started. We climbed the first hill and my thoughts went to the poet Francis Ledwidge, Slane's poet, who walked these roads and contemplated the life of this village:

> *"Above smokes the little town,*
> *With its whitewashed walls and roofs of brown*
> *And its octagon spire toned smoothly down*
> *As the holy minds within."*

St Patrick also had wandered these lands and lit his Paschal fire on the hill to my left. We had a piper who manfully led us up that first long hill. Henry Mountcharles reminded me of others who had travelled these roads:

'One of the most famous folk to travel this road,' he told me, 'was King George IV. He travelled to Slane at least twice. You see he had a wild passion for Lady Conyngham who lived here. It is said that the long straight road from Dublin to Slane was built by him.'

I stepped up the pace as we approached Collon. This was a ploy I used on the first day of walks as it almost certainly dulled the competitive edge of the casual joiners. We climbed a tough, muscle-tweaking hill and passed Mellifont Abbey; this was the first Cistercian house in Ireland and at the time of the walk was home to the great scholar, an tAthair Colm Cille Ó Corbuí, who always signed himself Manach and Sagart. Mellifont Abbey is still a home of prayer and contemplation and its gardens supply flowers and plants to horticulture enthusiasts.

A young man strode effortlessly beside me. He was a REHAB trainee and hardly spoke to me. Then, he surprised me, 'Who are you?' he asked. I looked sideways. He was serious! I gave him my name. Silence.

'What are you doing here?'
'Walking,' I said, 'like yourself.' A long pause.
'So you're the man,' he smiled. He wondered where
I worked.
'RTÉ,' I said.
'One or Two?' he asked. I explained.
Neither of us talked for a mile or so
'I never listen to either, they're all news and weather, mostly bad,' he said.

A band greeted us on our entry into Dunleer. The late Pádraig Faulkner, TD, a former Minister for Education and Cheann Comhairle of Dáil Éireann, together his wife met me there as did an enthusiastic local REHAB Committee and several generous ladies from Monasterboice.

Castlebellingham is yet another rural jewel but, sadly, rain accompanied our arrival. It was a portent of wettings to come. This village and its castle were home to the Bellingham family from the seventeenth century to the 1950s. Colonel Thomas Bellingham acted as a guide to William of Orange. The churchyard is the resting place of Dr Thomas Guither who allegedly introduced frogs into Ireland after he brought frog spawn here. It's a good story but most likely apocryphal. The same graveyard is the permanent resting place of Napper Tandy, one of the founding members of the Society of United Irishmen, and comrade in arms of Theobald Wolfe Tone. It was pouring rain as we entered Dundalk. I was thankful to reach my bed, as it happens in the bridal suite in the Derryhale Hotel. I slept far more soundly than any bride.

We walked through day after rain-soaked day and each night there was a gig or gigs to raise more funds, so it was always late when I finally crawled between the sheets. The walk was gathering momentum and we were on a high as we crossed the border. Portadown was the first town where we experienced the darker side of the North and its troubled times. I spoke at several Sunday Masses and afterwards Walter Love of Radio Ulster, told the world, and especially the local population, that I was coming their way. This was compounded by it being a Sunday, bringing out even greater crowds.

The Troubles in the North were at their thunderous worst at this time. I set out from the church flanked by Ted Berry from RTÉ and my son, Dónal. A sudden downpour caught us badly and we were cold and wet as we ventured along the way. A Hiace van was parked on the roadside with its backdoor open and the occupants visible inside. Cold stares were the only response to my hearty, but nervous greeting. The road had UVF painted on it and close to the van, behind a low wall, three armed men stood. They were togged out in paramilitary gear and said nothing. We hurried on.

We came upon a group of young men playing flutes and beating bodhráns. Our greeting this time was acknowledged but with a, "F*** off, you Fenians." A dark-eyed girl asked us if we were collecting. I affirmed and again I was told to, "F***off, you Fenian." We speeded up, trying not to show our fear as insult after insult accompanied us. The young men played The Sash and chanted "The Queen" while others banged the back and sides of their van. It was intimidating.

Opposite: In Armagh with great friend, Cardinal Tomás Ó Fiaich.

With Monsignor Horan and GAA President, Dr.Mick Loftus, when the building of Knock Airport was well underway.

The genesis of Ireland West Airport, Knock, formerly known simply as Knock Airport.

The Mayor of one small town greeted us on live radio with a "Welcome to our country." I told him that I'd been in this country since I was born, but thanked him anyway. The good point was that he donated £100 – money has no politics. I got a welcoming phone call from my friend, Cardinal Tomás Ó Fiaich.

The strangeness followed through the North. In one council, I think it was Enniskillen, Sinn Féin was the majority party and we were invited into the council chamber. I remember that half of the seats were facing the wall while the other half faced the central table. Donncha junior, who had joined us at that stage, asked in all innocence, why this was so. We were told that this was because the Unionist councillors refused to face the Sinn Féin ones and preferred to carry on business facing the wall!

We walked on and I admit that I felt a certain lightness as we made our way through Fermanagh and eventually headed for the border. Mayo is a big county and I recollect that we seemed to be walking endlessly there. We hit Knock on the Feast of the Assumption, August 15th. Monsignor Horan, the man who masterminded the building of an airport near that small town, greeted us. The runway was laid but the airport was yet to open. Only learner drivers taxied along the apron. The Monsignor was clear that we couldn't collect at Knock Shrine but he invited us in for tea and cake. He made the point that he'd be away for three hours and so wouldn't be watching us. It reminded me of a time that I made a programme on poitín and the local guards told me that they'd be away for a few hours – giving me time to make my programme. We seized the opportunity in Knock and passed around our buckets in the reverend's absence. 'Twas a great day of giving.

Things came to a head on the nineteenth day of the walk when I developed a shin splint in my left

leg. It is a nasty injury that results from excessive use of your muscles. The papers carried the story with the headline, *"Donncha limps into Nenagh."* "Limps" hardly describes it and words like struggle, staggers or even falls might have been a more accurate description of my state. Ossie Bennett, my ever-ready masseur maestro from Johnstown in Kilkenny, came to my aid. He set about his business in a Nenagh pub corner late that evening. I remember that I couldn't eat; I couldn't face it. I was truly concerned that I wouldn't be able to continue.

It was still dark at 5.30 a.m. when I arose the next morning in Nenagh. My leg was relatively quiet and Ossie's ministrations seemed to have worked but he had warned me that I'd have to take it easy. A *Cork Examiner* van driver gave me a copy of "the paper." 'You're one of our own, boy,' he said. It carried news of my "limp." Frank Flannery of REHAB, who would walk with me all day, covered up against the torrential rain and the great gusts of wind that whipped the backs of our legs. My rain gear split at the zip – a case of everything going wrong at the same time.

A couple drove by in that early morning rain stopped and returned. They asked the question that was to dominate the next few days of the walk, 'How's the auld' leg?' They donated a £1. I walked gingerly but we made progress towards Killaloe and this brought us into Co. Clare and across the Shannon, over the Twelve-Arch bridge where patriots are remembered in stone, and up the hill to the dark, windswept church and the rippling, accordion playing of Martin Connolly. A lady in a passing car, somewhat misguidedly called me "a little saint." Jim Turnbull, who dealt with our money matters, brought the good news – the day's takings were up to scratch.

Betty Purcell and Jim Jennings from RTÉ stopped to talk to us on their way to Lisdoonvarna. They tramped with me for a mile or so. When they had gone, Nell McCafferty and Nuala Ó Faoláin stopped and were cheerfully encouraging. Charlie Haughey stopped briefly, too, and made a contribution – I can't recall how much it was.

There was music as we climbed towards the turn-off for Castleconnell, and Martin McCabe, President of Comhaltas, offered tea and welcome. It was mid-afternoon in the village of Mick Mackey and the men of Ahane.

At four o'clock, a regular pattern developed. My shin-splint woke up and I lapsed into my usual painful silence. Frank Flannery, cheerful companion on a wet day, began to show signs of distress. The morning walkers and talkers became the afternoon hobblers. Conversation was a thing of the past. I began to hate signposts. Were they always wrong? Eamon de Stafort, Gaelic Leaguer and indefatigable worker for all things good and Irish in the Shannon region, and Máire offered support and encouragement. Later he told me that when he saw the look on my face, he wasn't sure whether or not to talk! I was speechless with pain and Limerick was still more than an hour away.

On the outskirts of Limerick I was joined by the spry and lively Willie "Whack" Gleeson, a walker and giver of blood without parallel. He favoured the odd pithy and thought-provoking phrase like describing my walk as "child's play", adding, 'Sure I'd walk from Nenagh to Limerick before breakfast!' He meant no harm and I am sure he would, but before I could do anything I visualised the heading in the paper on the following day, *"Injured Broadcaster Strangles Octogenarian!"* I always remember him with affection. Michael Noonan, then Minister for Justice, joined us and led us into Limerick on this, my first full day walking with a shin splint. We all talked unknowingly on a local pirate radio station. Imagine, a Minister of Justice, a member of RTÉ staff and Frank Flannery, a member of the RTÉ Authority, breaking the law in rainy unison!

We continued meeting celebrities and politicians along our route. Charlie Nelligan, the great football goalie met us in Kerry and Maureen Quill TD met us in Co. Cork. The walk finished finally in Brittas, Co. Dublin, just across the border from Wicklow, and in the last county on our itinerary. I had now walked through all of the counties in Ireland. That evening I joined a wedding party and enjoyed their celebrations, giving them a few renditions of my favourite songs, spurred on by a sense of completion. We had our official ending on O'Connell Street in Dublin where Jim Tunney, the then Mayor of the city, met us and accompanied me to breakfast in Barry's Hotel, near Parnell Street. After that, it was a leisurely walk from there to Croke Park for the All -Ireland hurling final between Offaly and Galway which Offaly won. At last I could relax.

10 NEW HORIZONS

... We drove the planned route over the following days. It started in Nazareth where we would begin following the route Jesus took to Cana, then on to Tiberias, Capernaum and into the Jordan Valley to Jericho. Our final destination was the Holy City itself, Jerusalem. We sealed our plans while sitting by the Sea of Galilee ...

Jerusalem, the Holy City of Judaism, Christianity and Islam.

MY GENERATION IS THE last that has a direct oral connection with the Great Famine that destroyed our people and country in the 1840s. It killed or drove away over half of the population and left great swathes of land without anyone to work it. Those surviving were weakened and further impoverished; worse still they carried guilt simply for having lived. Famine undermined our native tongue – something from which it has never recovered. I say mine is the last generation with a direct oral connection in that, as a young boy, I met and heard stories from elderly men and women who were born during or shortly after the famine. They had experienced the pain and agony of this terrible visitation and carried that mark with them to the grave. For me, the famine was a real "living" event and not something of great historical significance as it has now become. Thus, I am always touched and saddened when I hear of famine and starvation in other, far-off lands, for I know the despair that they must feel and their utter dependence on others to come to their aid.

There is one footnote in Irish history that has always intrigued me. It was the donation of $170 for famine relief in Ireland, made by the Choctaw people in the United States. That would be worth approximately $5,000 in today's terms. This gift is rich in symbolism and represents an act of true generosity from a people who had only recently suffered death and dispossession and who, on learning of the miserable plight of fellow beings in Ireland, gave all that they could to help spare some from the suffering that they had endured.

The "Trail of Tears" commemorates a great and tragic event in the life and history of the Choctaw nation as well as other American native peoples in the United States. It records the ethnic cleansing and forced migration of the indigenous people of South-eastern US, mainly to lands in Eastern Oklahoma. I was keen to, and eventually managed to, walk the greater part of it. It was a walk like no other that brought us into contact with the pain of a people dispossessed, that echoed across the years to the present day. It evoked the sin that was committed against the Native Americans by the colonisers of that great nation. That stain remains on the soul of the United States. The name "Trail of Tears" remembers the first forced migration of the Choctaw people.

The Choctaw's removal was typified by cruelty, administrative bungling, incompetence and arrogance. The Choctaw's lands were in what is now Alabama, Louisiana and Mississippi. Some people were allowed to remain but the majority were forced to cede their homeland. There were three phases to the Choctaw eviction. The first was in November 1831. Those taking part in the exodus faced harsh winter weather, with rain, snow and flash floods. The intention was to transport the people in wagons but these became bogged down in the mud and mire. They were then supposed to be transported by river, but ice prevented this. An incompetent guide led some of the group astray. Disease was rampant and the travellers were exposed to cholera, dysentery and other illnesses brought into the area by settlers – diseases for which they had no immunity. About half of those who travelled died and they had to be buried where they dropped by the exhausted survivors. Freezing weather, a lack of food and proper clothing compounded the misery for the group as they trekked towards their final destination.

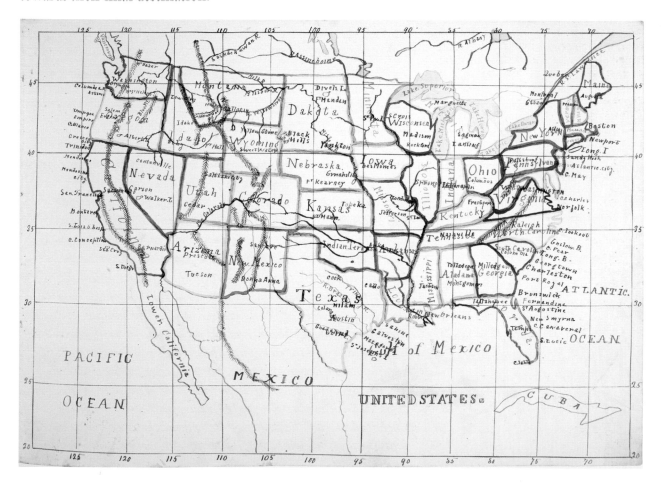

I may be accused of exaggerating the depth of this people's suffering and the callous indifference of those responsible for the move, but a contemporaneous account from the great French philosopher, Alexis de Tocqueville, who witnessed the Trail, recounted it as follows:

"It is impossible to conceive the frightful sufferings that attend these forced migrations. They are undertaken by a people already exhausted and reduced; and the countries to which the newcomers betake themselves are inhabited by other tribes, which receive them with jealous hostility. Hunger is in the rear, war awaits them, and misery besets them on all sides. To escape from so many enemies, they separate, and each individual endeavors to procure secretly the means of supporting his existence by isolating himself, living in the immensity of the desert like an outcast in civilized society. The social tie, which distress had long since weakened, is then dissolved; they have no longer a country, and soon they will not be a people; their very families are obliterated; their common name is forgotten; their language perishes; and all traces of their origin disappear. Their nation has ceased to exist except in the recollection of the antiquaries of America and a few of the learned of Europe.

"I should be sorry to have my reader suppose that I am coloring the picture too highly; I saw with my own eyes many of the miseries that I have just described, and was the witness of sufferings that I have not the power to portray.

"At the end of the year 1831, while I was on the left bank of the Mississippi, at a place named by Europeans Memphis, there arrived a numerous band of Choctaws (or Chactas, as they are called by the French in Louisiana). These savages had left their country and were endeavoring to gain the right bank of the Mississippi, where they hoped to find an asylum that had been promised them by the American government. It was then the middle of winter, and the cold was unusually severe; the snow had frozen hard upon the ground, and the river was drifting huge masses of ice. The Indians had their families with them, and they brought in their train the wounded and the sick, with children newly born and old men upon the verge of death. They possessed neither tents nor wagons, but only their arms and some provisions. I saw them embark to pass the mighty river, and never will that solemn spectacle fade from my remembrance. No cry, no sob, was heard among the assembled crowd; all were silent. Their

calamities were of ancient date, and they knew them to be irremediable. The Indians had all stepped into the bark that was to carry them across, but their dogs remained upon the bank. As soon as these animals perceived that their masters were finally leaving the shore, they set up a dismal howl and, plunging all together into the icy waters of the Mississippi, swam after the boat."

The Choctaw were condemned to leave their own lush land, in truth a vast country, of their ancestors and sentenced to eke out a living in a small reservation, Little Rock, deep in the desert. It is especially surprising then that group of the survivors of this ordeal gathered in Skullyville, Oklahoma, in March 1847 to raise money for the Irish famine relief fund.

One of hundreds of thousands of Bills of Sale for parcels of land belonging to the Choctaw Indian tribe.

I wanted to follow the Trail on behalf of Afri, a charitable organisation that fights against famine, poverty and injustice, and in some way to thank the Choctaw for the extraordinary kindness and love they had extended to our people.

We walked in summer and while the original Choctaw experienced desperate cold, my abiding memory of that time is of blue skies and fierce unrelenting sunshine. It is this element that will remain in my mind as long as it can cast back to these memories. From around 10 o'clock until the evening, the sun sits above you like a giant, white beaming ball. It highlighted the harshness of this environment and the difficulties that those poor souls must have endured. We didn't follow the original route but walked it from end to beginning seeing what that they saw in reverse. Our group was small, just about twenty people, and there wasn't a great interest in what we were doing or the reasons behind it. We set out from Broken Bow in Oklahoma and spent three weeks heading down to Mississippi, where these people's ancestors had farmed and traded, much like people anywhere in the world.

There were events along the route that brightened the days. On one occasion, we were trudging along when the police stopped us and an officer approached me with a solemn frown and apparent menace on his mind. He told me that we were distracting the trucks passing us as we walked. He then said that he'd have to take us in for further questioning. I was incensed and told him that there was no way that he was going to arrest me or any of the group for that matter. The officer's face changed and creased in laughter. 'I can't keep it up,' he said. Then he spilled the beans. He was of Irish origin and the local parish priest, also of Irish origin, told him to see if he could wind me up a bit and, for a time, he did so. The priest himself had arranged lunch for us further down the road and we had a chance to share a laugh at his prank. The police themselves stayed with us for three further days giving us a courteous and restrained escort through their patch.

Not all of our meetings were so pleasant. On another occasion, we were queuing for coffee in a small roadside place. There were three black women in front of me when I was called and asked for my order. I said that the women were ahead of me, but the serving woman still wanted me to order. So I left without my coffee. Afterwards, the three women came out and gave me warm, friendly thanks. It was frightening to think that such racism endured even as we walked to commemorate another tragic event from a different century.

We completed our walk at Nanih-Waiya, the sacred mound of the Choctaw. There a woman named Wanda told me of the origination stories associated with that place. Choctaw legend says that two brothers reached this point and placed a pole in the ground on the mound. One remained and the other went in the direction that the pole fell. The remaining brother was the founder of the Choctaw while the other brother gave rise to another tribe. There was a strange sense of oneness among all of the people who gathered there for the end of this pilgrimage. Father Pat Clarke, who trekked with us, described the mound as filling the place with a spiritual energy that broke through the divisions and separateness to create a sense of oneness, and I would concur completely with those sentiments.

This was not the most successful of walks. I doubt if we raised much money as we encountered little interest as we travelled the route. It seemed that the Choctaw were suspicious of our motives and found it hard to trust us as they had had bitter experience of white men bearing gifts. They have left their mark though upon the landscape as the poet Walt Whitman recalled in his poem, *Starting from Paumanok*:

> "*The red aborigines,*
>   *Leaving natural breaths, sounds of rain and winds, calls as of birds*
> *and animals in the woods, syllabled to us for names,*
>   *Okonee, Koosa, Ottawa, Monongahela, Sauk, Natchez, Chatta hoochee,*
>   *Kaqueta, Oronoco, Wabash, Miami, Saginaw, Chippewa, Oshkosh, Walla-Walla,*
>   *Leaving such to the States they melt, they depart, charging the water and the land with names.*"

We left the Trail feeling sad for the people of the Choctaw. Cromwell's phrase "To hell or to Connaught" echoed in my ears. For what we witnessed was a people still struggling to overcome or come to terms with a wrong done to them many years ago. They had been cast out of their land and were still metaphorically adrift in the desert. It was a rapacious act as there was plenty of land available then and, indeed still, to allow settler and native to live alongside each other. It showed me just how fortunate we had been to take control of our own country and destiny.

Holy Land

The Holy Land exercised an almost irresistible draw for me. It is, an extraordinary melting pot – literally and metaphorically - a true trip of a lifetime. The idea to visit there and walk the route grew from pre-Christmas conversations in 1984 with friends of mine, Tom and Angela Phelan. We were chatting about possible new adventures, along with Susan Hamilton, when the latter proposed the Holy Land – "Walking the Bible". At this stage I hadn't even thought of walking outside of Ireland, and the Holy Land seemed an exceptional leap from rural Ireland. I left the thought hang in the air as an option along with other, seemingly, more practical suggestions. Susan had some connections with the Israeli embassy people and she didn't allow time for me to develop cold feet.

My fate was decided the following morning. I met Susan in the Shelbourne Hotel. She had already been in touch with the Israeli embassy at that stage. She pointed out that the then President of that country (Chaim Herzog) was Irish born and had lived in Bloomfield Avenue in Portobello only a short walk from where we were then sitting. Susan had brought travel brochures with her and these showed bronzed bodies lying, or walking around, in glorious sunshine under a cloudless blue sky. There was a distinct contrast with the cold, sharp and frosty weather that then reigned supreme outside on the capital's streets. My resistance was broken – my original reservations melted, as an ice cube in a cocktail, under the imagined heat of an imagined balmy Israeli mid-afternoon.

The trip organisation took off from this meeting. I had three charities in mind as potential beneficiaries. Phil O'Meachair and Peter Stokes, of the Irish Wheelchair Association, were clear and direct when Philo told me that I hadn't failed them so far, so they were with me on this one, too. Frank and Stephen of REHAB were equally enthusiastic, and signed up immediately. In fact, they were on the phones rounding up support before I had left the room. The third charity I wanted to include in this walk was my local hospital, St. Vincent's. I dropped in to meet John Duffy on my way home and was delighted to find that Margaret Heffernan, the hospital's honorary fundraiser, was in his office when I arrived. She went for the idea immediately. Ironically, as I write this, I find myself confined as a patient in the very hospital I was supporting nearly thirty years ago.

Our plan was a simple one. We wanted each walker to raise a minimum of £2,000 each for one of the charities, as well as paying their own fare. It was a simple idea but needed someone to look after the travel logistics. Here Susan Hamilton, once again, came up trumps. She advised me to contact Alan Benson of Easy Travel to be the tour agent. This was another inspired choice and helped ensure that the travel component was properly taken care of. There was now the route to plan and the practicalities to work out.

Luck favours the brave walker. I was scheduled to visit Irish peace-keeping troops stationed in Lebanon and this afforded the opportunity for a stop-off in Tel Aviv. The intention was to meet two people who would prove to be most important on a walk such as this: Zelda Harris and Linda Levine from the Britain/Israel Public Affairs Committee (BIPAC) in Israel. There can't be too many things more bizarre than for an Israeli woman to have what appeared to be a half-crazed Irishman descend upon you babbling about a march by a gaggle of other Irish people - all to aid Irish charities. Their rigorous questioning and helpful suggestions showed that they were more than a match for the task.

There were insights into the political situation prevailing there at the time. I had tried to cross the border between Israel and the Lebanon at one stage and the Israelis were having none of it. I recall getting a telephone call from a senior officer, too, telling me not to say too much in front of the lady working on reception. I asked was she an Israeli agent and was told that the army (Irish) thought I'd be safer elsewhere and so they sent a taxi to take me to Jerusalem which they felt was a better option.

Back home, I spent Christmas in a flurry of preparation and celebration. I needed to get back and plan the route in detail and start addressing the logistics on the ground there. I returned to the Holy Land early in the New Year. I travelled through London this time and can still recall the strict security measures there which, though inconvenient, were comforting. It set me thinking though about the meaning of our walk for me and others. Our aim was to walk in a troubled land, riven by war, prejudice and enmity while following in the footsteps of the greatest among peacemakers. This dichotomy, whereby we venerate a peacemaker while still waging war, was far more relevant to our own country in the mid-eighties than to a land where Christianity was a minority faith. I felt that our challenge was to find some way of helping to lay a paving stone, or even the screed, on the long road towards peace. Perhaps, if we could find some peace within ourselves and through our practical help make life more peaceful for others, then that maybe would be success.

I met Joe Brett, our guide for the trip. We drove to Netanya, a modern beach resort thirty kilometres north of Tel Aviv and on the Mediterranean coast. Here we met Zelda and Linda. I recall the weather being bright, clear and, by Irish standards, warm given the time of year, creating a sense of difference and distance. There we sat in this lovely resort town and worked out every aspect of our route and our travel arrangements.

We drove the planned route over the following days. It started in Nazareth where we would begin following the route Jesus took to Cana, then on to Tiberias, Capernaum and into the Jordan Valley to Jericho. Our final destination was the Holy City itself, Jerusalem. We sealed our plans while sitting by the Sea of Galilee and drinking a toast of excellent Carmel wine produced in a vineyard close by. It was here too that I tasted St Peter's fish for the first time. St Peter is said to have taken a coin from the mouth of one of these fish to pay taxes for Christ and himself:

> *"But so that we may not cause offence, go to the lake and throw out your line. Take the first fish you catch; open its mouth and you will find a four-drachma coin. Take it and give it to them for my tax and yours."*
>
> (Matthew 17:27)

If only paying tax were as easy as that nowadays. The fish is known locally as Musht and is found only in the Sea of Galilee.

The planning was meticulous, it had to be. The Israeli police would escort us at all times together with an ambulance in case of illness, accident or heat exhaustion. There were to be air-conditioned buses

Leader, 1987.

at our disposal at all times for those needing to rest, massage blistered or tired feet or simply needing to get out of the direct sun for short while. The red-and-cream coloured buses of the Nazareth Transport and Tourist Co. Ltd. were to become a familiar and often welcome sight as they were to ferry us to the walk's starting point each day, and to our accommodation in the evening. They also acted as our camels in the desert carrying cool drinking water which they dispensed every half hour en route.

The troubles that affect that region were never far from the surface. I was told that the Israeli army would escort us through the West Bank area where the Jordan Valley forms the border between Israel and Jordan, until we reached Jericho. All was in place; all that remained was to recruit the walkers and walk the walk.

I joined the three charities, Susan Hamilton and Alan Benson for at least weekly meetings in the REHAB offices to build the momentum, raise awareness and, most importantly, raise money too. Part of this involved raising our profile and getting publicity. We had good support in the print media and on *Donncha's Sunday* and in the *RTÉ Guide*. Sadly, from a personal point of view, RTÉ were not the most enthusiastic overall and coverage gradually trailed off. One striking piece of promotion came from Dermot Kelly, also known as the singing Bank of Ireland manager, in Limerick who, together with the willing assistance of Denis Allen, famed for his song *Limerick you're a Lady*, and with the accompaniment of the well-known pianist Maurice Foley, produced the rousing song, *Donncha in the Desert,* sung to the air of Percy French's *Slattery's Mounted Fut (Foot)*. The words went as follows:

> *You've heard of Ronnie Delany and Eamon Coghlan too,*
> *And how their feet were famous from here to Kathmandu,*
> *But there's another pair around, made famous by the sand,*
> *'Tis Donncha's size elevens that tramp the Holy Land.*
> *He walked to help the wheelchairs, St. Vincent's and REHAB*
> *To raise some funds and in between to dissipate the flab,*
> *And all the Arabs shouted as he went marching past:*
> *Here comes the new Messiah, Donncha's here at last.*
> (Chorus)
>
> *And into the desert went the gallant motley crew*
> *Doctors, Sisters Nurses and a couple of Gardaí too*
> *Twenty goats from Dingle and an ass from the County Clare,*
> *Hand in hand through sea and sand, just for love and care*
> *They reached the Sea of Galilee so wondrous to behold*

The Lord walked on the waters there, or so the story goes:
There were no boats or timber floats to get the crew across
What will we do? It's up to you, Donncha you're the boss.
He put his agile brain to work and suddenly he said:
Line up ten thousand camels and put them tail to head.
They climbed upon their backs that stretched across the stormy sea
And humped it all the way across the Sea of Galilee.
(Chorus)
They walked for days through sun and haze, the going it was tough!
A bursar from St. Vincent's said, "Boss, I've had enough!"
Me feet is sore, me clothes is tore, I think I'll take a rest."
Till Donncha found him lying down and jumped upon his chest.
"Look here my man, this is no time for sittin' on your ass,
The Lord was here for 40 days so surely you can last
Till we reach Jerusalem, a sight so fair to see,
Any more lip you're off the trip and home by CIE."
(Chorus)

Green, white and oranges in the Holy Land.

In all, we walked in the Holy Land three times and these walks have influenced me profoundly. I find my mind wandering to those days and reliving the joy and pain of the walk. Sometimes I feel I can still smell the spices and feel the heat of that extraordinary place. Our groups grew with each walk and the reflections that follow mix my different trips there to give a sense of the reality of those days. One joy among many that these visits gave me is that my daughter, Sinéad, my wife, Vera and our youngest son, Donncha, had the opportunity to join me on the road through the Holy Land.

Nazareth was our starting point. This place seems unchanged from biblical times. There is heat and dust; vibrant colour and the noise and crush of the marketplace. It was here that I experienced the scents and sounds of the souk before we climbed to the great Basilica of the Annunciation. It dominates the skyline. It is richly decorated with mosaics and iconic imagery. Indeed, Our Lady of Knock greets you at the entrance gate. We were taken through the history by our guide, a patient, quiet Arab man, who retold the story of Jesus, Mary and Joseph and their life in that town. We learnt that the Basilica is built on the site where the holy family lived on their return to Nazareth. Jesus lived here for twenty-seven years, earning his appellation "The Nazarene." People then lived in houses built over caves. Nothing remains of the family house but the cave that was the lower part of it – cool in summer and warm in winter.

The first day of a walk is always testing. As part of this walk I recall additional burdens: I had to deliver the opening piece for *Donncha's Sunday* and pose for photos for the ever attentive Lucy Johnson. Oliver O'Brien, an old friend from Cork and now the technical maestro of the first Holy Land walk, gave me the thumbs up and I began: 'Fáilte romhaibh isteach, you're very welcome to *Donncha's Sunday* which comes to your today from a hill over Nazareth...', this was followed by a pre-recorded piece entitled "Donncha in the Desert." It was hard not to think of the listeners enjoying their Sunday afternoon in the quiet of their homes, so very different from where we were and what we were experiencing. It struck me, too, that many had probably

attended their church that day and heard tales of the places where we were now walking.

This walk made real to me the man that was Christ and I came to understand and share the experience, to an extent, of the mundane things he had done in his own time – walking from place to place, stopping for a chat and a drink of water with a neighbour or stranger, seeking out the cool, shady side of a narrow street, watching the merchants, mothers and beggars eke out their existence in the hard heat of the day.

We walked on to Cana where the locals were warm and welcoming; the walkers were hot and sweaty. We relished the shade found in the narrow cobbled streets. On our first journey I led our procession enthusiastically on the wrong path, taking them to the Greek Orthodox Church rather than the one run by the Franciscans, but where we were shown two of the six water pots used at the wedding feast in this town. The church was cool and the monk there gave me a glass of sweet, earthy wine before we bustled back to the Franciscans.

Later we passed through the Golani crossroads where, not too far away, is to be found the de Valera Forest, named after Éamon de Valera who, along with Cearbhaill Ó Dálaigh, judge and President, the Israeli people remember as being among a minority of great statesmen who were always prepared to extend a hand of friendship to their fledging State.

DONNCHA'S HOLY LAND WALK

MARCH 18th to 27th 1988

One of the great highlights of my times on this pilgrimage came when we first caught a glimpse of the Sea of Galilee. This sea of wonder, miracles and great beauty stretched out a blue mantle before us. It sent cooling breezes and fresh air to inspire us towards it banks. The poet, Henry Wadsworth Longfellow's words came to mind as we gazed at this natural beauty snuggling between the Golan Heights to the East and rough-hewn hills of Galilee. His poem, *Christus: a Mystery,* captures the meaning and emotion of that place much better than I could ever hope to do:

> *"...And Him evermore I behold in Galilee,*
> *Through the cornfields waving gold,*
> *In hamlet, in wood, and in wold,*
> *By the shores of the Beautiful Sea.*
> *He toucheth the sightless eyes;*
> *Before Him the demons flee;*
> *To the dead He sayeth: Arise!*
> *To the living: Follow me!*
> *And that voice still soundeth on*
> *From the centuries that are gone,*
> *To the centuries that shall be!*
> *From all vain pomps and shows,*
> *From the pride that overflows,*
> *And the false conceits of men;*
> *From all the narrow rules*
> *And subtleties of Schools,*
> *And the craft of tongue and pen;*
> *Bewildered in its search,*
> *Bewildered with the cry,*
> *Lo, here! lo, there, the Church!*
> *Poor, sad Humanity*
> *Through all the dust and heat*

Turns back with bleeding feet,
By the weary road it came,
Unto the simple thought
By the great Master taught,
And that remaineth still:
Not he that repeateth the name,
But he that doeth the will!"

Indeed, as the poet proclaims, this was the place where Jesus Christ lived out much of his public life. The land here is New Testament country. Soldier, pilgrim, and tourist have all experienced it as we had, yet there is no doubt that this first sight of the Sea of Galilee is inimitable, indescribable and, for me, the most precious memory of the Holy Land.

Our route took us close to a strictly orthodox kibbutz named Lavi and I was fortunate to be invited to visit it by its head, C.B. Kaye. He had arrived in Israel with many Jews from North Africa. He recalled the excitement and unrestrained emotion of his fellow passengers as they stood on Israeli soil for the first time. For C.B., though, it wasn't quite the same, as he had travelled from Ireland, 'Much as I loved coming here,' he told me 'I wasn't coming here for freedom. In Ireland, where I came from, we had our freedom. Jews were never oppressed there. We were lucky. When almost the whole of European Jewry was being wiped out, we were quite literally living the life of Reilly.'

The word for kibbutz is derived from the Hebrew verb to gather together and so its best translation is "togetherness." It calls to mind the Irish word "meitheal" which we often use for neighbours who gather together to help each other out. The kibbutz is a much more structured affair with the children, as C.B. described it, being the most important crop.

C.B. was a cheerful, outgoing man, strong in his faith and traditions, but in no way borne down or solemn with the weight of his beliefs. During our first visit to the Holy Land, the Jewish community were celebrating the annual feast of Purim. The outward signs – children in fancy dress and masks – reminded me of Halloween at home. C.B. explained, 'This feast celebrates the victory of Queen Esther and her Uncle Mordechai over the wicked Hammam in Persia. Hammam wanted to destroy the Jewish people, but he himself was defeated. To this day, we commemorate that event. It is a joyous occasion, so much so that we are told that we must drink until we cannot tell the difference between Hammam and Mordechai. This is something I do very religiously!'

The River Jordan had enormous significance for our walkers. Many chose to renew their baptismal vows and walked straight into the water until they were totally immersed. The dry air of the Jordan valley made the drying out much more bearable. I brought some of this water back to Ireland. Under Catholic rites, it doesn't need blessing to be used in baptism. I'm delighted to recount that my sample was used for the baptism of Mary Farrelly, the daughter of Rita and Stephen.

It was hot and dusty as we walked along the valley. We crossed the river on the third day and, from there on in, we were in the West Bank and we carried on to Bet Shean and the road to the desert. We were escorted into the town by a band decked out in red caps, white tops and blue shorts. We sat on a low wall before a fine ochre building and were gazed at in wonder and with curiosity by the very young and very old. Someone suggested that we repay the musical welcome that we had received and it was proposed we give them a few verses of *The Banks*. As we finished the second verse, a white-bearded very senior citizen shook, and then held, my hand and I swear he had tears in his eyes! Up the Rebels!

Our walk took us through true desert, just as Christ himself had walked. Our police escort had given way to a heavily armed military escort and they were to accompany us to Jericho as we had now entered a restricted military zone. There was a real risk of dehydration while walking in the desert and so we had to stop every second mile to replenish our water supplies. I noted an air of tension frequently between soldiers and some locals. The troops were constantly on the alert, scanning the surrounding countryside with binoculars. It was a reminder of the immediate conflict that afflicts this great land. It also made real the many wars, crusades, invasions and resettlements that have cast their shadows over the millennia.

I loved the silence of the desert; even with hundreds of companions, there is still a strange primeval atmosphere of stillness. There is no breeze or clouds, just an unmoving blue sky. The desert is a place for reflection; for reflecting that the sandaled feet of the Master walked here; that the Apostles, probably strung out behind, were silent. He must have been silent, too, on His last Passover journey to Jerusalem. He alone knew that he was walking these roads for the last time. His mortality, pain, insults, suffering, agony and terrifying death lay before Him. How the Apostles must have longed for the cool of Jericho, the greetings of friends in Bethany and a triumphal entry into the Holy City. He knew the reality though, and out of love to his companions, bore this burden alone.

A member of the Israeli military escort.

Jerusalem beckoned throughout the walk. It is a city that is almost beyond human comprehension; as well as being unique and commonplace, it is all things to all people; Christianity, Judaism and the world of Islam are all at home here. My exploration of that city began on the long flight from London to Israel when an elderly Jewish lady from Manchester enthused about "our country." She made me envious of her Jewish sense of identity. Now, I was here, in that amazing city, spending the final day of our walk exploring its beauty and diversity.

We entered the Old City by the Jaffa Gate and before long were

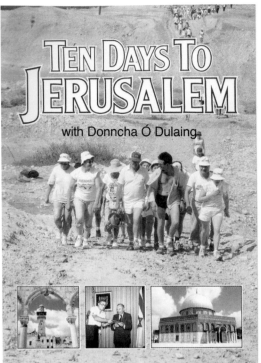

Donncha's 1987 book telling the story of his first Holy Land walk.

swallowed up in the timeless atmosphere of David Street. The streetscape is alive with traders and shoppers and the sound of bargaining and their striking at the end fills the air. Of course, you are offered all sorts of goods and hear a variety of entreaties – all with the sole purpose of creating a distance between you and the money in your pocket. We passed by St Stephen's Gate, now quite inaccurately called the Lion's Gate. This was a scene of strife during the Six-Day War in 1967, when Israeli paratroopers stormed it.

We reached the Golden Gate. It is sealed. It faces down to where a sign in English, Hebrew and Arabic reads "Gethsemane." The gate was erected in the seventh century. The Arabs call it Bab er Rameh, the Gate of Salvation, for this will be, both Jews and Arabs believe, the site of the Last Judgement. The Jews hoped that the Messiah would enter through this gate, so the Arabs, for this reason and for others, sealed up the entrance and buried their dead in front of it.

We crossed the road to enter the Garden of Gethsemane passing by the tomb of the Virgin. This brought us to lower slopes of the Mount of Olives. A railing protects the Garden from souvenir hunters. We passed through the Garden to the Basilica of the Agony of Christ, also known as the Church of All Nations. In the central apse of this church is the isolated block of rock which projects above the floor into the central nave. Tradition has it that this is the place where Jesus's agony took place. The name Gethsemane has never changed. Jesus and his disciples frequented this place and as a consequence three shrines were built there.

Through the afternoon silence, I heard the insistent song of tree crickets. Their woody serenade broke through the stillness like the tune of demented timpanists hammering out a burning beat when all other music ceased. Their unending, unchanging cacophony filtered through the peace of the Mount of Olives, until it seemed that the glare of the sun and the rhythm of the crickets were the only reality. Then the unique dome of the Church of Dominus Flevit (The Lord has wept) rose gently before us, a reminder that somewhere near here Jesus wept over that beloved city.

The chapel of the Ascension stands within the precincts of a mosque. The Arab "guardians" were friendly and one shekel saw us into the tiny chapel. I wondered if this was the place of which Luke, the Evangelist, wrote: *"He led them out as far as Bethany, lifting up His hands, He blessed them. He parted from them and was carried up into heaven."* My visit was brief, but the sight of the candle burning on the rock from which it is said Jesus ascended, more than compensated for a fast enveloping exhaustion.

Everyone in the Holy Land advised me to meet Larry Elyan and this I did in David Birkahn's home in Jerusalem. He was as lively as a cricket and as outspoken as only a true Corkman can be. He told me about his birth in Cork in 1902 in a place known as "Jewtown," an area around the Hibernian buildings and Albert Road. There were ninety houses in a block and although there are few Jews left in Cork, the name remains. He described a poor, but happy, childhood where he mixed and played with both Catholic and Protestant neighbours. On retirement, Larry came to Israel and described his amazement at finding himself as part of a majority after years in the minority.

Larry had worked in London and had become an actor – almost by mistake. He was a member of the Irish Literary Society which met for lectures once a month. One of the members was an actress named Úna O'Connor. She auditioned him for a part in a play and he was so successful that he got a second part in another production. He was working with the British Civil Service but he kept in close contact with the birth of the Irish State. He was drawn back and a letter of introduction to Lennox Robinson brought him to the Abbey Theatre. He could remember Yeats' presence there as he also recalled Lady Gregory who was nicknamed the "The Old Lady." It was this nickname, according to Larry, that gave Denis Johnson the title for his play *The Old Lady Says No.* He presented it to the Abbey first and

Donncha meets Irish-born Israeli President Chaim Herzog.

the reply he got was, "The old lady says, 'no'", and so that became the play's name. Other explanations were incorrect.

Larry wasn't the only Irishman I met in that country. We were received twice at the Presidential Palace by the Irish-born President Chaim Herzog, the sixth President of the State of Israel. On the first occasion I remember the great wave of emotion that swept over me as I stood up before our great and generous walkers and, with all the formality I could muster, tried to express with some coherence, our happiness, excitement and pride at being received by "one of our own."

It was cool in the great hall as I began my few words, first in Irish and then English, my nerves forced out a few beads of perspiration despite the cool air. It was marvellous to see the homemade Irish tricolour that our walkers had proudly carried from Bethany to the Holy City, laid side by side with the blue and white Star of David flag of Israel. I managed a few formal phrases on behalf of some of the greatest, bravest and most generous people in the world:

'We have walked all the way from Nazareth to Tiberias, to Capernaum and Bet Shean, through the burning desert, down the long hot road to Jericho, on to Bethany. Now today, unlike many of the Jews in the Diaspora, we are here – not as they crave "next year Jerusalem" – but this great day is ours.'

I paused for breath and also, if the truth be known, for a little ripple of applause. It never came! For once, the Irish seemed transfixed! I pressed on grimly:

'We come, representatives of a great and ancient nation, proud to be here, to greet another great and ancient nation and especially to greet you Mr President, one of our own.'

Then came the applause – plenty of it and President Herzog replied:

> *'First of all, let me assure you that I understand practically every word of Gaelic you said. I am still full of memories of a very historic visit to Ireland – the first state visit by a President of Israel to Ireland – and I can only say that I am looking forward, sooner or later, to returning the wonderful hospitality to President and Mrs Hillery. We wish to express our kindest appreciation to everyone for the wonderful reception we received in Ireland. Tell Ireland that we look forward to receiving many more groups like yours in Israel. You will always be welcome. And I hope you will always feel at home.'*

My thoughts always go back to a darkening twilight when the Holy Sepulchre was almost empty, only a whisper of prayers, foreign but familiar, disturbed the peace. It was here that Jesus suffered indescribably, here he died and from here he rose again. There is no despair here, only hope and belief. The best of humankind is rooted here. If you sit and close your eyes, faith, imagination and Jerusalem will do the rest. For me though, looking back on those days now, I cannot but think of the anguish of Jesus's mother, Mary. Now, I can appreciate the pain and anguish that a parent feels seeing a grown-up child taken before their time. My mind quickly goes to that terrible personal time in November 2010 when my dear Sinéad passed away after a long illness, courageously borne, constantly and lovingly supported by her husband, Eddie.

This land of the Gospels is rooted in the heart. It is not a place for theological, dry discourse but one where the raw emotions of two millennia echo through the heat and dust and settle in the souls of those who pause and let them touch them.

The Little Flower

The Reliquary of St. Thérèse of Lisieux, the "Little Flower," toured Ireland in 2001 and was a phenomenally powerful spiritual experience. Thousands visited churches all around the country to share in the joy, hope and faith inspired by her life, writings and spirituality.

My journey on that happy summer was among the most peaceful and enjoyable experiences of more than fifty years of broadcasting.

The relics of Saint Thérèse.

My role, which surprised and delighted me, began on a sunny day outside a cathedral in the Diocese of Ferns, County Wexford. I stood, tape machine poised, surrounded by those who were there to welcome the "Thérèse -mobile" and a relic lay in the front, watched over by Father Linus Ryan, the wonderful Carmelite, who presided over all the events and journeys of Thérèse.

The cathedral was, of course, in Enniscorthy where a voice suddenly convinced me further in my participation in the historic events. It was the voice of Bishop Brendan Comiskey, inviting me into St. Aidan's Cathedral, the stately Pugin masterpiece. I was about to begin a series of journeys and broadcasts that I never believed could happen.

What you would read now is as surprising and as amazing as it was to me and is not in any great order!

We begin our story in the infant class of the Presentation Convent in Tuam, County Galway. Sister Martina kept a large and lively class of boys and girls in order and I was stunned when a little boy described me as 'Saint Thérèse's radio man.' Then the whole class sang a great song for the saint. I am diverted, too, by Father Linus and his vivid account of the Lisieux Stud in County Kildare where the Collins family had vivid reasons to be great devotees of Saint Thérèse.

My shortest journey brought me down the road to St Mary's Centre where tender echoes stir me as I remember the late Sister Gerard, who introduced me in the chapel to various members of the blind community, and where Nellie O'Mahoney reflected on her joy in addressing the relics and talked of weeping for joy, and when I shared a meal with the kindly Gardaí Síochána on duty. This is truly the inspiration that became a reality, truly reflected in the tears of the blind as they sat and reflected on a unique happening in our lives.

A day of warm sunshine and vast crowds assembled in the Army base in The Curragh of Kildare when I met the then chief of staff of the Army, Lieut. Col., Mangan, whose joy was personal as he remembered his childhood home when pictures of "The Little Flower" dominated family walls and inspired by which his sisters became Carmelite nuns whom I would later meet in Knock, County Mayo.

Talking of meeting, later that day and often since, I've met Margot Coogan who was to become chieftain of the Lalor clan and the statue of whose distinguished ancestor, James Fintan Lalor, is in Portlaoise.

On our Theresian day in The Curragh, she was accompanied by the late Fr Gerry O' Mahony, PP, Mountrath, Co. Laois, and also by the parish priest of Abbeyleix, Fr Paddy Kehoe.

I got a great welcome in the Whiteabbey were Father Linus now rests. The hospitality was overwhelming and I met the lady who had baked three thousand, five hundred scones for thousands of guests

among whom were three friendly young lads who were slightly confused. One got off his bike and said: 'I suppose you're here for herself.' He was so right but then ran out of knowledge when he said: 'Sure she's one of our own coming here in a van. She's Saint Thérèse of Leixlip.' We forgive him. Thérèse might have been flattered.

How do you bring them altogether? Donncha do not even try. It's a bank holiday Monday and I'm on the road to Sligo near Castlegeal near the Bunduff River. It's mid-afternoon. Kathleen Shearer and her family are bringing lilies of welcome and a papal flag. I can still smell the flowers. Later at 6.45p.m. I'm in the cathedral in Sligo where an altar of lighted candles welcomes the young woman from Lisieux. And it's a strange kaleidoscope of prayers and hymns and peaceful people. There is a wonderful rendition, like I said, light-shot and a private and mystical experience as young nuns welcome me with the song: *May the road rise with you. Go néirí on bóthar leat.* All from the contemplative daughters of St. Teresa of Calcutta.

My dear friend Bishop John Buckley welcomed me and thousands to the 'North Chapel' in Cork city when a pilgrim tenderly

With Margot Coogan in Portlaoise.

asks Thérèse to hug her late father in heaven and almost before I know it, I've travelled the busy road to the Cobh cathedral where, as I wearily climbed the hill, the great bells ring out a welcome across the summer harbour. I think of all those who went away and never came back in the days when Cobh was their last view of Ireland. Fr Michael Fitzgerald was my overnight host.

On this great day of Thérèsian arrival, the sadness of departure still lingers even when Dympna Collins recites the exiles' return over this great sea of sadness.

St Peter's Cathedral in Belfast hosted the relics, but as we walked to the Cathedral, a helicopter flew threateningly low over us. The Divis Flats were in sight. Some things never change. We had to rise in the mobile and Fr Paddy Cassidy told me precisely where we were on this wonderful day. Saint Thérèse kept me and thousands of others awake all night. Ní bheidh a leithéid ann arís. The Falls Road was great. The shrine in Knock was unique. The late Bishop Aherne told of the saint's face after her death, how she was a young girl, the most documented saint in history. The Carmelite sisters welcomed me to a time of joy especially Sister Josephine from Cork. I didn't get to bed till 4.00 a.m.

Next journey reflected a short visit to Avila Church in Dublin when in early morning the Prior, Fr Willie Moore, read extracts from

The late Gerry Ryan, a dear friend, with Gerry's daughter, Charlotte.

the works of my favourite writer, Canon Sheehan of Doneraile. This inspired reading from the Canon ensured that I was in Doneraile for the saint's visit. I was welcomed by the parish priest, Father Casey, who drew my attention to the glorious Thérèsian window over the grave of the great Canon. Thousands visited the relics there. It was a unique day. Imagine a guard of honour of ladies wearing the name *Thérèse*. Well, this happened in Athboy, County Meath, when I heard some of the best singing of our journey.

Then can I forget the day our saint came in by helicopter? Of course I can't! She was flown into Ireland's pilgrim island in Lough Derg, accompanied by Carmelite Fr Eugene and I made a live broadcast from there to my great friend Gerry Ryan on 2FM. This was a day of sun, rain and barefoot pilgrims all welcoming our distinguished guest. Peace, calm and serenity of pilgrimage reflected in this amazing place of high spiritual achievers when I wore my shoes but not my socks. It was, perhaps, the most unforgettable adventure of my travels.

For once, prison bells' toll welcomes as we enter Mountjoy jail with the Little Flower. Her visit was much appreciated by all present. Kevin Barry and the young saint from Lisieux are joined in time and history.

When I talk of journeys, I remember our pilot, Pat Sweeney, his skilful driving, good humour and his late friend, Jim Doyle, as we made to the Carmelite sisters in Tallow, County Waterford, to meet Sister Patrice, sister of the chief of staff of the Army. Oddly enough I remember the sweet smell of rhododendrons on a lovely day. I had with me, my wife, Vera, our lovely daughter and our friend Nell McCarthy from Carrigtwohill, County Cork. Nell who has since died was a towering heroine in the world of camogie.

And now I come to Wexford Park to the last Thérèse experience in my broadcasting work or was this a prelude to a new world for me? Indeed it was, and like all other days, a day of vast crowds and Bishop Comiskey and the Papal Nuncio were present and the kindness which is so important to me was everywhere.

Fr Linus, the ever present inspiration and leader of journeys thanked me for my own part and invited me back to Lisieux with the relics of Saint Thérèse and the start of another journey which I was glad to be part of. Saint Thérèse, the little French Saint, had enriched all our lives and always will.

11

THE EVENING IS SPREAD OUT AGAINST THE SKY

... More importantly, we captured parts of our folklore and culture on film that hadn't been recorded before. The world of County Cavan, courtesy of John Clancy of Derrygarragh Inn, introduced me to cures, skittles, ploughing, helicopters and a land that microphones had never before recorded. ...

Cutting turf on a bog near Ballycastle, County Mayo, during the filming of *Donncha's Travelling Roadshow* in September 1979.

252

Pages 248-9: With former Minister Gerry Collins, TD, and Ned O'Keeffe, TD at Glenbrohane, Co. Limerick, for the retirement of Patrick Maher in November 2001.

Danny Maher, a native of Killacolla, Ballyagran and director of Cricklewood Homeless Concern with Donncha at a function in the Crown Moran Hotel in Cricklewood.

Donncha launches the first ever CBS Charleville Yearbook, with Tony Connolly, chairman Charleville Credit Union and Tom Clarke, principal, CBS Charleville, in 2002.

Celebrations after the Wheelchair Association Walk in Donegal 2010.

Great friend, Mainchín Seoighe, from Bruree, who first introduced him to Éamon de Valera, with Fr Bertie Troy.

With fellow broadcaster and great friend, Maxi.

Hurling legend, John Fenton, with a group of Christy Ring admirers and aspirants outside the GAA Stadium at Cloyne.

Interviewing Sisters for *Fáilte Isteach* at Holy Family Convent in Newbridge, Co. Kildare.

MY RADIO BROADCASTS LED almost inevitably to television work. The radio format had worked well and we recreated it as closely as possible, taking into account the peculiarities of the new medium. Essentially, in *Highways*, I arranged the interviewees, musicians and other participants in a circle around me and moved from one to another in order. Time management was of the essence. I had to coax the shy ones to speak up and contribute; the more vociferous had to be kept in check. In radio, all of this happens without the listener being aware of it. Indeed, I tried to create an atmosphere that allowed those listening to imagine us in a setting that matched their idea of what the programme was – a village hall, a pub, a theatre or a fireside – whatever made it real for them. Television brought new challenges. The shows had to be staged properly, with careful attention to the atmosphere that the setting created.

The challenge for my television producer was to recreate my radio personality in visual form. John Williams saw me as a form of Irish "country gent", complete with a dickie bow, waistcoat and a Stetson. At other times I dressed in a white dinner jacket, black tie and trousers giving a more serious persona. It was these images that I projected in shows such as *Donncha's Travelling Roadshow*, *Donncha's Diary*, *Donncha's Adare*, and *Donncha at Bantry House*.

John crafted our series from Adare Manor and we were ably assisted by a skilful crew whose skill was only equalled by their good humour and patience. The best performers in the land were among our guests and me and my Irish wolfhound became national figures. Robert White, the great American tenor, Bernadette Greevy, the Garda Band and many others graced the beautiful sets and my friend, Thady Quin, the Earl of Dunraven, and his wife, Geraldine, mingled with guests and crew during that time we would never forget.

We filmed the shows during the summer and my family travelled with me and often helped out where needed. My family had always been part of my summer entourage. They'd all pile into the car and we'd set off for some distant part of the land, Vera keeping control while I steered us towards our final destination. I suppose it gave them an unusual insight into their native land as they met the famous, infamous and unknown, but interesting characters that make up our great people. What was surprising was the ease with which they adapted to and accepted this lifestyle, hanging around old houses, living in hotels and stepping in to perform their party pieces when required.

Television suddenly made me visible and recognisable. People approached me as I walked along the street and believed that they knew me – not my television persona. Gone now were the days when people who had only heard me on the radio would tell me, 'You don't look at all the way you sound on the wireless.' I was now public property. The television world is far removed from that of radio. Everything took longer and was more intricate. Interviews that I could have dispatched with speed and accuracy on the wireless now became slow and lugubrious. The lights, cameras, make-up and sound, conspired to push the subject into the background. These intrusions were all necessary but took time to adapt to and accept. The crews were professional and made everything happen, but I realised that I was only a small part of a much wider production.

The Travelling Roadshow was the closest in television terms to *Highways and Byways*. We explored different places and brought television cameras to parts of Ireland that had never featured before. More importantly, we captured parts of our folklore and culture on film that hadn't been recorded before. The world of County Cavan, courtesy of John Clancy of Derrygarragh Inn, introduced me to cures, skittles, ploughing, helicopters and a land that microphones had never before recorded. It was Fiach Ó Broin who first brought me to this place where time lay dormant and generosity was endless.

Generosity was the component that linked many of the stories and programmes together. In Tooraneena, a village in west Waterford, Tommy and Kathleen Hickey told tales through many a long night of superstition, folklore and the strange cure of Cahill's Blood – a folk treatment for shingles. It was here that we recreated the story of Master McGrath, the great greyhound from Co. Waterford. A weak pup, his trainer despaired of him and gave him to his handler. His faith in the dog was rewarded when he won the Waterloo Cup three times in 1868, '69 and '71. We also heard of "Petticoat Loose", a frightening woman who lived across the border in Colligan, Co. Tipperary, and died in a drinking competition. She was later to haunt the district and curse the locals until she was exorcised and condemned to the bottom of Bay Lough, to empty it with a thimble for evermore.

Pages 248-9 In 2012 with former President Mary Robinson at the official opening of the Titanic Memorial Park in Lahardane, Co. Mayo.

With Cllr. Lettie McCarthy and Charlie Kelly up in the Dublin Hills.

Interviewing Paddy Murray about the RAF bomber which crash landed in Charleville in 1942.

Signing the Wall of Remembrance with Minister Jimmy Deenihan TD, at the 2013 Remembrance Run in the Phoenix Park.

With acclaimed actress of film, stage and screen, Fionnula Flannagan, and friend, at Annacurragh.

A group of young people and their leaders at Canon Sheehan's memorial, outside Doneraile Church, 2014.

With Mixie O'Toole who is featured in the film, *Forty years of Charleville Credit Union*, at the Schoolyard Theatre in 2003.

Bishop John Buckley, Bishop of Cork and Ross. "Two Working men" outside Cork city's County Hall.

Waterford often brought a warm welcome. In particular, I enjoyed the hospitality of the Dean in Saint Mochuda's town of Lismore, the Cistercians in Mount Melleray and Mary Ryan and her family and a great many others in the wonderful Déise. I recorded the Christy Ring documentary during the *Roadshow*. Places such as Dingle, the home now of another late evening weekend radio programme, *The South Wind Blows,* stand out as wonderful evenings and great programmes.

My forays into television were not confined to Ireland. I made the acquaintance of the Mardi Gras in Venice where John Williams, Margaret Costelloe and I visited for the annual festival of excess and excitement. I recall describing the scene for the viewers at home without a script or prompts. All went well until several finely-formed, nubile young women deposited themselves in front of me. They were unclad and I could hear a co-presenter from Japan describing the scene with high and rising excitement. I struggled for words where words were needed. Finally, I explained, 'That's something we're seeing now, that you wouldn't see most weekends around Buttevant or Doneraile!' A statement that has yet to be disproved.

The roadshow ventured to France through the good auspices of Irish Ferries on a never-to-be-forgotten visit when the Hennessys of Killavullen introduced us all to the wonders of brandy. This was a night on which the wild geese truly came home.

A show that stands out in my memory was a Christmas special called *Joy to the World.* This was a major undertaking and featured some of the greats of Irish entertainment in the early eighties. The show was broadcast on Christmas day 1983, if I recall correctly. It was recorded the previous November and featured the late great Frank Patterson, Red Hurley, Tony Kenny, the Furey Brothers, Eileen O'Grady, Dana, Johnny McEvoy, Noel Kelehan, a musician and conductor who sadly passed away recently, Maureen Potter, The Billy Barry kids and Twink. John McColgan produced the show and managed to bring the diverse components together successfully. I remember him as a very pleasant young fellow and it's fantastic that he has gone on to such great success. I sang *Baby It's Cold Outside* under the heat of the studio lights – thankfully it wasn't obvious and we had a hugely positive reaction after transmission.

Of course, radio broadcasts and walking and other charity events continued unabated. The walks were long and short, varying in difficulty, location and scenery. I've walked the Camino route to the Galician city of Santiago de Compostela. This is one of the oldest and certainly one of the most beautiful pilgrim walks. It crosses the northwest of the Iberian Peninsula from the border with France, through the Basque country to finish in Galicia. There are other routes

coming from central Europe, Southern Spain, Italy and beyond. We chose the route that most Irish people now take but also the one that medieval Irish monks and lay pilgrims followed. The pilgrimage, the Way of St. James, commemorates the belief that St. James's remains were brought by boat to Spain and laid to rest in Santiago.

On *Joy to the World* with comedienne, Maureen Potter, Christmas 1982.

There is a belief that St. James appeared to the troops in the battle of Clavijo when a much smaller force of Christian soldiers defeated the larger and better equipped Moorish forces. This battle never took place, but belief in it now is ensconced in Spanish lore. The scallop shell is the symbol of the pilgrimage and its adoption as such is buried in the myths and mists of time, with at least two different legends explaining its use. These shells are carved into the stone in churches and buildings along the route. Excavations in Mullingar found the shells in monastic ruins there. St. James's Gate in Dublin was the traditional departure point for pilgrims, from whence they sailed to the north of Spain.

I was struck by how similar the women and men of these regions are to those I had met in my earlier years of broadcasting on Ireland's Atlantic coast. These were strong, silent people, radiating dignity, often despite obvious hardship and poverty. We passed through pastoral and farming land. Much of the land was mountainous and poor; the farms were small holdings echoing those in Ireland's West. Vera joined me to explore the route by car before the actual walk, taking in the splendid beauty of this mountainous land.

The pilgrimage starts in Saint Jean Pied de Port, a UNESCO heritage site, and follows paths, tracks and roads for seven-hundred and seventy kilometres to the its final location. I've been fortunate to walk this three times and on each occasion it was different but beautiful in its own way. My son, Donncha, joined me in 2002 and added yet another generational dimension to this magnificent walk.

There have been a great many other walks over the years – far too many to mention now, let alone describe in any detail. I've kept up my walks and charity events since my retirement, some of the more recent being those I've carried out on behalf of the Irish Wheelchair Association. These series of walks commemorated the Flight of the Earls, and their epic journey across six countries - Ireland, France, Belgium, Germany, Switzerland and Italy. These walks led to me being appointed Grand Master of the St Patrick's Day Parade in Brussels in 2011.

There were other less spiritual but more colourful events and one which I recall with great fondness was the day I took part in Dublin's 1988 Millennium Parade. I was reminded of this by the recent celebrations organised to mark the millennial anniversary of the Battle of Clontarf held in April 2014. My role in the Dublin '88 festivities was to lead a group of the great and good from Clontarf's GAA Club, advertising the fact that I would soon be marching from Inagh in Co. Clare to commemorate Brian Boru's great march to do battle at Clontarf. I led, indeed commanded, the group mounted on a

With Mary O'Hara at Adare Manor.

magnificent white horse named "Carrigaline". No longer in the first flush of youth, my charger was a perfect mount for a king and I was attired as the great man himself - even if I was only King Boru for a day. Morgan Llewellyn, the author who wrote a wonderful children's book on Brian Boru, led me through the streets.

The parade took several hours to wend its way across the capital. I was and am grateful to Captain Billy Ringrose from the Army Equitation School who provided me with my steed. If there is a horsey heaven in the firmament then "Carrigaline" deserves a special place. I was awarded a beautiful Cúchulainn statuette splendidly inscribed: "Dublin Millennium St Patrick's Parade, 1988." I made the front page of *The Irish Times* in an excellently constructed photograph shot by Pat Langan. It's not often that a medieval king is captured making a call on a mobile telephone outside the Shelbourne Hotel while astride a white steed. The picture captures the rider's nervousness as well as the overall incongruity of the situation. I was somewhat embarrassed, but consoled myself that it was for a good cause, the Irish Wheelchair Association, and our march was a great success, financially and otherwise.

I recall that I left for my third Holy Land walk the following morning. If I strode out like John Wayne for the following days, the other walkers were too kind or modest to comment.

I should point out that the Dublin Parade was not my first such appearance. As early as the sixties, I had acted as joint Grand Marshal for the New York event – a city that knows how to celebrate our national saint's feast day.

"Brian Boru" in a live radio broadcast on Radio 2 outside the Shelbourne Hotel, St Patrick's Day, 1988.

12 FÁILTE ISTEACH

... People had offered me new opportunities in broadcasting and I had the chance to be part of the new world. The unfamiliar soon became the familiar. I was ready for the off ...

The *Fáilte Isteach* team, Aidan Butler, producer, Jarlath Holland, Meabh Mooney and Neil Doherty.

264

WRITING FOR SOUND IS NOT like writing for anything else. Words must be sure, uncomplicated and accurate, aural, transient and often lost in a breath. Radio writing must involve the listener when hearing is often more important than understanding. The listening mind is often locked in the complex process of thinking, understanding and feeling.

Radio is often like a short story when the verbal is aural and often concealed in half-heard and half-told things.

I think of the strange and half-told repeated words of Tommy O'Brien, the grand musical reflector from Clonmel, when non-grammatical stops and half-heard stops rolled into musical meanings. Seán Ó Faoláin put it so well, *"Broadcast words are laden with meanings edged with the gold of time,"* Beware of long words. Fifty years of verbal thinking reflect a multitude of meanings.

In the early years of the new millennium, it came to pass that I would marry my love of the spoken word with my love of music.

"Disc jockey" is defined in the *Oxford English Dictionary* as: *"Presenter of a selection of usually recorded popular music, especially in a broadcast."* I could never see myself in this role and certainly not every Saturday night after 10 o'clock. I had, however, found that I was redundant in an area in RTÉ that I had all but invented. The problem was not with my broadcasting colleagues but with the shadowy ranks of the middle managers in the Radio Centre. Bill O'Donovan suggested relocation within the RTÉ labyrinth to the Light Entertainment area. It was a stroke of genius and a world into which I was welcomed and made to feel at home. I didn't see myself as a DJ, though, and didn't give the idea a second thought.

However, through constant pressure and hints from producer Peter Browne, I had to give it a second thought. He believed that the *Fáilte Isteach* slot on Radio One might suit me and the interests that I had. I was sceptical. Playing records every Saturday night was not my idea of a radio career. Still, he persisted and Bill O'Donovan, his manager, was obliquely encouraging. What they did not realise was that my objections were not just to playing records, but playing them *myself.* I had never played a disc in my life and certainly never in a live situation.

Then one day I asked my friend Mick McKeever to show me around. We looked at a studio that was totally alien to me. It was my first introduction to the dreaded compact disc machines. I was told that these discs contained the sound, digitally recorded, and then reproduced by the reflection of a laser. I nodded in what I hoped was a wise way – something that has got me out of a great many scrapes. Mick told me that these CDs were the future and immediately I began to wonder where my own particular future therefore lay. Vinyl was to become a thing of the past and up until now, that had been my technology. Still the technical quality of these compact discs astounded me and I began to see the future in terms of new technology. Wet and dry batteries were never even mentioned! I was impressed with the progress but was certain that it wasn't for me.

Still, my mother never reared a jibber and I decided to have a go. I spent nights alone in these comp. op. studios, which to the untutored means "compere-operated broadcasts." One person, completely isolated, introduced the material. To make matters worse, or more precisely scarier, comperes or presenters controlled the technical aspects of the programme. It was a far cry from my days in Raidió Éireann in Cork. Yet I was expected to deliver with the same warmth as before. Life for the listener improved without the realisation that it was a quite different matter for presenters. We sat alone! No hands were held. I felt like young Giocante de Casabianca, the boy who stood on the burning deck when all but he had fled. It was all changed.

For reasons, largely unknown, I decided to "go with the flow." After all of the heart searching, *Fáilte Isteach* became part of my life. Being of a certain age, the decision to join the worlds of DJaying, digital broadcasting and comp. op. looked a very long shot. Still, it was hardly peak listening. Some described my new slot in the schedule as "the sump of the week." I didn't care. People had offered me new opportunities in broadcasting and I had the chance to be part of the new world. The unfamiliar soon became the familiar. I was ready for the off.

The core difference with my old life was that this programme was completely "live". What the listening public hadn't perhaps always realised was that my broadcasting life had consisted of recordings. I had a few memories of live commentaries and occasional editions of *Highways and Byways* in live format. My broadcasts from walks were usually live but with the support of a highly professional, dedicated team. I had to deal with the sweaty hands and palpitating heart.

Bloomsday 2014 at Cavistons, Glasthule, from left: Donncha, Evelyn Cusack, Deputy Head of Forecasting at Met Éireann and RTÉ weather forecaster; Robert Gahan, former Deputy Director General of RTE; PJ Brady, poet; Liam Mulcahy, professional photographer, former pictures editor with *The Independent* and *Evening Herald*; Tim Pat Coogan, author and former editor of the *Irish Press*; Peter Caviston, fishmonger, Glasthule.

Ceoltóirí óg at Kilrush in the summer of 2013.

Mary McAleese, Uachtarán na hÉireann, and husband, Dr. Martin McAleese, welcome Donncha to the Áras.

In the Palace Bar with Mick Wallace, Liam Aherne, and Louis Fitzgerald, August 2014.

Donncha interviews An Taoiseach, Enda Kenny, after he officially opened the Titanic Memorial Park in Lahardane, Co. Mayo, built in honour of the Addergoole victims and survivors of the RMS Titanic.

Mick Foster, Daniel O'Donnell,
Tony Allen and PJ Murrihy,
with Donncha on *Fáilte Isteach*
Christmas Show 2012.

The first night stays clear in my mind to this day. I had loaded the discs in the players and all was ready and waiting. The night's running order included many of the listeners' favourites. I was unfamiliar with most of the music, but Daniel O'Donnell, Foster and Allen, who had their first broadcast in *Highways and Byways*, and others were all lined up and ready to go.

Peter Browne clucked at my elbow. I cued myself into the national network and waited for my introduction from the Presentation Department. Peter told me, 'It's is too late to go anywhere now. Good luck.' I know that he often felt that these preliminary moments were like the horses lined up at the Aintree Grand National. Then I was on.

This was the first time I had ever spoken directly to listeners in this way. I read extracts from letters and cards, played music, ran a quiz and generally kept the show on the road until we hit the pips at 11.00 – they were sacrosanct. I wanted to create a sense of familiarity. My listeners were generally at home, wherever that was, and I wanted to them to feel that I was sharing this experience directly with them. I gave the programme a second name, "The Parlour of Dreams", to capture that homely feeling and certainty in a rapidly changing word. Peter Browne had a tiny dog called "Scooter" and he was recruited as part of my mythical menagerie, later renamed "Rebel." The dog joined a cat and shared the virtual hearth with "Daisy", the cow and "Gandalf", the goose. Despite operating from a hi-tech fortress, I wanted to weave dreams of an idyllic homestead.

Then there were the listeners. They wrote letters at first, some still do, and then, through the wonders of the internet, they emailed. The correspondence snowballed and I was soon hearing from people living in all parts of the country, all ages and facing the full gamut of life's challenges. Their letters shaped the programme's content and brought it into new and different places. We had created the *Fáilte* family.

The date of my retirement, the 15th of March 1998, approached inexorably. There were rumours of change, dire futures, truths, half-truths and bizarre concoctions whirling around the station. I tried to ignore these but it was hard not to become entangled in the speculation. There were those who claimed, or implied, they knew what my broadcasting future, if any, was, but they coyly kept this information to themselves. I received half-hints and vague banalities. I became jittery.

I did then what I should have done a long time before, I arranged to meet Helen Shaw, the recently appointed director of radio. She was kindness itself and readily agreed to my continuing as the DJ for *Fáilte Isteach* and she also suggested new avenues of work based on the vast archive of *Highways and Byways*. I was now to become a freelancer, a free agent after years of being a permanent and pensionable employee. It brought new freedoms – I worked on Saturday evenings in studio seven in the darkened and almost deserted radio centre. I met only those who were working on the evening shift – sports, news and variety presenters generally. It was a quiet, reflective world.

I soon developed a routine around the programme. I walk to the Radio Centre having completed my preparation earlier on the Saturday morning. Some programmes practically prepare themselves but others need extensive background research to bring them together. I use the walk to clear my head and get into my broadcasting frame of mind. Indeed, I keep active while I'm on the premises by walking the deserted corridors and counting my steps as I go. It has developed into something of a ritual at this stage.

The audience for *Fáilte* has become an international one aided by the arrival of the internet. People listen to the show in almost every country in the world and are able to get in touch immediately by email or text if there is something that interests or annoys them. There is always someone with an additional nugget about virtually any topic under the firmament and they gladly share these with me, and ultimately, the listeners. Now I have listeners barbecuing their lunches on the West Coast of America while tuning in, having a late breakfast in Australia or New Zealand or nodding off in the cities and towns of Europe. There is a great depth of support for the programme in our neighbouring isle, too. There, pockets of people in London, Birmingham, Manchester, Carlisle or across the border in Glasgow and Aberdeen, join the *Fáilte* family for the hour. I have lots of nuns listening, too. One said to me, 'It's a great comfort to go to sleep with you talking to me.' Well, I'm happy with that, too. If I help nuns have a peaceful night's sleep, that's a bonus.

I was astounded and humbled by the great flow of letters, emails and texts that flowed into the studio when the listeners learnt of my recent illness. They came from near and far, bringing good wishes and blessings. One even wended its way from a bishop with kind words and blessings. I'll never have the opportunity to thank all of those good people individually but I acknowledge them now sincerely, and let them know that they gave me great consolation during that unfortunate time.

With the late Fr. Robert Forde, historian, at Tullylease Holy Well in County Cork.

Fáilte Isteach Christmas party 2004.

What heartens me most is that the show is now reaching out to new generations, people for whom many of my stories and ramblings represent history and an opportunity to glimpse a past, fast-disappearing world. It was wonderful, for example, to have received a letter from an Academy Award winner, composer, film star and musician, Glen Hansard, who wrote: *"Donncha, I'm sending you my record because your radio show means most to me. Big love and respect always."* These letters mean much – knowing that my programme is crossing generational divides and finding new hearts to warm.

I've made my own moves, too, to cross the generation gap and challenge some of the ageist attitudes that exist in RTÉ – as they do in most institutions. What may surprise many is that I built a great friendship and respect for the late and much missed Gerry Ryan. Gerry was unique and a bit of a maverick in RTÉ's hallowed halls. Indeed, he loved to test the limits in a way that reminded me of how I did the same in my early days. This was on 2FM which was a complete novelty for me and I'm sure for the listeners, too. I had hardly ever listened to the station as RTÉ One is very much my station and if not that, Raidió na Gaeltachta or Lyric. Vera prefers the latter.

I started with Gerry by reminiscing on what I had done over the years and then was able to work in some of the material that I had recorded in my previous life. Later, he sent me to pilgrimage sites around the country. I headed off to Knock with a busload of Dublin pilgrims. I reported live from Lough Derg, having to fill fifteen minutes for Gerry. Pilgrims normally do this pilgrimage barefoot and I was challenged on a number of occasions for wearing shoes. I told them I was a worker not a pilgrim!

Gerry and I did have one scrap that brought the attention of the authorities to what we were doing. I had brought a bottle of Midleton whiskey into the studio in connection with an item we were doing. Somehow, during the broadcast, the bottle was opened and whiskey consumed live on air. We survived. Gerry was a warm, intense character with a massive sense of humour and he is someone I miss greatly now.

Time moves on so swiftly. It seems like a few days ago since I made my first tentative steps in broadcasting but I've now passed the fifty-year milestone and I'm still going relatively strong. There were celebrations and special programmes but modesty forbids me from reproducing the many wonderful and kind words written and spoken to mark that event. I'm not too modest, though, and I will include some comments that Labhrás Ó Murchú, Director General of Comhaltas Ceoltóirí Éireann and member of Seanad Éireann made during our live Christmas show in 2012:

> "...I know that your listeners not just in Ireland but worldwide, look forward to you every single week but at the moment this is a very special time of the year. There's a lot of nostalgia and a lot of sentiment, and many of your listeners, I have no doubt about it, would be reflecting, I suppose, on their own environment, their own lives, maybe their own homes as well. There have been a lot of changes in Ireland over the years but nevertheless, down at community level, people are still the same, and listening to Fáilte Isteach each single week they get the opportunity, not only of reminiscing, but of celebrating excellence and celebrating community activity. When I think of your own career, if I may say this, for decades over a half a century, you have traversed not just the Irish countryside but the Irish mind as well. You have been seeking out people who otherwise would not get the spotlight and yet they were labouring away at community level helping people who were less fortunate in life, a ballad maker, the story teller – all of those people. I think that the Irish people and the Irish world owe you a huge, huge debt of gratitude and I'm delighted to be here to say that to you tonight."

I was tickled, too, to have a song penned about me and performed live on that Christmas show. It was a very different type of tribute to Labhrás's words but welcome and enjoyed nonetheless. PJ Murrihy composed the ballad entitled, *There's life in the old dog yet* an apt summary of my condition, approach to life, and philosophy. Daniel O'Donnell and Foster and Allen joined him for this. Daniel and

Foster and Allen have been great participants in and supporters of my shows over the years and so it was fitting that they were there to take part in the celebrations. I couldn't possibly list all of the other participants, whether balladeers, storytellers, authors, musicians, singers, performers of all sorts, and if I did I'm bound to leave some out. But to all of them I send my thanks and best wishes. Go raibh míle, míle maith agaibh go léir.

The Songs of My Life

The songs of my life began by the fireside in our first home in Convent Road in Doneraile, Co. Cork. My mother, Helena, introduced me to my first song *The Minstrel Boy*, on one of those happy pre-school days. Songs I learned and loved were always about stories and words. I can never forget:

> *"The Minstrel Boy to war is gone*
> *In the ranks of death you will find him…"*

With Susan McCann on *The Susan McCann Show,* in Castlebar, County Mayo, October 1983.

She brought Thomas Moore's sad and immortal words into the kitchen of a small house in North Cork and into a child's heart from where they would never leave. In a way and, perhaps quite unintentionally, she led her only son, Denis, gently and kindly into a world that was at once unique yet commonplace.

Since then, and during my broadcasting career, I have always belonged to the likes of Percy French whose *Mountains of Mourne* and *The Darlin' Girl from Clare,* were sung by the late Detective Garda John Roche. Incidentally, John, from the Garda Technical Bureau in Dublin, photographed my son, Donal, and myself in the early miles of our first Dublin City Marathon. So the world of songs and our physical rendition of them were one.

Singers and their songs invited me into that wonderful world of the performer when Kate O'Connor of Cork taught me the subtleties of the singer's life. Every Thursday afternoon in early manhood, I would travel by train from Charleville to Cork for a singing lesson from Kate. Five shillings bought me a return on the train and Kate's fee was five bob. I would often meet many of her other students. Among them was Michael Murphy, a great tenor from Cobh, Anne Brennan, a sweet soprano and Terry Cashman, a bass, with whom Paul Robeson would feel entirely at home and whose winding words brought me home to *Old Man River.*

I was, I suppose, a baritone for whom the fireside world of Convent Road was as real as that of a wonderful singer, Mario Lanza, who suddenly emerged from the wireless world and whom I listened to every week in the home of my friend, Noel Tarrant, in Charleville who owned a fine gramophone. Here, for the first time, I listened to the glorious voice of Mario Lanza, and his singing of *Be My Love* became a young singer's national anthem. I joined, too, the real world of the ballad singer. I remember the young man who at the Charleville Fair day sang *Bould Robert Emmet, the Darling of Éireann,* which ballad, apparently, I sang at the end of many an evening during Comhaltas tours of America.

This event is well remembered by the great Clare singer, Séamus MacMathúna. Will I ever forget the ballad singers who performed at Munster hurling championships in Limerick in the fifties? The answer is, 'Never! Never!' Except that we never see or hear them now, carefully treading their way down, row by row, collecting from the spectators.

However, only a few years ago when walking down Grafton Street in Dublin, a man ceased his accordion playing to say, 'Donncha, will you sing one?!' I did, but had no collection. 'Thady' was unique.

The world of the ballad singer is always in my heart, as are those

about whom ballads were written like Kevin Barry and Seán South of Garryowen.

Then there is the singer of singers, Seán Ó Sé, whose *An Poc ár Buile, The Town of Fermoy, Cnocáinín Aerach Cill Mhuire, The Ballad of Christy Ring,* have inspired and roused people across the globe.

Could I mention here what I consider to be the greatest Wexford song? I will. It is, of course, *Boolavogue,* as sung by the great Art Sinnott. Art sang for JFK in New Ross in 1963, and for me in 1978. A CD by the Sinnott family brings to life the immortal words of Thomas Davis:

"But, hark! A voice like thunder spake:
The West's awake! The West's awake!
Sing oh hurrah! Let England quake.
We'll watch till death for Erin's sake."

1980s single commemorating the visit of US President Ronald Reagan to the home of his forebears in Ballyporeen.

And add Paddy Berry's rendition of every Wexford song to your record collection.

The Old Refrain, sung by the great Derry tenor, Michael O'Duffy, is utterly moving and unforgettable. Michael once launched one of my walks from Dungarvan in the presence of Anne Mulqueen. At once Charleville Fair Day returns to my memories as I recall a great rendition of Delia Murphy's *If I were a blackbird.*

What a strange world is that of song and readings! *Donncha Entertains* was a long play record featuring seventeen tracks including poems, among them Patrick Galvin's *On Bandon Hill* and *Shancoduff* by Patrick Kavanagh.

Shay Healy emerges from the shadows with a satirical, *Protecting the Reagans in Ballyporeen,* where I perform in *My Lagan Love, The Isle of Inisfree, Bould Thady Quill* and several other well-known ballads.

Much of the credit for my songs and music belongs to Vera, including two surprising classical symphonic elements. The sound of such music in my life began on an evening in the Savoy Cinema in Cork when, a little confused and nervous, I joined Vera and heard the wonderful Bamberg Symphony Orchestra. A new love affair entered my life, that of the work of Brahms, far removed from the Brahms'

Lullaby which little translation in Irish I had learned from Brother Redmond in Charleville CBS. The world of Brahms' *Piano Concerto No.1* enchanted me. Does love of a beautiful woman lead one quickly into that of the classical world? Obviously! Ach sin scéal eile.

Let us take a few classical steps to the Limerick City Savoy Cinema for progress into the magical world of classical music. We pause now to listen to the angelic violin-playing of Yehudi Menuhin, when a voice, unique, well-known and extraordinary, interrupted a slow movement to leave us in no doubt that we were in a unique world of Menuhin-playing competing with the conversation of a musical man from Clonmel. It would be as simple to say "ssshhh" to Yehudi as to silence Tommy O'Brien. This was a unique broadcasting legend I would get to know and be happy to know in the years ahead. Tommy would be as familiar as The Bells of Shandon or the Homes of Tipperary. Ar dheis Dé go raibh a anam.

A book called *Munster and the City of Cork* by Richard Hayward, illustrated by Raymond Piper and launched in Bunratty Castle by Bryan McMahon, led me to a labyrinth of wonderful CDs. It seems a long time since the lovely September day in 1964. The beautiful book was poignantly signed very near the end of his life by Richard and by Raymond: *"For Donncha, his book! Sep. 4 1964."*

Waltons, with whom we always "sang an Irish song", were ever on *Fáilte Isteach*. My life-motto emerges in a PJ Murrihy special, "Don't give up till it's over." Another regular was Johnny McEvoy with, *You never learned to dance.* There were, of course, The Dubliners, especially in Siamsa Cois Laoi and on a famous day when An Taoiseach, Charlie Haughey TD expressed a desire to sing with Ronnie Drew and the boys. To their and my surprise, before the thirty-thousand present, he suggested he didn't know any songs except a verse or two of *Meet me up in Monto,* which he, The Dubliners and I sang to huge applause.

Ironic in that it was the time when my friend, Jack Lynch, hurling star and TD, was removed from centre stage. Jack and I often sang *The Banks* together, but not on that strange day in Páirc Uí Chaoimh.

Memories flood back from the world of *Fáilte!* Philomena Breslin and *My Wild Irish Rose;* Bing Crosby and *Galway Bay*, as only he could.

Richard Hayward was a regular on *Fáilte Isteach*, especially his *Three Flowers* recorded in 1938. Its CD rests comfortably beside *Terence's Farewell to Kathleen* by John McCormack, *The Road by the River,* by Frank O'Donovan and, perhaps the most popular recording on *Fáilte Isteach, What Will You Do, Love?* with Delia Murphy and Richard Hayward. *The Merry Ploughboy* with Dermot O'Brien I played on the radio the day that our Sinéad was born – for her and for Vera. Then there was a performance not generally accorded much applause of *Bould Thady Quill* in the Pavilion Ballroom in Charleville with Dermot long ago.

I'm sure PJ Murrihy from Co. Clare is my most frequent guest on *Fáilte Isteach*. He has proved over and over again that there's life in the old dog yet. He's right. He introduced us to the sad but heroic world of Jane Hogan, a Lusitania survivor from Co. Clare. The ship was sunk by a German U-boat off the Cork coast in 1915. He wrote the heroic song of the courageous Clare woman, who not alone survived, but made her way home.

PJ has also sung with the true heroes of the radio on his many appearances on *Fáilte Isteach*. Among them are Daniel O'Donnell, whose late mother I met years ago in Donegal, and old friends Foster and Allen who lit up my radio world, as did PJ himself and his lovely wife, Mary.

All my songs began with the late John McCormack and of course, he is always remembered as is Canon Sydney McEwan and his wonderful and unique *Song of the May* which I first recorded with him in Glasgow.

Let me, however, reflect on the written words of Senator Labhrás Murphy: *'Donncha, the faithful son of Doneraile, and the much revered author Canon Sheehan had much in common. They were both the voice of those who had no one to speak for them.'*

Go raibh maith agat, Labhrás, and you, too, Michael, our inimitable publisher. Ní fheicfear bhúr leithéid arís. Up the Rebels!

"The Parlour of Dreams" has sheltered many, I think, especially Gandalf, the Gander, Rebel, the dog, Kilkenny the cat, all of whom were invented for my own comfort. I think particularly of my constant driving companion, Aidan Murphy and his wife, Frances. Listeners, generous, kind and constant, here through my memoirs and my dreams. May I mention a few:

Sister Conleith, now in her nineties in Leeds; Bishop John Buckley from Cork; Margot Coogan, also chieftain of her clan, the famous Laois Lalors, whose Australian echoes touch our Irish hearts, James Fintan Lalor and Peter Lalor. I'm hospitably led to the home of Fr Jack Walshe in Rath, Co. Laois. Echoes of the thoughts and friendship of Sally Mulready and the London Centre in Camden Square in London with her wonderful cohorts, Irish Elderly Advice Network are in many ways closest of all. Michael McGrath and Kay bring me home to Charleville where his dad, Michael, was a very dear friend. More, more and more surge to my life. They surge like a classic *Highways and Byways*, a voice magical if never as famous as his feet. I refer to the one and only Gene

Sally Mulready, founder of the Irish Women Survivors Support Network and member of the Irish Council of State.

Farmyard conference,
Knockfierna, County Limerick.

Kelly, one of the greatest screen dancers who I met and interviewed long ago in Tipperary.

He was then neither dancing nor singing in the rain, but sitting by a fireside listening to me and a show I wrote, *Where now, Kathleen?* He was even kind enough to invite me to Hollywood. I didn't go but Gene Kelly, I thank you.

My Whole World

I've called this book *Donncha's World* and that is a constantly changing planet. My world originally was the tiny one of Doneraile and its environs. It expanded gradually through Charleville to Cork. It moved more quickly to the capital cities of London and Dublin. From there Ireland, particularly rural Ireland, became my world. And onward over the years I've added countries and continents to my travels and brought back tales of these to Irish audiences. More recently my world has become virtual as my broadcasts span the entire planet and, who knows, maybe even beyond. I may well be heard on space craft and certainly my broadcasts bounce off telecommunications satellites before returning to earth. I confess that I've never had a request, letter or text from space but there's always a first time.

There is another world though and that is the personal one. Vera and I have been married for fifty-three years. She has been my loyal companion, support and mother of our wonderful children. She is the co-creator of my family world and, to paraphrase John Lennon, the other half of my sky.

Our boys have grown into young men with their own families. Feargal graduated in law in 1984 and is married to Dervilla Evans. He practised as a solicitor in Ennis, Co. Clare. They have two daughters Sinéad and Bláthnaid. Ruairí graduated in horticultural science (1989) and is married to Anne McDonald. Rúairí now works with Fingal County Council. They have two children, Cian and Aisling. Dónal graduated in Arts (1989) and is married to Lorraine Ní Bhroin. He is Principal of St. Conleth's College, Ballsbridge, very close to me here in Donnybrook. They also have two children, Caoilfhionn and Diarmaid. Donncha graduated in Arts (1990) and is married to Lorraine Crawford. Donncha works in the Railway Procurement Agency and was recently in the news for organising the removal of the statue of Molly Malone from its home at the end of Grafton Street to make way for work on the Luas Cross City Link. Molly was installed clean and reinvigorated in her new site just around the corner on Suffolk Street. Again, Donncha and Lorraine have kept the Ó Dúlaing symmetry in having two children, Rúairí and Finnán.

Thus, I have a complement of eight grandchildren, growing up fast and quickly establishing themselves as competent young adults. Our boys have brought us great joy and are a constant source of pride for Vera and myself. Our one regret and it is a small, but significant, one is that, despite their county of birth, they grew up supporting the Dubs. Such is the wheel of life!

I have left mention of our daughter, Sinéad, until last. Sinéad, like two of her brothers, graduated in Arts and did so in 1990. I was delighted when Sinéad joined me in RTÉ where she started working in production. She worked for a time in children's television, as well as in current affairs. Her life was blossoming but she began to notice that she was feeling tired and out of sorts. Her GP sent her to Beaumont hospital where she was diagnosed with cancer. It was a bolt from

Feargal and Dervilla's wedding at Our Lady of the Wells Church, Sixmilebridge: Ruairí, Donncha, Donal, Donncha Óg, Dónal, Vera, Feargal and Sinéad.

the blue and shook us to our foundations. Sinéad bore this cross with courage and humour. Together with her husband, Edmund Johnson, she carried on, working and living life to the fullest extent possible. She died on the 25th of November 2010 at her home, with her husband and the rest of the family caring for her at the end.

It is hard to describe the intensity of the feelings that I felt as I realised that our own daughter was gone from us. It was the hardest and bleakest time of our lives. Sinéad had been a great companion to me on a number of our walks. I regretted now that I hadn't talked to her more on these walks – especially the sixteen days of the O'Sullivan Beara March. My practice is to concentrate on walking rather than talking and I deeply regret I missed the opportunity those walks presented.

To live in the hearts we leave behind
   Is not to die.

Go raibh míle maith agaibh

Tá saol na nGael bualite linn- saol a mhaireann briomhiar agus beo i gconaí. Paróiste agus paróiste as leo tír na hÉireann, mar a dúirt Dev liom fadó.

> *As Dev said to me long ago: 'The life of the Gael has come to us and lives strong and alive. If you love your parish, you love your country'.*
> *And we certainly do!*

Nobody can achieve anything without the support of many somebodies.

I am blessed to have been surrounded by hundreds if not thousands of people who have supported my life, my career, and my journey along the highways and byways. Together they form one great world-wide family made up of many.

Ballycotton Harbour, Co. Cork, 1979.

I thank in particular my RTÉ family of Aidan Butler, producer, Meabh Mooney, Neil O'Doherty and Jarlath Holland; my Comhaltas family, of which the chief is my great friend Senator Labhrás Ó

Murchú; my Charities family, of which the chief is another great friend Peter Stokes of the Irish Wheelchair Association who persuaded me to take my first walk for charity. Later, thousands of members in Concern, Rehab and others joined in to become members. Then, there is my Listening family, those who may be alone, forgotten, exiles, members of the hidden Ireland who enter the 'Parlour of Dreams' on *Fáilte Isteach* on RTÉ Radio One on Saturday nights and who have been followers of *Highways and Byways* for generations.

Numerous people suggested that I produce a memoir giving an account to date of my life and times. I succumbed to the notion eventually. And here, two years later, following hours and hours of reflection and research is this magnificent book.

Writing a book is not just a job of work. It can be the hardest of work but it was made so much easier by a team of people who listened while I talked. I thank in particular a number of people who made this book possible.

Vera and the Ó Dúlaing family; Vera has been my meticulous archivist and curator of every photograph, newspaper article, poster, review, book, magazine, record, eulogy, encomium and interview about my career and adventures, none of which would have been possible without her ardent guidance and support. She has provided an extraordinary pool of source material from which we have drawn.

My writer, Declan Lyons interviewed me for hours and hours over a year and succeeded in recording and distilling my life of fifty years in broadcasting and my life before RTÉ in that short space of time into about 90,000 words. He gently helped me recall of parts of my life that I had forgotten about and helped me bring back many happy memories.

Liam Mulcahy, former photographic editor of the Irish Independent, was at Cahirmee Fair when I visited in 1976. I would not have guessed then that many years later Liam would become a great friend and researcher of photographs that have recorded my life in newspapers and magazines across Ireland and in this book.

Helen Ashdown, Clonleigh, Palace, Enniscorthy, former newspaper sub-editor, editor of this book and editor of numerous other acclaimed books, pored over files of photographs and press cuttings and researched and edited every word. Helen is a director of Enniscorthy Athenaeum, of which I am honoured to be a patron.

Sinéad McKenna of Sin É Design, Rush, Co. Dublin, one of Ireland's foremost book designers, translated the thousands of words and photographs and images into a stunningly visual and colourful book that will be enjoyable and enriching to you the reader and to all your family and friends.

Editing at The Elms, Donnybrook: Sinéad McKenna, Helen Ashdown and Donncha.

Phil Murphy, editor of my favourite magazine *Ireland's Own*, an old friend, and who has been with me on *Fáilte Isteach* numerous times over the years, gave me wise opinion.

Aidan Murphy, my great friend and "logistics manager" of Limerick, Cork and Inchicore lineage, to whom I am grateful for arranging my trips and gigs and for often transporting me to so many events, as though I was the king of Ireland. Aidan provided photographs from his vast collection.

Michael McGrath of Charleville, newspaper columnist, *The Corkman*, former public relations manager with Dairygold, who is known to journalists everywhere and who, like his father, is my long-time friend. Michael provided photographs from his collection which goes back to the year dot.

Paddy Whelan of Ballyruane, Ballycullane, Co. Wexford, researched background and guided me around Co. Wexford and gave wise counsel to my producers.

John Joe O'Shea of Ballyhogue gave directions and Emily Rafter of Killurin, photographed me for the cover in the sublime surroundings of the beautiful Bellevue Church by the River Slaney.

Peter O'Connell of Peter O'Connell Media, Dublin, publishing expert and guide, gave enthusiastic approval to *Donncha's World* when first proposed and then managed, publicised and promoted it to the media and the book trade of Ireland and throughout the world.

Pearl Quinn and Emma Keogh in RTÉ Still Library Archives, Irene Stevenson in *The Irish Times* and Berni Metcalf and Nora Thornton in the National Library researched photographs at short notice.

The An Post Corporate Communications team kindly facilitated the national launch of the book at Ireland's sacred national place, the GPO in O'Connell Street, Dublin, which was home to me when I made my early Radio Éireann broadcasts from the third floor there back in the '60s.

Jennifer Boyle, managing director of Seefin DM in Listowel and Joanne Dignam transcribed my talks.

Maurice McCarthy, 'the Sixth Beatle', of MJ Flood's , scanned many outsized images for us.

Researching: Donncha and Michael Freeman.

My publisher Michael Freeman of Three Sisters Press in Co. Wexford, without whom this book would not have happened.

Go mbeirimid beo ar an am seo arís.

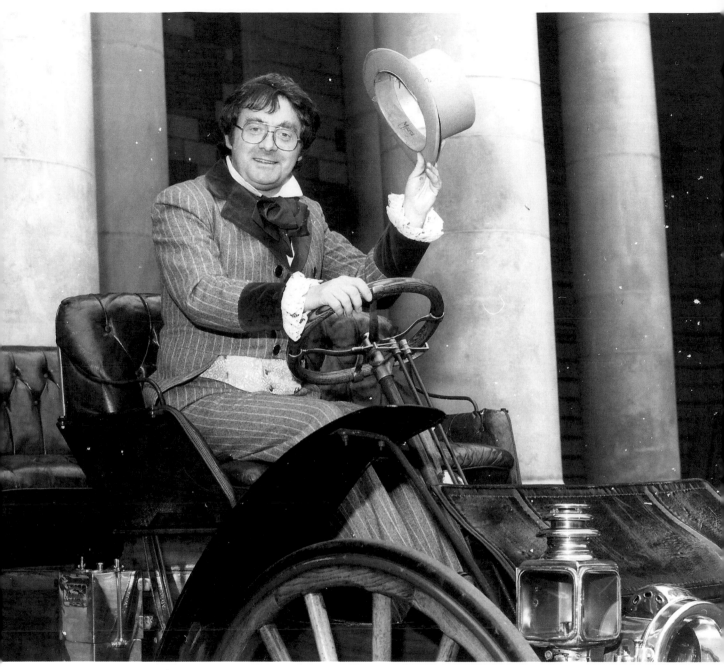

At the Bank of Ireland, College Green, with Tom O'Neill's vintage car for "Tipperary Remembers Kickham" 1982.

The Limerick Show 1985.

Words and Pictures

Writer: Declan Lyons is author of several books including the cycling bestseller, *Cycling the Canal du Midi*. An avid radio listener, he grew up in a time when Donncha was a colossus in Irish radio broadcasting. A well-known management consultant, he delivers training in communications, interpersonal skills, editing, writing and publishing to state, semi-state, public and private bodies in Ireland, the Balkans and Europe generally. His home is in Dun Laoghaire. He works from his offices in a village near Béziers in France and in Arthurstown, Co. Wexford.

Photographic research: Liam Mulcahy, a native of Cork, living in Dublin, is former group photographic editor with Independent News and Media. He produced the acclaimed bestselling photographic book *Images of Dublin*. He is former president of the Press Photographers' Association of Ireland.

Photo Credits

The publishers thank the following sources for their kind permission to reproduce the photographs and illustrations in this book. Every effort has been made to contact the copyright holders, but we would be happy to correct any errors or omissions in future editions.

The Irish Times
Cork Examiner
National Library of Ireland
RTÉ
Miley Carroll
Michael McGrath
Liam Mulcahy
Aidan Murphy
Vera Ó Dúlaing
Emily Rafter
Garda John Roche
REHAB
IStock

First published in 2014 by Three Sisters Press, Galbally,
Enniscorthy, Co. Wexford.

Text copyright © Michael Freeman, Donncha Ó Dúlaing
and Declan Lyons.

ISBN: 978-0-9573162-5-6

Trade enquires to Gill & Macmillan Distribution
Hume Avenue, Park West, Dublin 12
 Tel: +353 (1) 500 9534
Sales@gillmacmillan.ie

This book is typeset in Foundry Wilson.

Design by www.sinedesign.net

Printed in Ireland by Naas Printing, Naas, Co. Kildare.

Air Corps helicopter organised by President Éamon de Valera to take Donncha and his radio crew to County Clare for the opening of a new school in the early 1960s.

And as you leave 'The Parlour of Dreams' for now,
make sure to pull out the door after you. It is imperative.